"A necessary and prophetic text for those interested in the unsettling yet essential work of reconciliation between settlers and Indigenous people. L. Daniel Hawk is a compelling storyteller, myth buster, Bible expositor, and bridge builder. Hawk's book brings the 'receipts' of colonization—receipts of settler violence, broken treaties, missionary missteps, and stolen land. If the church is courageous enough to take Hawk's stories seriously, it may yet restore the integrity of its presumed destiny to manifest good news, living in right relationship with Indigenous people and the Creator."

T. Christopher Hoklotubbe, director of graduate studies at NAIITS: An Indigenous Learning Community and coauthor, with H. Daniel Zacharias, of *Reading the Bible on Turtle Island*

"'Fake news!' some might react upon seeing the title of L. Daniel Hawk's book. Yet echoing the voice urging St. Augustine before biblical scrolls to 'take up and read,' I dare any considering *Undoing Manifest Destiny* to do the same and then prove the Scriptures wrong that 'the truth will set you free' (John 8:32)! What truths? Settler truths! Government truths! Native and Indigenous American truths! Each of these voices resound concretely through Hawk's pursuit of justice so that—and here be forewarned!—you and I as readers will be unsettled from the blinders of our preferred 'testimonies' and impelled by the Spirit of truth to bear ever more authentic witness to the coming divine reign that promises, finally, to undo all earthly colonial regimes, even the ones that we are complicit with because of the benefits gained."

Amos Yong, professor of theology and mission at Fuller Theological Seminary

"The importance of L. Daniel Hawk's *Undoing Manifest Destiny* dare not be underestimated. This is an incredibly important book. Hawk counters the persistent tendency for Christian folk to justify their use of violence against American Indians in their conquest of Indian homelands, and he adds his theologian's voice to the unending cry of Native peoples for justice and truth in remembering that past. Too many turn American history into a romance of the European Christian conquest and the Indians who lived here into merely minor impediments to that winning of the West. Hawk demonstrates the falseness of that romance."

Tink Tinker, member of the Osage Nation and emeritus professor of American Indian Cultures and Religious Traditions at the Iliff School of Theology

"This book is a well-crafted overview of the history, ideology, and legacy of settler colonialism's 'logic of elimination,' which clarifies how, as Dr. King put it, 'our nation was born in genocide.' Historian and biblical theologian L. Daniel Hawk grounds each chapter in the regional lore of his home place, interrogates devised and dismembered public narratives, and concludes with suggestions for, and a call to, decolonizing discipleship. A highly recommended primer that meets this moment!"

Ched Myers, coauthor of *Healing Haunted Histories: A Settler Discipleship of Decolonization*

"Get ready for a disturbing yet hopeful journey as L. Daniel Hawk, writing not just as an academic but as someone whose heart beats for genuine reconciliation, walks us through the painful truths behind Manifest Destiny and the doctrine of discovery. *Undoing Manifest Destiny* challenges the descendants of settler colonists to question the stories that formed them, to see with new eyes, and to join the work of truth-telling and restoration. I hope the reader will hear the call to walk alongside those who long to see harmony and balance restored."

Terry M. Wildman, lead translator, general editor, and project manager for the *First Nations Version* and *First Nations Version Psalms and Proverbs*

"The destructive power of a warped imagination lingers throughout the American story. The lack of awareness about the doctrine of discovery and Manifest Destiny reveals the inability of the church and American society to deal with reality. In this thoroughly researched text, L. Daniel Hawk offers an essential study of American history. With clarity and precision, Hawk exposes the White settler narrative that needs to be dismantled. This text exemplifies the type of truth-telling that is required if the healing that all sides of the narrative desperately need can occur."

Soong-Chan Rah, Robert Boyd Munger Professor of Evangelism at Fuller Theological Seminary and coauthor, with Mark Charles, of *Unsettling Truths*

"This book is exceptionally timely. With the return of the imperial idea of Manifest Destiny to the highest level of the US government, the whole idea of one nation manifestly having the right to take over another's land needs a fresh challenge. L. Daniel Hawk forcefully provides this challenge in *Undoing Manifest Destiny*. Drawing on both history and Scripture, Hawk unmasks the appeal and un-Christian logic of 'destiny' ideology and calls for a return to the ways of Jesus. This book deserves study in classrooms and churches across the country."

Howard A. Snyder, author of *Jesus and Pocahontas* and *The Community of the King*

UNDOING MANIFEST DESTINY

L. DANIEL HAWK

UNDOING MANIFEST DESTINY

Settler America, Christian Colonists,
and the Pursuit of Justice

An imprint of InterVarsity Press
Downers Grove, Illinois

InterVarsity Press
P.O. Box 1400 | Downers Grove, IL 60515-1426
ivpress.com | email@ivpress.com

©2026 by Lewis Daniel Hawk

All rights reserved. No part of this book may be reproduced in any form without written permission from InterVarsity Press.

InterVarsity Press® is the publishing division of InterVarsity Christian Fellowship/USA®. For more information, visit intervarsity.org.

All Scripture quotations, unless otherwise indicated, are translated by the author.

The publisher cannot verify the accuracy or functionality of website URLs used in this book beyond the date of publication.

Cover design: Faceout Studio, Spencer Fuller
Interior design: Daniel van Loon
Images: DigitalVision Vectors via Getty Images:
　　© clu; © ilbusca; © GOLDsquirrel; © FingerMedia

ISBN 978-1-5140-0864-5 (print) | ISBN 978-1-5140-0865-2 (digital)

Printed in the United States of America ∞

Library of Congress Cataloging-in-Publication Data
A catalog record for this book is available from the Library of Congress.

32　31　30　29　28　27　26　　|　　13　12　11　10　9　8　7　6　5　4　3　2　1

To my brothers,

Dave, Randy, Rob, and Jeff

I am proud to be counted among you.

CONTENTS

1 THE INDIAN MAID OF FORT BALL   1

2 DISCOVERING THE INDIAN   25
   The Doctrine of Discovery and the Creation Mandate

3 EXTORTING THE INDIAN   50
   Treaties, Legislation, and Executive Orders

4 EXTERMINATING THE INDIAN   72
   Frontier Violence and Military Conquest

5 EXPELLING THE INDIAN   105
   Removal and Relocation

6 ERASING THE INDIAN   131
   The Civilization Project

7 CONSTRUCTING THE INDIAN   161
   Five Mythic Tropes

8 MIRRORING CONQUEST   191
   Reading Joshua and the American Settler Narrative

9 BEYOND INNOCENCE   213
   Dismantling the Settler Narrative

ACKNOWLEDGMENTS   237

FOR FURTHER READING AND RESEARCH   239

GENERAL INDEX   243

SCRIPTURE INDEX   246

1

THE INDIAN MAID OF FORT BALL

Voted, that the earth is the Lord's and the fullness thereof; voted, that the earth is given to the Saints; voted, that we are the Saints.

MILFORD, CONNECTICUT, TOWN MEETING, 1640

ON THE WEST BANK of the Sandusky River, the Indian maid keeps watch over the city of Tiffin, Ohio. She stands atop a granite pedestal, with a serene countenance and one arm folded at the waist. A blanket is draped over her left shoulder and falls over her arm. Her pose and raiment evoke the statuary of ancient Greece and Rome, the classical civilizations that inspired the Founding Fathers of the United States. A plaque on the pedestal contains a bas-relief that depicts the maid giving water to a settler. Above the relief is an inscription: "This Indian maid keeps ceaseless watch where red men and sturdy pioneers drank from a spring, whose sparkling waters flowed within the stockade of old Fort Ball."

Tiffin citizen Meschech Frost donated the funds for the statue, which was unveiled on October 11, 1926. Frost was the embodiment of the American dream. He worked his way up from humble beginnings to become a successful entrepreneur and real-estate developer. Frost is remembered for bringing several industries to Tiffin, including the Sterling Grinding Wheel Company, the Beatty Glass Company, Brewer Pottery, and the National Machinery Company, which he reorganized, managed, and eventually purchased. Under his leadership, National Machinery introduced significant innovations that led to the rapid expansion of the factory and contributed to the prosperity of the city. A generous philanthropist, Frost also has the distinction of building the town's first electric street railway.

The citizens of Tiffin thus unveiled the statue of the Indian maid amid the energy and optimism that fueled the prosperity of Tiffin during the early twentieth century. The unveiling took place during the 102nd year since the city's recognition and its designation as the seat of Seneca County. Sadly, Frost was not present for the ceremony, having died four years before. The city nonetheless expressed its admiration and gratitude by renaming the street next to the statue Frost Parkway.[1]

The statue commemorates a young, unnamed woman who assisted a detachment of US soldiers during the early days of the War of 1812. American general William Hull had recently surrendered Detroit to the British, along with a force of twenty-five hundred soldiers, leaving Ohio open to invasion. To prepare for that eventuality, General William Henry Harrison ordered the construction of three forts along the Sandusky River for the purpose of establishing a supply line for the defense of the Lake Erie coastline. Fort Ball, the southernmost of the three forts, was to serve as a supply depot. When soldiers arrived to construct the fort, they encountered a young Seneca woman. She showed them the location of a spring that could be enclosed within a stockade, therefore providing the fort with a protected water supply in the event of a siege.

Why did the citizens of Tiffin choose to celebrate their prosperity by erecting a statue of an Indigenous woman? Why not the city's namesake, Edward Tiffin, the first governor of Ohio? Or one of the early pioneer families? Why an anonymous Indigenous woman who probably lived in a Seneca town a few miles downstream, a town that has not existed for almost two hundred years? Why mark the city's dynamic growth by erecting the statue of an Indigenous woman to watch over the city? In short, why did the citizens of Tiffin commemorate the city's origins with a nostalgic account of a time when "red men and sturdy pioneers" shared the land together?

Ohio Hawks and the Settler Story

My forebears were part of an immigrant wave that settled Seneca County in the 1830s, not long after the Senecas left the last of their lands in Ohio. My

---

[1] "Meschech Frost," Find a Grave, www.findagrave.com/memorial/6069859/meshech-frost; "History," National Machinery, www.nationalmachinery.com/history.

great-great-grandfather, Ludwig Hack, migrated from the German kingdom of Baden-Württemberg to the United States about ten years earlier. Our family doesn't remember much about him, aside from the fact that he was a blacksmith, and we don't know why he decided to emigrate. His journey may have been precipitated by antiquated inheritance laws, which had so divided estates among heirs that many no longer possessed enough land to sustain themselves. Or he may have been drawn by the freedoms enjoyed by the citizens of the United States. Or he may simply have been captured by a spirit of adventure.

Whatever the reason, Ludwig entered the United States through the port of Philadelphia in the early 1820s, settled in Lehigh County, Pennsylvania, married a young woman named Eva Ferber, and began to raise a family that would eventually number nine children. In the early 1830s, the family migrated to Seneca County, Ohio, and took up farming. There have been Hawks in the county ever since. (The change of spelling occurred, so the story goes, when a clerk heard German "Hack" but wrote English "Hawk" on a property deed.)

Present-day Tiffin is a city of approximately twenty thousand. My formative years there were shaped by the cadences of small-town America: attending church and youth group every Sunday, camping with my fellow Boy Scouts, attending sports events on the weekend, and playing saxophone in the Tiffin Columbian High School Marching Band. (Only the second and third activities were my choice. My parents were devoted Christians, and my father was the director of the high school marching band.) My education included the formation of the values of integrity, truthfulness, honesty, perseverance, and fairness, and more fundamentally, love for God and country. These values were exemplified by William Harvey Gibson, whose statue stands in front of the county courthouse. Gibson, Tiffin's most illustrious son, was a renowned orator during the latter half of the nineteenth century and well-known for declaring that the two most important things in life are piety and patriotism.

I also learned values from the TV westerns of the 1960s and from the version of the American story they presented. The Westerns reiterated seemingly inexhaustible variations on stock themes. Courageous pioneers overcame hostile savages and made a home for themselves in a new land by hard work and sheer determination. Indians attacked wagon trains and isolated settlers. Righteous gunslingers outgunned lawless villains, delivered hapless citizens, and brought order to a lawless land. Disputes were often settled at the point of a gun. Looking back, I am amazed at how often gun violence was sanctioned and celebrated in the Westerns. The Westerns taught me that American violence is righteous violence. Violence brings order. Violence was thus necessary to tame the land and to impose law and order.

I don't recall thinking much about the people who lived in Seneca County before my ancestors arrived. It never occurred to me to wonder why we White people live in the land and the Senecas do not. In the world of my childhood, Indians were characters from the past, gone and largely forgotten, save for presentations about Indian lore at the local library, a portrait in the Seneca County museum depicting the death-by-torture of Colonel William Crawford at the hands of murderous Delawares, and campfire tales about an Indian ghost named Oscar, who roamed the countryside on weekend nights, looking for young campers to terrorize.

Indians populated my imagination but not the place I called home. The stories that shaped my formative years were stories about people like me—who looked like me, thought like me, and shared my values and experiences. The history that I learned in the classroom was likewise populated by people like me. That history shaped my sense of who I am and how I was expected to live as a citizen of the United States, an exceptional nation and a beacon of freedom, opportunity, and progress.

In the landscape of my youth, the Indian maid represented the nostalgic tropes of Tiffin's origin story, harking back to a time when "red men and sturdy pioneers" together enjoyed the nourishing resources of the land: the red man destined to vanish into the mists of history and the sturdy pioneers destined to transform a forest wilderness into fields of corn and soybeans as well as factories that manufactured glass and machine parts. In her classical bearing and toga-like dress, the Indian maid looks more like a Roman goddess than an Indigenous woman. In a sense, she symbolizes the land, not as it once was but as it has been remade in the image of a pioneer people. The maid plays a brief but pivotal role in Tiffin's story, helping the first settlers and then vanishing from the scene, along with her people.

The Seneca of Sandusky

Before I go further, I should explain some of the terms I am using and why I use them. I employ the term *settlers* as shorthand for White Christian settlers, that is, for European colonists and their descendants. Adopting a comprehensive term for the original peoples of the land is difficult because, as Thomas King observes, "There has never been a good collective noun because there never was a collective to begin with."[2] I have chosen to employ the term *Indigenous*, mainly as a way of highlighting the connection between the colonial program of the United States and the experience of colonized peoples around the world. I will, however, use the term *Indian* sometimes when I want specifically to accentuate the colonial perspective. When referencing specific tribes or nations, I've sought to employ the community's preferred name. In some cases, this is attested by wide use in contemporary discourse (for example, Lakota, Lenape, Haudenosaunee). When multiple names are well-attested, I adopt the name that appears on the nation's website. In a related sense, I try to use the terms *nation*, *tribe*, and *band* as the community designates itself, while employing a general preference for *nation*.

Now back to the story of the Ohio Senecas and settlers.

Bands of Seneca began migrating to Haudenosaunee (Iroquois) land in the Ohio Country beginning in the 1740s.[3] Their aim was to escape the frontier violence that their kindred and other Indigenous nations experienced as a consequence of colonial expansion. The first bands settled near the Ohio River in what is now southeastern Ohio. Over the next few decades, the Senecas were joined by a larger number of Cayugas, along with a small number of Mohawks and Onondagas.[4] Ohio settlers called them Mingos, a pejorative meaning "treacherous."

Settler violence, however, stalked the Senecas. The most notorious instance involved a respected Cayuga leader named Tachnechdorus, who was

---

[2]Thomas King, *The Inconvenient Indian: A Curious Account of Native People in North America* (University of Minnesota Press, 2012), xiii.
[3]The Ohio Country was a colonial-era name for the land between the Ohio River and Lake Erie, and west of the Appalachian Mountains.
[4]The website of the Seneca-Cayuga nation also lists Conestogas, Eries, and Wyandots among those who joined the Senecas in Ohio. See the history posted on the tribal website at https://sctribe.com/history/.

known to the colonists as Chief Logan.[5] Tachnechdorus was a respected advocate for peace during and after the French and Indian War, which raged from 1754 to 1763. On October 10, 1774, a number of his family and friends were murdered by a group of Virginia settlers at Yellow Creek, near present-day Steubenville, Ohio. Accounts of what happened vary, but most agree on the following details. The Virginians invited a group of approximately twelve Senecas to join them at their camp and offered them whiskey. At some point, the settlers challenged the Senecas to a shooting match. After the Seneca men fired their guns, however, several colonists arose from hiding places and shot most of them dead on the spot. The Virginians pursued the survivors and killed all but one of them. The dead included Tachnechdorus's wife and pregnant sister. The settlers strung the young woman up by her wrists, cut the unborn child from her body, and scalped her. The lone survivor was her daughter, who had been carried on her mother's cradle board.

Tachnechdorus sought revenge, resisted pleas to refrain, and dispatched war parties to raid settlements in western Pennsylvania, joining Shawnees who were defending their lands from Virginia settlers (a conflict commonly known as Lord Dunsmore's War). After a climactic battle at Point Pleasant in present-day West Virginia, the Shawnees sued for peace and ceded their land south of the Ohio River. In return, they received a promise that Virginia would not settle Shawnee land to the north. Tachnechdorus refused to attend the treaty negotiations but sent a response to the council.

Thomas Jefferson later published the following transcript of the speech in his *Notes on the State of Virginia*:

> I appeal to any white man to say, if ever he entered Logan's cabin hungry, and he gave him not meat; if ever he came cold and naked, and he clothed him not. During the course of the last long and bloody war, Logan remained idle in his cabin, an advocate for peace. Such was my love for the whites, that my countrymen pointed as they passed, and said, Logan is the friend of white men. I had even thought to have lived with you, but for the injuries of one man. Col. Cresap, the last spring, in cold blood, and unprovoked,

---

[5]Logan's Cayuga name is uncertain. Daniel K. Richter, *Facing East from Indian Country* (Harvard University Press, 2001), and Colin G. Calloway, *The Indian World of George Washington* (Oxford University, 2008), refer to Logan as "Tachnechdorus." "Tahgahjute" is also a strong possibility. See Thomas McElwain, "Then I Thought I Must Kill Too," in *Native American Speakers of the Easter Woodlands*, ed. Barbara Alice Mann (Greenwood, 2001), 83-106.

murdered all the relations of Logan, not sparing even my women and children. There runs not a drop of my blood in the veins of any living creature. This called on me for revenge. I have sought it. I have killed many. I have fully glutted my vengeance. For my country, I rejoice at the beams of peace. But do not harbor a thought that mine is the joy of fear. Logan never felt fear. He will not turn on his heel to save his life. Who is there to mourn for Logan? Not one.[6]

Jefferson praised the speech as equal in eloquence to any work of European oratory, prompting other editors to reprint the speech hundreds of times under the title "Logan's Lament."[7]

Questions have been raised, however, about the accuracy of Jefferson's transcript, beginning with the fact that the speech attributes the atrocity to Michael Cresap, a notorious Indian hater, rather than to Daniel Greathouse, who was the likely ringleader of the Virginians. Furthermore, rhetorical analysis of the speech suggests that it more closely conforms to the structure, vocabulary, and content of English rhetoric than to the conventions of Iroquoian oratory.[8] Whether an exact transcript or not, Jefferson's version went viral in part because it reflected an image of the Indian constructed by the settler imagination, just as the Indian Maid does for the present-day citizens of Tiffin.

By 1760, most of the Senecas had moved north and established towns along the Sandusky River, where they became known as the Senecas of Sandusky.[9] Along with other Ohio nations, they defended their land during the Revolutionary War, as well as in the conflicts that ensued when the newly constituted United States claimed the Ohio Country and began to settle it. The wars came to an end with the defeat of a coalition of tribes at Fallen Timbers in 1794 and the subsequent Treaty of Greenville in 1795. The treaty ceded all but the northwest quadrant of Ohio to the United States. The Seneca towns lay north of the treaty line and thus remained on unceded territory.

---

[6]"Logan's Lament," American Rhetoric, www.americanrhetoric.com/speeches/nativeamericans/chieflogan.htm.
[7]Carol Eastman, "The Indian Censures the White Man: 'Indian Eloquence' and American Reading Audiences in the Early Republic," *William and Mary Quarterly*, 3rd series, 65, no. 3 (2008): 535-36.
[8]McElwain, "Then I Thought," 117-20.
[9]By this time, Cayugas constituted the largest group within the communities.

The War of 1812 brought renewed conflict. While most of the Ohio tribes sided with the British during the war, the towns along the Sandusky River adopted a neutral stance, although some individuals assisted the United States. The war was precipitated in part by a smoldering dispute over possession of the Ohio Country. Although the British relinquished their claim to the Ohio Country at the Treaty of Paris in 1783, they nevertheless continued to provide covert assistance to the Indigenous nations who resisted American expansion into the area. The Treaty of Ghent, which formally ended the War of 1812, put a stop to that assistance. In the treaty, Great Britain again agreed to relinquish all claims to the Northwest Territory (encompassing all land north of the Ohio River and east of the Mississippi), and the United States agreed to end hostilities with the Indigenous peoples and to restore "all possessions, rights, and privileges, which they may have enjoyed or been entitled to" before the war.[10]

The end of British support left the Indigenous peoples of the Old Northwest without an effective counterbalance to American power. Shortly after the treaty was ratified, the US government launched a vigorous effort to acquire more Indian land for settlement, propelled by what one historian has called an "inordinate demand for lands . . . fueled by an explosive spirit of nationalism."[11] Between the end of the War of 1812 and the inauguration of President Andrew Jackson in 1829, the US government made thirty-nine treaties with twenty-four tribes and bands in the Northwest Territory and areas just west of the Mississippi. Almost all of them entailed cessions of Indigenous land.

The federal government coveted the parts of Ohio still in Indigenous hands as settlers flooded into the state. In 1800, shortly before statehood (1803), the White population of Ohio stood at 45,000. By 1820, that number had grown to more than 581,000, and by 1830 to 938,000. The rapid expansion of settlers into Ohio generated considerable pressure on the federal government to acquire the remaining Indigenous land.

---

[10]"Treaty of Ghent (1814)," National Archives, accessed March 25, 2025, www.archives.gov/milestone-documents/treaty-of-ghent.

[11]Francis Paul Prucha, *American Indian Treaties: The History of a Political Anomaly* (University of California Press, 1994), 135.

In 1814, General William Henry Harrison and Indian agent Lewis Cass negotiated "a treaty of peace and friendship" with the Senecas of Sandusky and other nations. The Indigenous parties agreed to acknowledge themselves under the protection of the United States, and the United States, in turn, affirmed the boundaries established by prior treaties. Another treaty followed in 1815, which required all tribes Ohio tribes to accept the terms of the Treaty of Greenville, a treaty that reserved the northwest quadrant of Ohio for the Indigenous nations. Under pressure from federal authorities, Indigenous representatives agreed to the terms of a third treaty in 1817 at Fort Meigs. The treaty required the six Ohio nations to sell almost all of their remaining lands in Ohio—more than 4.5 million acres—in return for annuities and compensation for damages suffered by those groups that had assisted the United States during the War of 1812.[12]

The last treaty, supplemented by a fourth in 1818, established small reservations for the remaining Ohio tribes. Two were established for the Senecas, the first of thirty thousand acres along the Sandusky River and the second of ten thousand acres near Lewiston. The federal government viewed the reservations as places where the Indigenous peoples could learn American agricultural practices, make progress toward civilization, and eventually assimilate into the mainstream of the new nation.

To many in the government, the Senecas demonstrated the efficacy of the policy to assimilate Indigenous people into the new nation. A visitor to the Sandusky reservation in 1827 noted, "The men were well dressed, with their rifles strapped across their shoulders and their wagons drawn by fine oxen, and were living in comfortable houses with sash windows and shingled roofs."[13] The reality, however, was more complex, as the Senecas adopted some of the practices of civilization but struggled to preserve their traditions and ceremonies. Especially troublesome were harangues by Methodist preachers, who regularly entered the reservation uninvited, intent on converting tribal members to the Christian God.

The immigrants who established settlements near the reservation did not share the government's outlook. For the most part, they had little love for

---

[12]Transcripts for all four treaties can be accessed online at the Tribal Treaties Database, https://treaties.okstate.edu/treaties/.
[13]Mary Stockwell, *The Other Trail of Tears: The Removal of the Ohio Indians* (Westholme, 2014), 183.

the Senecas and wanted them gone. Tensions flared. Settlers stole and killed the Senecas' horses, hogs, and cattle. They passed through the reservation at will. Although the sale of alcohol to Indians was prohibited by law, liquor merchants ringed the reservation, and local officials turned a blind eye to whiskey sales to young Seneca men and women. Unscrupulous merchants replaced Indian agents as trading partners, jacking up prices. Settlers depleted the game in the Senecas' hunting grounds.

In 1819, Indian agent John Johnston appealed for a subagent to provide protection for the Senecas, arguing that the "character of the Government of the U.S. requires that they should not be left thus exposed to the inroads of the wicked and abandoned portion of our species."[14] President James Monroe granted the appeal and appointed James Montgomery, a Methodist missionary, for the task. The appointment followed the adoption of the Civilization Fund Act, which Congress passed earlier that year. The legislation enlisted missionaries, church leaders, and "capable persons of good moral character" to "introduce the habits and arts of civilization" to Indigenous communities located near frontier settlements.[15]

Montgomery investigated the depredations, kept a record of them, and petitioned the government for compensation for lost and vandalized property. He was able to recover only a fraction. The situation so deteriorated by 1824 that Tall Man, the principle leader of the Senecas, along with fourteen other leaders, appealed directly to President Monroe for help, writing, "Our hearts are often made sick. . . . Whitemen passing through our Land often say this land is too good for Indians—We fear that we will soon be driven from this country unless you help us."[16]

By 1829, the situation had become intolerable. Seneca leaders reluctantly petitioned the federal government for land west of the Mississippi in exchange for their Ohio reservations. The administration of newly elected president Andrew Jackson was all too happy to comply. Jackson had made Indian removal a central plank of his presidential campaign. He subsequently appointed James Gardiner, a former senator and ambitious office

---

[14] Quoted in John P. Bowes, *Land Too Good for Indians* (University of Oklahoma Press, 2016), 124.
[15] "29. Civilization Fund Act March 3, 181," in *Documents of United States Indian Policy*, 3rd ed., ed. Francis Paul Prucha (University of Nebraska Press, 2000), 33.
[16] Quoted in Bowes, *Land Too Good*, 124.

seeker, as special commissioner to the Ohio Indians, and directed him to negotiate a treaty with the Senecas. About the same time, and unaware of the Senecas' petition, a group of seventy-eight Seneca County settlers sent their own petition to Jackson, demanding that the Senecas "be removed to a country better adapted to their habits of life."[17]

The treaty Gardiner negotiated was signed at Little Sandusky in 1831. In exchange for the forty thousand acres the Senecas occupied in Ohio, the US government granted the tribe sixty-seven thousand acres adjoining a previously established Cherokee reservation west of the Mississippi. The US also agreed, among other things, to defray the expenses of removal from Ohio, advance $6,000 to cover the funds needed to establish farms and build homes, and provide one hundred rifles, four hundred blankets, and an assortment of plows, hoes, and axes.[18]

The Senecas were the second group to sell their lands and migrate west of the Mississippi after the passage of the Indian Removal Act in 1831 (a band of Choctaws being the first). The federal government was eager to make their removal as positive an experience as possible, as an inducement to nations who resisted removal. Jackson appointed another office seeker, John McElvain, to oversee the removal. The journey, however, was a tragic fiasco from the beginning. The Senecas did not trust McElvain, and most declared that they would not make the trek under his leadership. McElvain, in turn, did not trust Henry Brish, the subagent assigned to the Senecas. A plan to travel by canal and steamboat had to be modified when most of the Senecas refused to travel by water. This necessitated dividing the people into two groups. About a third of the tribe took the journey by water, but the rest joined those who were driving the community's horses and livestock by an overland route. Neither group departed until late fall.

A harsh winter slammed into the Senecas. The roads became impassable for the land party, which eventually could make only about five miles a day. The group ran out of provisions near present-day Muncie, Indiana. Distemper killed eighteen horses. Four people died, including two children. Some among the group refused to go any farther. Others returned to Ohio.

---

[17]Stockwell, *Other Trail of Tears*, 201.
[18]"Treaty with the Seneca, 1831," Tribal Treaties Database, https://treaties.okstate.edu/treaties/treaty-with-the-seneca-1831-0325.

Those traveling by steamboat fared no better. With removal costs mounting, Brish sold the best of the Senecas' horses to buy provisions, breaking a promise that he would not do so. Winter conditions grew so severe upon the group's arrival in St. Louis that the travelers could go no farther. They pitched camp eight miles outside the city, while Brish remained in St. Louis to secure provisions. When he rejoined them, the group resumed their westward trek but could go no more than forty-five miles. They pitched camp again near the town of Troy. By this point, several were dying, and many others were frostbitten and sick. Then measles broke out among the children. To make matters worse, McElvain never sent the blankets and rifles promised by the treaty.

After securing more provisions for the water group in Missouri, Brish traveled back across the Mississippi in search of the land party. He found them near Muncie and stayed with them for the rest of the winter. In May, the group resumed its journey, with six of its number near death and another sixteen so ill that they had to be transported in wagons. By the time the two groups met up at the land reserved for them in Oklahoma, on July 4, 1832, at least thirty Senecas had died, and many more had suffered serious illnesses. In a final indignity, the tribe learned that the land the government promised them had already been given to the Cherokees. The situation required yet another treaty, which resulted in an exchange of the sixty-seven thousand acres promised to the Senecas for sixty thousand acres adjacent to the Missouri border.

In a report to William Clark, the region's superintendent of Indian Affairs, Brish wrote, "I charge myself with cruelty in forcing these unfortunate people on, at a time when a few days delay might have prevented some deaths, and rendered the sickness of others more light, and have to regret this part of my duty."[19] Clark, however, had a different take. He wrote that the Seneca had "been more ungovernable, by far, than any others of this superintendency, and certainly, by their own misconduct at times, very much increased the real difficulties which occurred in their removal."[20] This was the same William Clark who, along with Meriwether Lewis, had been the beneficiary of Indigenous hospitality and assistance when the Corps of

---

[19] James H. O'Donnell III, *Ohio's First Peoples* (Ohio University Press, 2000), 124.
[20] Bowes, *Land Too Good*, 130.

Discovery explored the Louisiana Purchase in 1804–1805. Appointed superintendent in St. Louis in 1822, Clark subsequently played a key role in dispossessing the peoples within his district from their ancestral lands.

Why was it necessary to remove the Senecas from their Sandusky reservation? How did their land become the rightful possession of the present citizens of Tiffin? Early historians of Seneca County had answers. One wrote:

> The dignity which poets and untraveled persons ascribe to the red man vanished the moment the European appeared. From this time he lost all the noble qualities of the child of nature, and measured his evil doings by his opportunities. . . . With the few exceptions [the Seneca] were animated monuments of moral deformity and physical decay, growing weaker and weaker, dying in their young days with a curse for the white race lingering on their lips. Only a short time and their history will alone remain to acquaint the future with their existence; the traveler will never find the camp of Ohio's Red pioneers. . . . May we not hope that before they pass these children of nature may learn from the past; may arrive at a high state of civilization and then come among us to realize the barbarous condition of their fathers, and conceive the littleness of their tribal glories?[21]

Then there is this even darker turn, from the pen of another Seneca County historian:

> For more than a century [the Seneca] had been in contact with the white race, in peace and in war; and instead of deriving the benefit which naturally ought to have followed, from this intimacy, they deteriorated to more abject barbarism still, and dwindled down to a handful of dirty, stupid, superstitious, worthless rabble. Had not this county once been their home, and been named after them, nobody would care to read or learn anything about them.[22]

Why are there no Senecas in the county that bears their name? Because they did not adapt to the "high state of civilization" White settlers brought to the land. Behind this explanation lurks the myth of Manifest Destiny, the conviction that, whether by Providence or the inexorable tide of human development, the Anglo-Saxon race was destined to overspread the continent and to establish a higher and purer form of European civilization for the benefit

---

[21]Michael A. Leeson, *History of Seneca County, Ohio* (Chicago, 1886), 217.
[22]A. J. Baughman, *History of Seneca County Ohio* (Lewis, 1911), 1:33.

of all humanity. The conquest of the Indigenous nations and the occupation of their lands opened the necessary arena for this higher civilization to develop its salient virtues of freedom, prosperity, and progress.

In the eyes of the county historians, the Senecas were barbaric, stupid, and worthless. Their presence in the land impeded the progress of civilization and an unfolding destiny. Their inability to adapt therefore justified their dispossession. Civilization could not flourish until these primitive occupants had been removed from the land.

As the historians tell the tale, the Senecas had every opportunity to become part of the civilization the White race was developing in the New World. Yet they refused to do so. Instead of "deriving any benefit which naturally ought to have followed" from their contact with the White race, they clung to their barbaric ways and became even more barbaric. They therefore became "animated objects of deformity and decay," growing weaker and weaker, until one day they vanished altogether. In this sentiment, the historians echoed that of Oliver Wendell Holmes, who wrote, "(The Indian's) instincts lead to his extermination, too often the sad solution of the problem of his relation to the white race.... So, the red-crayon sketch is rubbed out, and the canvas is ready for a picture of manhood a little more like God's own image."[23]

In the eyes of the settler historians, the Senecas' futile resistance to the advance of civilization sealed their doom, a fate that settler society could only lament with sympathy and nostalgia. One could only hope that those who remained would "learn from their past" and realize the "littleness of their tribal glories" before it was too late. The historians' assumption, of course, was that it *was* too late. Were Seneca County not named for them, "nobody would care to read or learn anything about them"; nobody, that is, among the descendants of settlers who occupy the land the Seneca once inhabited.

The accounts of the Seneca County historians represent local iterations of a national narrative that had become well established by the end of the nineteenth century. No one articulated this narrative with more panache and enthusiasm than Theodore Roosevelt, whose multivolume *The Winning of the West* constitutes both a celebration and a defense of US colonial

---

[23]Quoted in Sonia Reid, "A 'Bracketed Year' Approach to American Literary History: What Can We Learn?," *Pacific Coast Philology* 28, no. 1 (1993): 47.

conquest and dispossession.[24] American national mythology casts Roosevelt as the epitome of the energetic, can-do spirit the nation prizes. Teddy is a larger-than-life figure, an American icon, who exemplifies optimism, perseverance, initiative, achievement, self-reliance, and above all *winning*. The mythic Roosevelt is a man of the people with a broad grin and a fondness for exclaiming "Bully!" This is the courageous leader of men who led his Roughriders to victory at San Juan Hill, Puerto Rico, during the Spanish-American War. He is the visionary president who preserved the West's breathtaking landscapes for future generations and laid the groundwork for the rise of the United States as a global power.

The Winning of the West, however, reveals a Roosevelt of less noble sentiments. Convinced of the transcendent destiny of the United States, Roosevelt writes, "The conquest and settlement by the whites of the Indian lands was necessary to the greatness of the (white) race and to the well-being of civilized mankind." Indeed, "it was all-important that [the land] should be won, for the benefit of civilization and in the interests of mankind."[25] Roosevelt regarded Indians as a selfish people who impeded the advance of civilization. He therefore had little patience with those who challenged the American myth or the righteousness of its conduct.

> It is indeed a warped, perverse, and silly morality which would forbid a course of conquest that has turned whole continents into the seats of mighty and flourishing civilized nations. All men of sane and wholesome thought must dismiss with impatient contempt the plea that these continents should be reserved for the use of scattered savage tribes, whose life was but a few degrees less meaningless, squalid, and ferocious than that of the wild beasts with whom they held joint ownership.[26]

The United States, Roosevelt writes, acquired its land fairly and justly by treaties that had more than compensated the Indians for the loss of their homelands.

> In these treaties we have been more than just to the Indians; we have been abundantly generous, for we have paid them many times what they were

---

[24]Theodore Roosevelt, *The Winning of the West*, 6 vols. (New York, 1889–1896).
[25]Roosevelt, *Winning of the West*, 6:388, 3:44.
[26]Roosevelt, *Winning of the West*, 3:45.

entitled to; many times what we would have paid any civilized people whose claim was as vague and shadowy as theirs. . . . No other conquering and colonizing nation has ever treated the original savage owners of the soil with such generosity as has the United States.[27]

Roosevelt's narrative expresses an unquestioned belief in the superiority of the White race and an unveiled disdain for Indians. This is the Roosevelt who famously riffed on the well-known quip that "the only good Indian is a dead Indian" by declaiming, "I don't go so far as to think that the only good Indians are dead Indians, but I believe nine out of every ten are. And I shouldn't like to inquire too closely into the case of the tenth."[28] Roosevelt believed that "the English-speaking race" was "the mightiest race on which the sun has ever shone" and declared that the pioneers who forged the path westward had "accomplished a task of great 'race-importance' in killing off the Indians, a weaker and inferior race."[29]

Roosevelt justified settler violence by asserting that "the most ultimately righteous of all wars is a war with savages."[30] The Sand Creek massacre—during which the US military killed more than one hundred peaceful Cheyenne—"in spite of certain most objectionable details, was on the whole as righteous and beneficial a deed as ever took place on the frontier."[31] And Logan's famous lament? "A strangely pathetic recital of his wrongs, and a fierce and exulting justification of the vengeance he had taken."[32] Even the conservation initiatives that many consider Roosevelt's greatest legacy are not untarnished. Roosevelt vigorously pursued the privatization of reservation lands and confiscated eighty-six million acres of those lands for the newly formed National Forest Service, leading one biographer to remark, "The rise of conservation dovetailed with a national closeout sale on the Indians' landed heritage."[33]

---

[27]Roosevelt, *Winning of the West*, 1:42.
[28]Quoted in Wolfgang Mieder, "'The Only Good Indian Is a Dead Indian': History and Meaning of a Proverbial Stereotype," *The Journal of American Folklore* 106 (1993): 45-46.
[29]Quoted in Thomas G. Dyer, *Theodore Roosevelt and the Idea of Race* (Louisiana State University Press, 1980), 76.
[30]Roosevelt, *Winning of the West*, 3:45.
[31]Theodore Roosevelt, ed., *The Works of Theodore Roosevelt* (Charles Scribner's Sons, 1924), 8:157.
[32]Roosevelt, *Winning of the West*, 1:237.
[33]Char Miller, "Play, Work, and Politics: The Remarkable Partnership of Theodore Roosevelt and Gifford Pinchot," in *Theodore Roosevelt, Naturalist in the Arena* (University of Nebraska Press, 2020), 115.

Taken as a whole, *The Winning of the West* articulates the themes that configure the American settler narrative, the well-known contours of which may be summarized as follows. Colonial forefathers established a nation "conceived in Liberty, and dedicated to the proposition that all men are created equal."[34] Beginning in Jamestown and Plymouth, the nation's Anglo-Saxon forebears transplanted a purified form of European civilization onto the soil of a New World and, propelled by an inexorable destiny, steadily pushed westward and tamed a trackless wilderness. The destiny of the new nation was manifest by the unstoppable advance of its civilization, the settlement and development of the land, the vibrancy of the nation's ideals, and the progressive impulse of innovation. Inspired by a democratic vision and dedicated to the values of life, liberty, and the pursuit of happiness, an immigrant people established a new nation that would light the path of all nations.[35]

Settler Narratives and Settler Structures

Setting the historians' account against the backdrop of settler interactions with the Seneca of Sandusky hints at what has been suppressed, silenced, and embellished by the American settler narrative. The history that formed me as a child exalts hardy pioneers, lauds their exemplary virtues, and revels in the achievements of the great and exceptional nation they founded on the continent. As illustrated by the county historians' accounts, the settler narrative depicts the land's Indigenous people as primitive and violent, and it expresses a feigned sympathy for their disappearance. In so doing, however, the narrative masks memories of settler perfidy, violence, intimidation, land theft, and Indian hating. Above all, the narrative justifies a settler system constructed by White settlers for the benefit of White settlers.

The colonization of what became the United States did not follow the typical script of European colonialism. Beginning in the fifteenth century, European powers sought to expand their domains and enrich their coffers by discovering and dominating non-Christian lands and populations for the purpose of exploiting their labor and extracting their lands' resources. To

---

[34]Abraham Lincoln, "The Gettysburg Address" (November 19, 1863), Abraham Lincoln Online, www.abrahamlincolnonline.org/lincoln/speeches/gettysburg.htm.

[35]For an introduction to and elaboration of the settler narrative, see Anders Stephanson, *Manifest Destiny: American Expansion and the Empire of Right* (Hill and Wang, 1995).

facilitate these objectives, colonial powers constructed structures configured by unequal relationships that were designed to maintain colonial power and control. When the Indigenous population of a colony broke free and regained their polities, the colonizers left, and the systems were dismantled in whole or in part. This was largely the case in formerly colonized nations as diverse as India, Indonesia, and Zaire.

In a small number of instances, however, the object of colonial desire was the land itself. In these cases, colonists traveled to a newly discovered land with the intention of taking it, settling it, and transforming it into a source of productivity and profit.[36] The settler-colonial mode of domination thus developed along a different trajectory. Settler colonists were—and are—less interested in exploiting Indigenous labor than in erasing Indigenous presence, which impeded and complicated their ownership and development of the land. Settler modes of domination persist over time because settler colonists end up taking over, and they never leave.[37] As exemplified by settler nations such as the United States, Australia, and Canada, "invasion is a structure, not an event."[38]

Settler colonists thus destroy in order to replace. That is, they seek to eliminate Indigenous societies so that they can replace them with a new colonial society on the land they have taken. In a seminal essay on the topic, Patrick Wolfe speaks of the process of erasure as the "logic of elimination" and describes its implementation along three trajectories: physical displacement (forced removal), cultural erasure (cultural annihilation and assimilation), and legal and political marginalization (legal subjugation and the stripping away of rights and autonomy). By these means, he argues, settler regimes aim to eliminate Indigenous occupants of the land in order to replace them with the settler population.[39]

As in other forms of colonialism, settler societies develop structures designed to maintain unequal relationships, configured by "the organizing

---

[36]Lorenzo Veracini, "Introducing Settler Colonial Studies," *Settler Colonial Studies* 1, no. 1 (2011): 1-12, https://doi.org/10.1080/2201473X.2011.10648799.

[37]Veracini, "Introducing Settler Colonial Studies." See also, by the same author, "Settler Colonialism," in *The Palgrave Encyclopedia of Imperialism and Anti-Imperialism*, ed. I. Ness and Z. Cope (Palgrave Macmillan, 2019), 1-6.

[38]Patrick Wolfe, "Settler Colonialism and the Elimination of the Native," *Journal of Genocide Research* 8, no. 4 (2006): 388, https://doi.org/10.1080/14623520601056240.

[39]Wolfe, "Settler Colonialism," 388.

grammar of race."⁴⁰ The grammar renders colonizer and colonized identities in opposing terms. The settlers, for example, cast Indigenous communities as primitive, lawless, and indolent, and colonizing peoples as advanced, law abiding, and industrious. A related binary typically dismisses Indigenous title to the land, framing it in terms of Indigenous "occupancy" over against settler "dominion."⁴¹

An original displacement and the unequal relationship between colonizer and colonized thus constitute the two basic elements of settler colonial societies.⁴² These elements are reproduced over time and eventually become invisible, as do the Indigenous people themselves. Indigenous invisibility enables the settler society to maintain the fiction that it has resolved the contradictions generated by its seizure of Indigenous land. The settler-colonial state, in short, "forever proclaims its passing, but it never goes away."⁴³

The settler structure persists in large part because it is masked by a narrative that justifies the settlers' occupation of the land and their displacement of its Indigenous peoples. The narrative renders settler regimes innocent of land theft, abuse, and violence and cloaks settler domination, past and present, with a myth of innocence. By asserting the legitimacy of the colonial project, the settler narrative deflects challenges to entrenched settler supremacy and the system of unequal relationships that supports it. And by silencing other voices and experiences, the settler narrative presents itself as the one, true, and correct account of the nation's identity. Dominion over the indigenous peoples and dominion over the narrative thus go hand in hand.

A Settler Reckoning

Today the American settler narrative is under assault. Its proponents are no longer able to suppress silenced voices, which articulate opposing narratives, remember episodes of mendacity and violence, and expose the settler narrative's mechanisms of denial. The truth proclaimed by the settler narrative,

---

⁴⁰Wolfe, "Settler Colonialism," 387.
⁴¹Wolfe, "Settler Colonialism," 390.
⁴²Lorenzo Veracini, *The Settler Colonial Present* (Palgrave Macmillan, 2005), 9. For an elaboration of the diverse ways that settler structures exist in the present, see 68-94 as well as Veracini, "Containment, Elimination, Settler Colonialism," *Arena* 51/52 (2018): 18-39.
⁴³Veracini, *Settler Colonial Present*, 38.

in other words, is presently being contested by truths spoken by communities that have been on the receiving end of settler domination.[44] The voicing of these contrary narratives, in turn, exposes the unjust and unequal structure the settler narrative legitimizes.

These alternate narratives often indict Christian complicity in the colonial project.[45] Christian theologians constructed the ideological infrastructure that rendered colonization and dispossession as a divinely ordained mandate. Christian religious leaders cast the theft of Indigenous land as expansions of Christendom and as victories of Christian light over pagan darkness. Christian potentates claimed Indigenous lands in the name of God. Christian settlers committed atrocities against Indigenous people who occupied land they wanted. Christian leaders endorsed military operations to exterminate and remove resistant peoples. Christian missionary and educational programs demonized Indigenous cultures and attempted to erase Indigenous identities in warped attempts to civilize and Christianize Indigenous people. Christian settlers of European origin and descent, in short, participated with colonial powers in the construction, implementation, and perpetuation of colonial structures, and benefited by them. The whole operation was and is configured, in the American settler mind, by a conflation of Christianity and Euro-American civilization so thorough as to be inseparable.

I have written this book because I believe that settler Christians like myself have an obligation to dismantle the sinful structure that our Christian forebears established and that persists to the present day. The colonial structure, along with the narrative that justifies it, continues to aid and abet a system of unequal relations among the citizens of the United States. Dismantling that structure, I urge, constitutes an essential practice for the

---

[44]See particularly Steven T. Newcomb, *Pagans in the Promised Land: Decoding the Doctrine of Christian Discovery* (Fulcrum, 2008), as well as Roxanne Dunbar-Ortiz, *An Indigenous Peoples' History of the United States* (Beacon, 2014); David Treuer, *The Heartbeat of Wounded Knee: Native America from 1890 to the Present* (Riverhead, 2019).

[45]For example, George E. Tinker, *Missionary Conquest: The Gospel and Native American Cultural Genocide* (Fortress, 1993); Randy S. Woodley and Bo C. Sanders, *Decolonizing Evangelicalism: An 11:59 P.M. Conversation* (Cascade, 2020); Mark Charles and Soong-Chan Rah, *Unsettling Truths: The Ongoing, Dehumanizing Legacy of the Doctrine of Discovery* (InterVarsity Press, 2019); and King, *Inconvenient Indian*. See also Robert P. Jones, *The Hidden Roots of White Supremacy: And the Path to a Shared American Future* (Simon & Schuster, 2023).

pursuit of justice, the ministry of reconciliation, and the creation of a society that seeks the well-being of all members.

But how to start? How do settler Christians like me, and perhaps you as well, face our "complicity in narratives of ongoing colonization and aim at their undoing"?[46] The act of exposure I will undertake stands on the premise that the essential, first step must entail uncovering and rejecting the settler narrative's denials and fictions of innocence—thus revealing the settler structure as illegitimate. *The work of dismantling the settler structure and its legacy must, in short, begin by demystifying the American settler narrative.*

The task is not for the timid. The atrocity perpetrated against the family of Tachnecdorus is but one of a litany of offenses that the settler narrative covers over. The mechanisms of settler denial are powerful and deeply ingrained in the American psyche. The narrative I relate in this book will likely be painful, disturbing, and destabilizing. What you read may provoke horror and disbelief. I want to encourage you, nonetheless, that this is profoundly important work. Demystifying the settler narrative constitutes an indispensable starting point for bringing about "a recognition of the historical continuity of the logic of elimination" and thus of the ways its program of erasure influences settler thinking and commitments today.[47]

UNMASKING THE SETTLER NARRATIVE

I will begin, in the following chapter, by exploring the two arguments that European powers employed to cast the colonial program as a divinely ordained mission: the doctrine of discovery, which held that a Christian power had the right to take newly discovered non-Christian lands and to subjugate those who inhabited them; and the creation mandate, which asserted that Christian powers had a right, if not an obligation, to subdue and develop Indigenous land. Chapters three through six then identify the processes that, according to Wolfe, characterize the logic of elimination, with the addition of a fourth process: legal marginalization (the seizure of land through treaties, legislation, and executive orders), the use of mass violence, which is my addition (settler violence on the frontier and violence by settler

---

[46]Richard Davis, "Settler Colonialism," Political Theology Network, July 19, 2022, https://politicaltheology.com/author/richard-a-davis/.

[47]Patrick Wolfe, *Settler Colonialism and the Transformation of Anthropology* (Cassell, 1999), 212.

military forces), displacement (the forced removal of Indigenous peoples from their lands), and cultural erasure (programs to civilize and Christianize the Indian).

Chapter seven examines settler America's construction of mythic types and tropes, by which White settler America articulated its identity and that of the Indian. Chapter eight argues that the book of Joshua and the American narrative of Manifest Destiny share a common script that can generate Christian conversation as they are read in conversation with each other. Chapter nine lifts up manifestations of the settler structure in the present day and concludes with proposals for demystifying the narrative that supports it.

I begin each chapter with a vignette set in Ohio, as I have done in this chapter. I do so for three reasons. First, I want to emphasize the importance of excavating the history of settler/Indigenous interactions in your particular location: which people inhabited the land before settlement, how they were dispossessed, and how local histories depict them and justify their erasure. Second, Ohio serves as an apt place to introduce the threads of the narrative, because the state constituted the West at the time the United States was constituted as a nation; Ohio therefore is the site of many precedents that rippled westward as the nation expanded. That said, I do not begin with Ohio because what happened in the state is exceptional. Quite the opposite. I begin with Ohio not because Ohio is *unique* but because it is *typical*. The practices of erasure and dispossession that characterize the Ohio narrative are replicated, in myriad forms, in localities throughout the United States.

I write primarily to the descendants of White settlers—people who, like me, enjoy a position of privilege in the settler structure—although I will be pleased if other readers also find this study helpful. My privilege within the settler structure is augmented by my roles as a seminary professor and an ordained minister in the United Methodist Church. I write with the conviction that the pursuit of peace and justice is central to Christian mission in the world.

I argue that both settler and Indigenous people need healing from the warped thinking and practice that emanates from the settler structure and that manifests today in gun violence, toxic racism, a rapacious commodity culture, and a host of other maladies. I do not indict myself or others of my settler kin for the sins of the past. It is not my intention to blame and shame. We cannot be held accountable for what happened in the past. But we do bear responsibility, as I maintain above, for rejecting the enunciations of our colonial past in the present day, dismantling settler supremacy, and, specific to our task, exposing the mechanisms of denial that justify it.

The scope and scale of this project do not allow a comprehensive, exhaustive, or unbiased account of settler history. I seek mainly to trace the implementation of the logic of elimination by relating representative incidents and policies. I do so with the hope that readers will be prompted to excavate the settler stories of their own place and to expose the justifying fictions that mask them. I also limit the study to the forty-eight contiguous states and do not address many of the most egregious instances of violence and land theft, such as the California genocide and the overthrow of the Hawaiian monarchy. Finally, I will not, for the most part, include the stories of the many settler individuals and groups who challenged and condemned colonial policies throughout history. My focus is directed squarely toward exposure. I will, however, conclude by pointing to contemporary efforts, on the part of Christian bodies, to undo the damaging narrative of Manifest Destiny.

I write, live, and teach in Ashland, Ohio, in an area of Ohio that has been home to various Indigenous peoples, including the Erie Nation and bands of Lenni Lenape, Senecas, and Wyandottes. Ashland County's most prominent Indian story has to do with Greentown, a predominantly Delaware town of about 150 dwellings that existed in the southern part of the county in the early 1800s. The residents of the town sided with the United States when the War of 1812 broke out. The local military, however, feared that they would defect to the British and sent a detachment of regulars to move them east to an area controlled by US forces. The inhabitants of Greentown refused. Too small to remove them forcibly, the federal force enlisted the aid of John Copus, a local pastor trusted by the townsfolk. Copus persuaded the residents to leave, with the promise that their possessions would be inventoried, their homes would be protected, and their departure would be temporary. The residents had not gone far, however, when Ohio militia rushed into the town, plundered the homes, and burned the town to the ground. Greentown was never resettled.

Questions for Reflection and Discussion

1. What draws you to this book? What do you hope to learn through it?
2. Which peoples inhabited your present location at the time of settlement?
3. What is their story?
4. What has influenced the way you view Indigenous Americans? Have your perceptions changed? If so, what precipitated the change?
5. Do you believe that some aspects of the settler narrative—as recounted by Roosevelt and the Seneca County historians—have an element of truth?
6. Do you think that, broadly speaking, the structures of US society and government, for all their flaws, facilitate equitable relations?
7. Are efforts to demystify the settler narrative expressions of justice or of an unbiblical ideology?

2

DISCOVERING THE INDIAN

The Doctrine of Discovery and the Creation Mandate

The white race stood upon this undeveloped continent ready and willing to execute the Divine injunction, to replenish the earth and SUBDUE it. The savage races in possession, either refused or imperfectly obeyed this first law of the Creator. On the one side stood the white race in the command of God, armed with his law; on the other, the savage, resisting the execution of that law. The result could not be evaded by any human device.

Charles S. Bryant and Abel B. Murch, *A History of the Great Massacre by the Sioux Indians, in Minnesota*, 1864

Ashland County, Ohio, is divided into a grid of fifteen townships. Five of the townships constitute squares of six miles by six miles. Another six townships are smaller and irregular. The northern three townships measure five miles square instead of six. The delineation of the townships reflects various attempts by the Confederation Congress to set boundaries on land that the United States had recently acquired from the Indigenous occupants. The division of the land into township grids prepared the land for sale and settlement, transforming wilderness land into private property and (at least in principle) ensuring clear title and an orderly settlement.

All but the northern three townships were "Congress lands," that is, public land that was opened for settlement by an act of Congress in 1805 and that was sold directly by the US government. The northern three townships constitute a section of the Firelands, a tract of approximately 3.4 million acres, which Congress granted to the state of Connecticut to compensate citizens who had lost of homes and property during the Revolutionary War.

The American Revolution generated a huge public debt. Under the Articles of Confederation, adopted by the Continental Congress in 1777, Congress lacked the authority to tax or to regulate trade and commerce and could generate revenue only by appeals to the states, which the states routinely ignored. With sovereignty located primarily in the states, the Confederation government had no effective means of enforcing its decisions and resolving disputes between the states. Contributing to its relative impotence was the fact that many delegates attended sessions only when it suited them, so that sessions often failed to reach a quorum, leading to vexing and interminable delays.

Congress, however, considered the nation rich in land, which is to say, *Indian* land. The Ohio Country, as well as the larger region known as the Old Northwest (bounded by the land north of the Ohio River and east of the Mississippi), constituted a virtual land bank for the fledgling nation. By selling and settling Ohio land, Congress planned to resolve the national debt in short order, stimulate military enlistment with the promise of free land, and fuel expansion.[1] As Congress looked forward to the terms of peace between the United States and Great Britain, it anticipated that Great Britain would relinquish its claims to much of its land in North America. Congress therefore set about the task of mediating land claims among the colonies and establishing a system for the sale and settlement of the land.

Five states—Virginia, Massachusetts, Connecticut, Pennsylvania, and New York—held claims to parts of Ohio that were based on royal charters that set the western boundary of each colony at the Pacific Ocean. The five states pressed their case vigorously but were just as vigorously opposed by the rest of the colonies, who feared that granting the claims would create huge states with large populations and enormous power. They argued as well that British claims to Indian land had been transferred to the nation as a whole and not to individual states.[2] In 1780, Congress established a

---

[1] Patrick Griffin, "Reconsidering the Ideological Origins of Indian Removal," in *The Center of a Great Empire: The Ohio Country in the Early Republic*, ed. Andrew R. L. Cayton and Stuart D. Hobbs (Ohio University Press, 2005), 15.

[2] Virginia in particular argued that (1) its troops had taken British forts and quelled Indian resistance in the northwest, (2) it needed the land to fulfill bounties promised to its veterans, and

committee to resolve conflicting land claims and succeeded in doing so in 1781. Congress thereafter assumed the exclusive authority to sell Indian land and to create "free, convenient, and independent governments" on land gained "by the blood and treasure of the thirteen states."[3]

At the Treaty of Paris, which ended the Revolutionary War in 1783, Great Britain relinquished its claims to land south of the Great Lakes and east of the Mississippi River. The agreement came in the nick of time, as the United States teetered on the edge of economic collapse. Saddled with a debt of approximately $40 million, the United States had seen its currency depreciate virtually to the point of worthlessness. Congress therefore wasted no time drafting legislation that would facilitate the orderly sale and settlement of western land.

In land ordinances passed in 1784, 1785, and 1787, the Confederation Congress dictated the process by which Indian land would be incorporated into the United States. The Ordinance of 1784 stipulated that the land would generate new states (as opposed to expanding the territory of existing states), thereby inventing what has been called "a *new* species of empire."[4] The Ordinance of 1785, in turn, established the system by which Indian land would be sold and settled. It stipulated that western land would be surveyed into a grid of townships, measuring six miles by six miles (irrespective of geographical features) and subdivided into thirty-six sections of one square mile (or 640 acres). One section in each township was to be set aside for public education, another for "purposes of religion," and four others for land bounties to veterans of the Revolutionary War. Immediately after its passage, a team of surveyors led by Thomas Hutchins and individuals representing eight states began a survey of the Seven Ranges (vertical north-to-south rows of townships), beginning where the easternmost boundary of the Northwest Territory met the Ohio River.[5]

---

(3) Virginia land speculators had already defined significant land in the Ohio Country for sale. Those colonies without land claims argued, in addition to what has been noted, that all the colonies were making sacrifices and their own land speculators had also been marking claims in the Ohio Country. See "Editorial Note," "Motion Regarding the Western Lands, [6 September] 1780," Founders Online, https://founders.archives.gov/documents/Madison/01-02-02-0051.

[3] Griffin, "Reconsidering the Ideological Origins," 15.

[4] Francis Jennings, *The Creation of America: Through Revolution to Empire* (Cambridge University Press, 2000), 281.

[5] "Land Ordinance of 1785," History, Art & Archives: United States House of Representatives, https://history.house.gov/HouseRecord/Detail/25769822302.

The Ordinance of 1787 dictated that three to five states would be carved out of the Northwest Territory and stipulated the process by which they would be created. That process would begin with congressional appointments of a governor, secretary, and judges, who would oversee the process of survey, sale, and settlement of land until such time as the settler population reached five thousand "free male inhabitants of full age" who owned at least fifty acres of land. When this benchmark was reached, settlers could form a territorial legislature, which would work in conjunction with the governor. When the population of the territory reached sixty thousand free males, it would be eligible for statehood.[6]

Congress planned to sell western land at public auction, in sections of 640 acres, and with a base price of one dollar per acre. Few prospective settlers, however, could afford the terms of sale. As a result, land syndicates negotiated with Congress and were given huge grants of land at greatly reduced prices. Land syndicates generated an enormous return on their investment by parceling the land into smaller plots that were affordable for settlers. Surveyors, who knew where the best lands were located, also amassed fortunes by purchasing those lands and reselling them for significantly higher prices. As one historian aptly notes, "The Northwest Territory was a land of opportunity for the nation, for settlers, but above all for the land companies."[7]

Conspicuously absent in these deliberations were the people who inhabited the land. The Indigenous nations of Ohio were not party to or even mentioned in the Treaty of Paris, even though most had fought for the British or the colonists. The two colonial powers negotiated claims to land as if its Indigenous occupants had no right to the land at all. Likewise, the land ordinances did not acknowledge Indigenous rights to the land, save for one oblique declaration in article 13 of the Ordinance of 1787.

> The utmost good faith shall always be observed towards the Indians; their lands and property shall never be taken from them without their consent; and, in their property, rights, and liberty, they shall never be invaded or disturbed,

---

[6]"Northwest Ordinance (1787)," Milestone Documents, www.archives.gov/milestone-documents/northwest-ordinance. For a detailed account of the legislative process, see Farley Grubb, "Land Policy: Founding Choices and Outcomes, 1781–1802," in *Founding Choices: American Economic Policies in the 1790s*, ed. Douglas A. Irwin and Richard Sylla (University of Chicago Press, 2011), 259-89.
[7]Colin G. Calloway, *The Victory with No Name: The Native American Defeat of the First American Army* (Oxford University Press, 2015), 40.

unless in just and lawful wars authorized by Congress; but laws founded in justice and humanity, shall from time to time be made for preventing wrongs being done to them, and for preserving peace and friendship with them.

The declaration turned out to be more aspirational than realistic. Underlying it was the assumption that the Indians *would* one day cede their lands to the United States. The question was not whether but when and how.[8]

By what right and by what authority did the Continental Congress justify taking the land that Indigenous peoples had inhabited for countless generations? Why were they not included in deliberations regarding their homelands? How did principled individuals at all levels of society, many with strong Christian convictions, justify taking land that belonged to others? Why, in other words, did colonial regimes act as if they owned the land and could do whatever they wanted with it and with the people who lived on it?

The answer? The settler mind had long since resolved the conflict between its ideals and its theft of Indian land. In short, settler Christians claimed rightful ownership of Indigenous land by warping Christian theology to serve colonial ends. In particular, they justified the colonial project by casting it as an extension of Christendom (defined here as land dominated by Christian culture, rule, or religion). The justification for taking Indigenous land rested on two pillars. The first, commonly called the doctrine of discovery, dictated that a Christian power had the right to take land inhabited by non-Christians when discovered and to subjugate its Indigenous population. The second, commonly referred to as the creation mandate, held that Christians have been given a divine calling to take dominion over all the earth and to transform wilderness land into an ordered and productive territory. By the time of the nation's founding, few questioned these two beliefs. In sum, Christian theology provided theological cover for colonial violence, mendacity, and dispossession. It provided the fabric from which was woven the myth of innocence that masked "the diseased social imagination" of Western Christianity.[9]

---

[8]For a trenchant analysis of how the "just and lawful wars" declaration laid the groundwork for wars of "extirpation," see Jeffrey Ostler, "'Just and Lawful War' as Genocidal War in the (United States) Northwest Ordinance and Northwest Territory, 1787–1832," *Journal of Genocide Research* 18, no. 1 (2016): 1-20.

[9]Willie James Jennings, *The Christian Imagination: Theology and the Origins of Race* (Yale University Press, 2010), 9.

This chapter will discuss key individuals and documents, both religious and secular, that rendered the colonial seizure of land as a Christian right and a moral imperative. I will focus particularly on the early period of colonial settlement, when the framework of justification was constructed, and then cite salient expressions of the justifying narrative into the nineteenth and twentieth centuries.

Discerning the Work of Providence

In 1730, a group of Puritans gathered in Southampton, England, to embark on a journey across the Atlantic, with the aim of establishing a colony at Massachusetts Bay. As the time of their departure neared, they heard a farewell sermon delivered by John Cotton, a prominent Puritan clergyman. The sermon, titled "God's Promise to His Plantation," has been called "a promotional tract to encourage emigration, and a typological argument for possessing the wilderness."[10] Cotton based his sermon on 2 Samuel 7:10, where God tells David, "I will appoint a place for my people Israel." The sermon elaborates on the verse by explaining how the immigrants could recognize where God was preparing a place for them and how to discern God's purpose in transplanting them from England to New England.

Cotton asks, "Wherein doth this work of God stand in appointing a place for a people?" That is, how could the colonists know that their journey had been ordered by God, and how would they know what land God had appointed for them to settle? Cotton answers by identifying a three-part biblical sequence. First, God "espies or discovers a land for a people" that is fitting to them. Second, God carries his people to that land (Ex 19:4). And finally, God "makes room for a people to dwell there" (Ps 80:9).

Cotton observes that the first two points have been revealed. God is sending the congregation to Massachusetts Bay and is carrying them there via a flotilla of ships. But how would God "make room for a people to dwell"? This is the pressing question, and Cotton devotes considerable attention to answering it. He briefly lists two ways that need no elaboration: (1) God casts out the enemies of his people by "lawful war," undertaken "without

---

[10]Reiner Smolinski, ed., introduction to "God's Promise to His Plantation (1630)," by John Cotton, *Electronic Texts in American Studies* 22, https://digitalcommons.unl.edu/cgi/viewcontent.cgi?article=1022&context=etas.

provocation," and by "a special commission from God"; or (2) God moves the native people to sell some of their land, as the Canaanites sold Abraham a grave plot in Machpelah. Cotton then elaborates a third way: "when he makes a country though not altogether void of inhabitants, yet void in the place where they reside." Where there is a "vacant place," Cotton declares, "there is liberty for the sons of *Adam* or *Noah* to come and inhabit, though they neither buy it, nor ask their leaves."

Cotton develops this third point at length. He cites a number of instances in the Bible where God allows the chosen people to take land that is devoid of inhabitants. Appealing to "a principle in nature," he declares, "In a vacant soil, he that hath taken possession of it, and bestoweth culture and husbandry upon it, his right it is." And why do Christians have the right to take possession of vacant land? Because God has given Christians a mandate to fulfill "the grand charter given to *Adam* and his posterity in Paradise, *Gen 1.28*)," namely, to "*multiply, and replenish the earth, and subdue it.*"[11] Cotton's exposition thus offers a simple formula for discerning divine confirmation for the colonial enterprise. God "espies" a land via discovery for a Christian people and then sends them there to subdue and replenish it.

Cotton was drawing on more than a century of Christian thought on the subject of Christian colonies in newly discovered lands. Christians, the thinking went, had the right to enter and take possession of land occupied by non-Christian peoples. The thinking originated in a series of papal bulls (edicts) that together articulated what became known as the doctrine of discovery.

THE DOCTRINE OF DISCOVERY

Beginning in the fifteenth century, Portuguese mariners ventured into the Atlantic Ocean and along the coast of Africa, looking for new territories for agriculture, access to gold and ivory from West Africa, and a sea route to the lucrative eastern spice trade. By the 1440s they had established trading posts and forts along the African coast and began trafficking in slaves. Anxious to establish his rights over his African possessions, Portuguese King Alfonso V answered a call by Pope Nicholas V for assistance against the Turks, who

---
[11]John Cotton, "God's Promise to His Plantation."

were threatening Christian lands in the East. Sometime later, Pope Nicholas issued a papal bull titled *Dum Diversas*. The bull, published in 1452, authorized Alfonso and his successors "to invade, search out, capture, vanquish, and subdue all Saracens and pagans whatsoever, and other enemies of Christ," to take whatever they owned, and to subject them to "perpetual slavery."[12] It further decreed that his acquisitions had been "justly and lawfully" acquired and permitted him to appropriate the lands and goods "for his and [his heirs'] use and profit."[13]

Tensions between Portugal and Castille led Alfonso to appeal a second time to Pope Nicholas, who responded, in 1455, with a more expansive bull, titled *Romanus Pontifex*. The bull effusively commends Alfonso for his zeal to establish the Christian faith in lands he has subdued. Nicholas then confirms and expands the previous bull so as to "give, grant, and appropriate" to Alfonso whatever lands "shall hereafter come to be acquired."[14] In this way, Nicholas cast Portuguese colonialism as a Christian enterprise.

Nicholas grounded his authority over other nations in his position as the "successor of the key-bearer of the heavenly kingdom and vicar of Jesus Christ." In this capacity, Nicholas expressed his desire for "the salvation of all" and pondered the means "by which he may bring the sheep entrusted to him by God into the single divine fold." The Catholic kings and princes were, he declared, the "athletes and intrepid champions of the Christian faith" who defended and spread the faith by subjugating new lands and people.[15] Nicholas thereby cloaked imperial violence and dispossession with the language of Christian mission and claimed authority over all the lands of the earth.

When Christopher Columbus's first voyage vaulted Spain into the colonial picture in 1492, Pope Alexander VI expanded the scope of colonial authority by issuing a bull in 1493 under the title *Inter Caetera*. In the bull,

---

[12]"Saracens" refers to Muslims.

[13]"1452—Dum Diversas—Issued by Pope Nicolas V to Alfanso V of Portugal," The Complete Doctrine of Discovery, www.doctrineofdiscovery.net/1452-dum-diversas-issued-by-pope-nicolas-v-to-alfanso-v-of-portugal.html.

[14]"Romanus Pontifex," January 8, 1455, Papal Encyclicals Online, www.papalencyclicals.net/nichol05/romanus-pontifex.htm.

[15]In granting Portugal sovereign authority over colonized land, Nicholas overrode a moral principle established at the Council of Constance in 1414, namely that non-Christian peoples possessed inviolable rights and that their lands must not be taken from them.

Pope Alexander granted the Spanish monarchs the same authority Nicholas had given to the Portuguese and added a new wrinkle: discovery. *Inter Caetera* authorized Ferdinand and Isabella of Spain "to seek out and discover islands and mainlands remote and unknown and not hitherto discovered by others" and urged them "to lead the peoples dwelling in those islands and countries to embrace the Christian religion." Alexander, acting "on the basis of the fullness of our apostolic power . . . by the authority of Almighty God," thus reinforced the fusion between colonial programs and the church's missionary enterprise. Alexander awarded the Spanish "all islands and mainlands found and to be found, discovered and to be discovered towards the west and south," provided those lands did not already lie under the authority of a Christian sovereign.[16]

England entered the colonial enterprise when, three years after *Romanus Pontifex*, Henry VII of England issued letters of patent to Gioanni Caboto (John Cabot) and his son. Echoing the language of the papal bulls, the English monarch granted Cabot "full and free authority" to "find, discover and investigate" lands "which before this time were unknown to all Christians." When such lands were discovered, Henry authorized the explorer to "conquer, occupy and possess" them and to acquire "for us the dominion, title and jurisdiction of the same towns, castles, cities, islands and mainlands so discovered." Notably, Henry said nothing about bringing discovered lands or peoples to the Christian faith. Cabot's voyages were explicitly and exclusively mercantile endeavors, undertaken to acquire trade goods.[17]

The Protestant Reformation upset the colonial applecart. Protestant powers did not recognize the pope's authority, although they had no problem asserting that, as Christian rulers, they possessed the right of discovery. As more colonial actors entered the fray, European powers were forced to clarify the modes and procedures of discovery. This in turn generated the development of a large body of international law. Lawyers for the court of Elizabeth I of England, for example, argued that the claim of discovery meant nothing unless the discovering power occupied the land. A later

---

[16] "Inter Caetera," May 4, 1493, Papal Encyclicals Online, www.papalencyclicals.net/alex06/alex06inter.htm.

[17] "Patent Granted by King Henry VII to John Cabot," Doctrine of Discovery Project, https://doctrineofdiscovery.org/patent-cabot-henry-vii/.

principle held that a symbolic act (such as planting a flag) signified "the intent to occupy" and thus was sufficient to establish a claim.[18] When planted at the mouth of a river, the symbols of occupation were understood to claim all the land encompassed by the river's watershed.[19] A system for sorting through claims of discovery therefore emerged over time, as "it was more expedient for the individual nations to compromise their exaggerated claims than to fight over them."[20]

Colonial powers, both Catholic and Protestant, thus proceeded on the premise that a Christian power had the right to seize discovered land, ostensibly to promulgate the Christian faith. In most cases, the appeal to Christian mission was a thinly veiled ruse. Consider, for example, the charter that James I granted in 1606 to the Virginia Company, a joint-stock syndicate of wealthy London gentlemen. In the charter, James identifies himself as "Defender of the Faith," thus asserting his authority as a Christian monarch to grant and assign land to the company. Although explicitly a mercantile enterprise, James declared that the most important work of the colony would be "propagating of Christian religion to such people, as yet live in darkness and miserable ignorance of the true knowledge and worship of God, and may in time bring the infidels and savages, living in those parts, to human civility, and to a settled and quiet government."[21]

When the Jamestown colony failed to turn a profit, the Virginia Company rebranded it as a missionary enterprise and enlisted a number of respected clergymen in a bid to attract new investors.[22] A surge of "justification literature" consequently made the case for colonization on religious terms. One of the most notable examples is a sermon published by Robert Gray in 1609

---

[18]Robert J. Miller, "The Doctrine of Discovery in the English Colonies," in *Discovering Indigenous Lands: The Doctrine of Discovery in the English Colonies*, by Robert J. Miller et al. (Oxford University Press, 2010), 15-21.

[19]Jacinta Ruru, "Concluding Comparatively: Discovery in the English Colonies," in Miller at al., *Discovering Indigenous Lands*, 258.

[20]Wilcomb E. Washburn, "The Moral and Legal Justifications for Dispossessing the Indians," in *Seventeenth-Century America*, ed. James Morton Smith (University of North Carolina Press, 1959), 18.

[21]"First Charter of Virginia (1601)," *Encyclopedia Virginia*, https://encyclopediavirginia.org/entries/first-charter-of-virginia-1606/.

[22]John Parker, "Religion and the Virginia Colony, 1609-10," in *The Westward Enterprise: English Activities in Ireland, the Atlantic and America 1480–1650*, ed. K. R. Andrews et al. (Wayne State University Press, 1979), 245-70.

titled *A Good Speed to Virginia*. Gray, as did Cotton, drew parallels between the English colonists and the biblical Israelites. First, he argued that colonization would solve the problem of overpopulation, scarcity, and unemployment that beset England at the time, declaring, "We may justly say, as the children of Israel say here to Joshua, we are a great people, and the land is too narrow for us." Second, he cast the Indigenous people as idolaters who, like the giants Israel encountered in Canaan, were subject to God's judgment and unworthy of possessing the land.

As for the Indigenous inhabitants, Gray reported that "in Virginia the people are savage and incredibly rude, they worship the devil, offer their young children in sacrifice unto him, wander up and down like beasts, and in manners and conditions, differ very little from beasts." "Oh how happy," he proclaimed, "were that man which could reduce this people from brutishness, to civility, to religion, to Christianity, to the saving of their souls."[23]

THE CREATION MANDATE

The charter that Charles I granted in 1629 to the Massachusetts Bay Company (underwritten by another joint-stock syndicate) echoed the language of the Virginia Charter. The Puritans who migrated to the New World in 1630 assumed that they had the right to settle all the land within the boundaries of the area defined by the king because they were acting under the aegis of a Christian monarch. Cotton's sermon, as we have noted, articulated the conviction that Providence transports colonists to a new land and that colonists, in return, are to take dominion over, subdue, and replenish it. The claim that Europeans were taking land that was empty or undeveloped (signified by the phrases *terra nullius* or *vacuum domicilium*) provided an important corollary to the doctrine of discovery. The assertion derives from God's mandate to Adam in Eden: "And God blessed them, and God said unto them, Be fruitful, and multiply, and replenish the earth, and subdue it: and have dominion over the fish of the sea, and over the fowl of the air, and over every living thing that moveth upon the earth" (Gen 1:28 KJV).[24]

---

[23]Robert Gray, *A Good Speed to Virginia*, 1609, Early English Books Online, https://name.umdl.umich.edu/A02059.0001.001.

[24]God repeats the mandate to Noah after the flood: "And God blessed Noah and his sons, and said to them, Bring forth fruit, and multiply, and replenish the earth" (Gen 9:1).

The early Puritan colonists viewed the land in the New World as empty because, in their eyes, it was not *occupied*. The Indigenous peoples of the region typically moved their settlements according to the seasons and the kinds of bounty the land yielded. It was common practice to settle in one place during the spring and summer and to plant and harvest crops. Then, after the crops had been harvested and stored in bins, the community would move to hunting camps for the winter.

From the Puritans' perspective, however, Indigenous land was empty because no one *owned* it, occupied it permanently, or, in their words, improved it. Whereas Indigenous populations saw land as a resource that sustained the community, the colonists saw land as a commodity. Daniel Richter helpfully summarizes the differences between Indigenous and Puritan perspectives on the land:

> Native communities treated land as a "resource," which could not in itself be owned any more than could the air or the sea.... What people owned was the right to use the resources for a particular purpose.... Once a resource was no longer being used, ownership rights faded. Europeans, by contrast, treated land as a "commodity" that was itself inherently and irrevocably owned, along with all its resources. Use had nothing to do with it; a vacant lot was still the exclusive property of its owner, a fixed feature of the landscape.[25]

In the Puritan mind, ownership of the land established the condition for replenishing it, which entailed restoring the earth to the Edenic paradise it had been before the fall. Wilderness, on the other hand, constituted creation in its sinful, fallen state. As a result, the Puritans considered those who occupied it as living under the dominion of Satan. William Bradford, the first governor of Plymouth Colony, characterized the surrounding land as "a hideous and desolate wilderness, full of wild beasts and wild men."[26] Michael Wigglesworth, a Puritan preacher, described the land as

A waste and howling wilderness,
Where none inhabited

---

[25]Daniel Richter, *Facing East from Indian Country: A Native History of Early America* (Harvard University Press, 2001), 54.
[26]William Bradford, *Of Plymouth Plantation, 1620–1647*, ed. Samuel Eliot Morison (Alfred A. Knopf, 1963), 62.

But hellish fiends, and brutish men
That Devils worshiped.[27]

What did restored paradise look like? As it turned out, it looked a lot like England without the mess. Replenishing the earth meant *ordering* the land: putting fences around it, cultivating it, and populating it with domesticated animals rather than wild ones. The Christian paradise, in other words, looked like an English heaven, but not an Indigenous one. This was despite the fact that the Indigenous peoples worked the landscape considerably. Through controlled burning, they created spacious pathways through dense forests and edge zones that attracted an abundance of wild species. They cultivated the three sisters—corn, beans, and squash—in vast fields, employing techniques that were more beneficial for the soil than European-style plow agriculture. Indigenous people, in other words, also managed the land, just not in the way the English colonists did. In the colonists' eyes, Indigenous land was therefore available for the taking.

John Winthrop, the first governor of the Massachusetts Bay Colony, elaborated, "The whole earth is the Lord's garden and he hath given it to the sons of Adam to be tilled and improved by them."[28] Why, he asked, should "a whole continent as fruitful and convenient for the use of man to lie waste without any improvement?" As for the Natives in New England, Winthrop declared, "They enclose no land, neither have any settled habitation, nor any tame cattle to improve the land by, and so have no other but a natural right to those countries, so as if we leave them sufficient for their use, we may lawfully take the rest, there being more than enough for them and us."[29]

The subtext, of course, was that since no Indigenous land was improved according to English standards, virtually *all* Indigenous land was vacant. The surrounding people, in Puritan eyes, needed very little land to sustain themselves. Most of the land therefore awaited Christian workers to improve it. Winthrop made this explicit in another document. "We deny that the Indians

---

[27]Michael Wigglesworth, "God's Controversy with New England," in *God's New Israel: Religious Interpretations of American Destiny*, rev. and updated ed., ed. Conrad Cherry (University of North Carolina Press, 1998), 42.

[28]John Winthrop, "General Observations," Winthrop Family Papers, www.masshist.org/publications/winthrop/index.php/view/PWF02d073.

[29]John Winthrop, "Reasons to Be Considered, and Objections with Answers," Winthrop Family Papers, www.masshist.org/publications/winthrop/index.php/view/PWF02d079#sn=3.

here can have any title to more lands then they can improve, . . . all men by this have a like right, by virtue whereof any man may make use of any part of the earth, which another hath not possessed before him. . . . God gave the earth etc. to be subdued, ergo a man can have no right to more than he can subdue."[30]

During the early years of the Massachusetts Bay Colony, the colonists purchased land as needed from the surrounding peoples. But when a rapid influx of immigrants required more land, the colonists resorted to less noble means of acquisition. Their favorite tactic entailed releasing their cattle and hogs to roam freely into Indigenous cornfields and storage bins, even when they put up fences. The strategy enabled authorities to haul Indigenous offenders into court when they killed one of the invasive beasts and to demand a fine in the form of land. Other tactics included plying Indigenous people with liquor and getting them to sign a deed they could not read, or convicting Indigenous men of false charges and requiring them to sell land to obtain release from jail.[31] When the Indigenous peoples pushed back against colonial encroachment and the extension of colonial jurisdiction, the Puritans found ways to execute "just and lawful wars" against them.

Puritan ideas about vacant land corresponded to the thinking of political philosophers in the eighteenth century. The most influential were John Locke and Emer de Vattel, both of whose works were widely read by the Founding Fathers. Locke's *Two Treatises of Government* addressed such concepts as inalienable rights, religious tolerance, and government as a social contract. Germane to our discussion, however, is his discussion about the relationship between land, property, and civilization.[32] On the matter of property, Locke began with the premise that "God, who hath given the world to men in common, hath also given them reason to make use of it to the best advantage of life and convenience. The earth and all that is therein is given to men for the support and comfort of their being." God did not mean by this that the earth should always remain common and uncultivated. Rather, "he gave it to the use of the Industrious and Rational, (and *Labour* was to be

---

[30]"John Winthrop to (John Wheelwright)," Winthrop Family Papers, www.masshist.org/publications/winthrop/index.php/view/PWF04d089.
[31]Charles M. Segal and David C. Stineback, *Puritans, Indians, and Manifest Destiny* (G. Putnam's Sons, 1977), 48-49.
[32]John Locke, *Two Treatises of Government*, vol. 5 (London, 1823), www.yorku.ca/comninel/courses/3025pdf/Locke.pdf.

his Title to it.)" By mixing labor with land, individuals take the land out of its common state and make it their own, transforming land into *property*. "Thus labour, in the beginning, gave a right of property."[33]

With respect to land, Locke declares that labor takes the form of enclosure and cultivation. "As much Land as a Man Tills, Plants, Improves, Cultivates and can use the Product therefore, so much is his Property. He by his Labour does, as it were, enclose it from the Common." In short, by developing land through labor, one acquires a right to take the land as property. This, Locke argues, accords with God's command for creation: "Hence, subduing or cultivating the earth and having dominion, we see, are joined together. The one gave title to the other. So that God, by commanding to subdue, gave authority so far to appropriate. And the condition of human life, which requires labour and materials to work on, necessarily introduce private possessions."[34]

Locke argued that owning property motivates the owner to improve the land, which in turn increases the land's value. Labor also produces a surplus, which the owner may exchange for goods and services, thereby leading to the establishment of a market economy. The introduction of money into the equation makes it possible to develop large tracts of land and facilitates the development of civilization and the prosperity it brings. Locke therefore saw property, and particularly *land* as property, as indispensable for the establishment and advancement of civilization.[35]

Emer de Vattel's *The Law of Nations* addressed the matter of vacant and uncultivated land within the context of international law.[36] De Vattel drew on natural law and common sense to develop principles by which individuals and nations should define their rights and obligations relative to each other. Concerning the colonization of discovered lands, he asked the

---

[33]Locke, Two *Treatises*, II, pars. 5, 33, 45.
[34]Locke, *Two Treatises*, II, pars. 33-34.
[35]Some scholars argue that Locke's arguments were influenced by his position as secretary to the Lord Proprietors of Carolina and to the Council of Trade and Plantations. His arguments about land as property may therefore have constituted a defense of colonies during a time in which many were objecting that colonies would ruin England or that England had no right to take land that belonged the Indigenous peoples. On this, see Barbara Arneil, "The Wild Indian's Venison: Locke's Theory of Property and English Colonialism in America," *Political Studies* 44 (1996): 6-74.
[36]Emer de Vattel, *The Law of Nations* (1760; repr., Liberty Fund, 2008), https://oll-resources.s3.us-east-2.amazonaws.com/oll3/store/titles/2246/Vattel_1519_LFeBk.pdf.

"celebrated question, to which the discovery of the new world has principally given rise . . . whether a nation may lawfully take possession of some part of a vast country, in which there are none but erratic nations whose scanty population is incapable of occupying the whole?"[37]

His response proceeded on the premise that every nation must cultivate the soil in its possession in order to provide for its citizens.

> The whole earth is destined to feed its inhabitants; but this it would be incapable of doing, if it were uncultivated. Every nation is then obliged by the law of nature to cultivate the land that has fallen to its share; and it has no right to enlarge its boundaries, or have recourse to the assistance of other nations, but in proportion as the land in its possession is incapable of furnishing it with necessaries.[38]

Every nation, then, has an obligation to cultivate the land for the benefit of its citizens but may not possess any land in excess of what is needed. This being the case, de Vattel argued that those nations that "disdain to cultivate their lands" but instead "live by plunder" are "injurious to all their neighbors" and "deserve to be extirpated as savage and pernicious beasts." Likewise, nations that avoid labor but subsist by hunting have no right to complain when "more industrious" nations "take possession of a part of these lands."[39] Land available for cultivation must not be wasted.

When, therefore, an industrious nation discovers a land inhabited by "wandering tribes," that nation may lawfully take possession of it, provided that it establishes settlements that will develop the land. Land in possession of wandering tribes "cannot be accounted a true and legal possession; and the people of Europe, too closely pent up at home, finding land of which the savages stood in no particular need . . . were lawfully entitled to take possession of it, and settle it with colonies."[40]

Locke and de Vattel thus presented the ownership and improvement of land as a moral obligation. Land not owned, occupied, and improved was wasted land and available for the taking. Transformed into property through the labor of its owner, land was to be cultivated for the benefit of the nation

---

[37]De Vattel, *Law of Nations*, 216.
[38]De Vattel, *Law of Nations*, 129.
[39]De Vattel, *Law of Nations*, 129-30.
[40]De Vattel, *Law of Nations*, 216.

and, viewed as a commodity, generated the wealth necessary to fuel a developing market economy. Land as private property therefore stood at the heart of civilized society. Unsettled and unimproved land was wasted land, and the "wandering tribes" that inhabited it did not use it beneficially and productively. Such tribes possessed much more land than they needed, and therefore civilized settlers had every right to take, enclose, and develop the land. If they resisted, Locke declared that they should "be destroyed as a *Lyon* or a *Tyger*, one of those wild Savage Beasts, with whom Men can have no Society or Security."[41]

Discovery, Vacant Land, and Westward Expansion

During the first half of the nineteenth century, the concept of transforming wilderness into a source of wealth was folded into a developing national mythology, which included beliefs about the superior genius of the Anglo-Saxon race, America's mission to spread progress and liberty, and America's destiny to overspread the continent.[42] Thus, when Thomas Jefferson sent the aptly named Corps of Discovery to explore the Louisiana Purchase in 1804, he was not just sending Lewis and Clark to gather information about the territory the United States had acquired from the French. Jefferson was staking claim to that vast area and extending American sovereignty over the peoples who inhabited it. This was made explicit in the declaration the two explorers were to make when first encountering Indigenous nations, namely that those nations had a new father, the great chief of the seventeen great nations of the United States. As a symbol of dominion, Lewis and Clark typically presented tribal leaders with a peace medal bearing Jefferson's image.[43]

In 1823, the US Supreme Court established the doctrine of discovery as the basis for the settler nation's title to the land. At issue in the case of *Johnson v. M'Intosh* was the title to a tract of land that one Thomas Johnson purchased from the Piankeshaw nation in 1773. In 1818, William McIntosh,

---

[41]Quoted in Robert J. Miller, "The Legal Adoption of Discovery in the United States," in Miller et al., *Discovering Indigenous Lands*, 30.

[42]Richard Horsman, *Race and Manifest Destiny* (Harvard University Press, 1981), 81-97.

[43]The expedition's discovery of the Columbia River formed the basis for US claims to the Pacific Northwest. See Robert J. Miller, "The Doctrine of Discovery in United States History," in Miller et al., *Discovering Indigenous Lands*, 69-73.

purchased the same land directly from the US government, after the Piankeshaws had ceded the land by treaties in 1803 and 1809. Johnson's grandsons sued to reclaim the property. Who held title to the land, and for what reason?

The court ruled in favor of McIntosh and the federal government. Writing on behalf of a unanimous court, Chief Justice John Marshall begins with the premise that a nation has the right to make the laws that govern it. He noted that US law was guided by the principles that governed Christian nations. He then cited Henry VII's patent to John Cabot to argue that the relevant principle for determining title derived from an unquestioned statute of international (that is, European) law, namely that "discovery gave title to the government by whose subjects, of by whose authority, it was made, against all other European governments, which title might be consummated by possession." Discovery had given the British the original title to the land in question. When, therefore, the British relinquished its claim to the land now occupied by the United States (at the Treaty of Paris), Britain's title to the land was transferred to the United States.

In addition, since the idea of title assumed dominion, the discovery of a land rendered the Indigenous inhabitants as subjugated nations, who henceforth held only the right to occupy the land; discovery necessarily "diminished" their right to the land. Marshall writes, "They were admitted to be the rightful occupants of the soil, with a legal as well as just claim to retain possession of it, and to use it according to their own discretion; but their rights to complete sovereignty, as independent nations, were necessarily diminished." In a sense, then, the United States was something like a landlord, who could allow the native inhabitants to live on the land or evict them by lawful means if and when it so desired. Marshall summarizes the implications:

> The United States, then, have unequivocally acceded to that great and broad rule [discovery] by which its civilized inhabitants now hold this country. They hold, and assert in themselves, the title by which it was acquired. They maintain, as all others have maintained, that discovery gave an exclusive right to extinguish the Indian title of occupancy, either by purchase or by conquest; and gave also a right to such a degree of sovereignty, as the circumstances of the people would allow them to exercise.[44]

---

[44]Johnson & Graham's Lessee v. McIntosh, 21 U.S. (8 Wheat.) 543 (1823), Legal Information Institute, www.law.cornell.edu/supremecourt/text/21/543.

In essence, the Marshall court reasoned that (1) the court was bound by the rules and precedents that defined the US legal system, (2) international law acknowledged Great Britain's claim of sovereignty over the land by virtue of discovery, and (3) the United States inherited Great Britain's claim and sovereignty over the land when the British relinquished the land to the United States. In a nutshell, Marshall declared that the United States owned the land because its laws said that it did and because it exercised dominion over the land.[45]

The creation mandate, for its part, was cited often throughout the nineteenth century to validate American expansion. John Quincy Adams even had Genesis 1:28 read into the congressional record. Adams, a devout Christian, believed that God had given humanity a mandate to develop the earth and that the United States had a divine destiny to occupy the continent and redeem the world. Among the first to conceive of the nation in these terms, he wrote, "The whole continent of North America appears to be *destined by Divine Providence* to be peopled by one *nation*, speaking one language, professing one general system of religion and political principles, and accustomed to one general tenor of social usages and customs."[46] Adams believed that if the United States "cast away the bounties of Providence," the nation would suffer "perpetual inferiority." He therefore vigorously advocated the development of a transportation infrastructure that facilitated the rapid expansion of settlement. At the groundbreaking of the Chesapeake and Ohio Canal in 1828, he again cited the creation mandate and asked God's blessing on the project and "other similar work."[47]

A similar articulation of the creation mandate is reflected in the writings of Samuel Bowles, an influential newspaperman, who published a series of midcentury travelogues. Like Adams, Bowles was a vigorous proponent of western expansion, although he did not share Adams's belief that the United

---

[45]For a review of the ways that the doctrine of discovery has shaped federal Indian law, see Blake A. Watson, "The Doctrine of Discovery and the Elusive Definition of Indian Title," *Lewis & Clark Law Review* 5, no. 4 (2011): 995-1-24, https://ecommons.udayton.edu/cgi/viewcontent.cgi ?article=1049&context=law_fac_pub; and Miller, "Legal Adoption," 26-765.

[46]Quoted in Horsman, *Race and Manifest Destiny*, 87.

[47]Gary Scott Smith, "John Quincy Adams: A Republic of Virtue," in *Religion in the Oval Office: The Religious Lives of American Presidents* (Oxford University Press, 2015), 87-122, https://doi .org/10.1093/acprof:oso/9780199391394.003.0004.

States should deal fairly with Indians. In a travelogue about a trip to the Rockies, published in 1869, with the title *The Switzerland of America*, he writes the following:

> We know we are not [the Indians'] equals; we know that our right to the soil, as a race capable of its superior improvement, is above theirs; and let us act openly and directly our faith. The earth is the Lord's; it is given by Him to the Saints for its improvement and development; and we are the Saints. This old Puritan premise and conclusion are the faith and practice of our people; let us hesitate no longer to avow it and act it to the Indian. Let us say to him, you are our ward, our child, the victim of our destiny, ours to displace, ours also to protect. We want your hunting-grounds to dig gold from, to raise grain on, and you must "move on."[48]

The sentiments that Bowles expresses recall those articulated by Theodore Roosevelt, cited in the previous chapter. As the United States entered the twentieth century, developing the land for the good of humanity had become an oft-expressed justification for taking Indigenous land. Roosevelt articulated the formula succinctly when he wrote of the settlement of Ohio, "On the western frontier lay vast and fertile vacant spaces; for the Americans had barely passed the threshold of the continent predestined to be the inheritance of their children and their children's' children."[49]

As noted earlier, Roosevelt vigorously asserted the rectitude of Indigenous dispossession and settler occupation. Where there had once been a wilderness, there was now a thriving and progressive nation, which represented the apex of human civilization and technology. Indians, on the other hand, represented an "antiprogressive principle . . . the few who stood in the way of the many."[50] Roosevelt could therefore assert with unabashed confidence, "The truth is, the Indians never had any real title to the soil. . . . The settler and pioneer have at bottom had justice on their side; this great continent could not have been kept as nothing but a game preserve for squalid savages."[51] If the Indian could not adapt, then "let him,

---

[48]Samuel Bowles, *The Switzerland of America: A Summer Vacation in the Parks and Mountains of Colorado* (Springfield, MA, 1869), 124.
[49]Theodore Roosevelt, *The Winning of the West* (G. P. Putnam, 1889–1896), 3:1.
[50]Richard Slotkin, "Nostalgia and Progress: Theodore Roosevelt's Myth of the Frontier," *American Quarterly* 33, no. 5 (1981): 618.
[51]Theodore Roosevelt, *Winning of the West*, 1:90.

like these whites, who will not work, perish from the face of the earth which he cumbers."[52]

Roosevelt's bombastic assertions reveal the extent to which the justifying narrative of destiny and mandate had become self-evident in the settler mind. The future belonged to the industrious and progressive nation that would unlock the land's potential, freeing it from the wilderness state and its erstwhile occupants. "And thus," wrote an early historian of Ohio, "every foot of the soil of Ohio passed from the red man, who had so long roved its savage wilderness, into the hands of the white man, who was destined to make the wilderness bud and bloom as the rose."[53]

THE PERSISTENCE OF THE SETTLER STRUCTURE

The Supreme Court did not mention the doctrine of discovery again until it ruled on the case *City of Sherrill v. Oneida Indian Nation*, which was handed down on March 29, 2005. The case originated when the city of Sherrill, New York, levied taxes on property that the Oneida nation had recently purchased on the open market. The Oneidas refused to pay the tax, arguing that the land was located within the historic reservation that had been established by a treaty between the United States and the Haudenosaunee in 1794. The Oneidas argued that their acquisition of the land by purchase revived their sovereignty over it, rendering it immune to taxation. The city of Sherrill, however, attempted to foreclose on the parcels of land, whereupon the tribe sued the city in federal district court. The District Court and the Court of Appeals subsequently decided in favor of the Oneidas.

The Supreme Court, however, ruled 8-1 for the city of Sherrill. The opinion, written by Justice Ruth Bader Ginsburg, begins with a review of history. Ginsburg notes that the historic Oneida reservation, established by the Treaty of Canandaigua in 1794, originally constituted three hundred thousand acres (out of an original six million) in upstate New York. The treaty guaranteed the "free use and enjoyment" of the land to the Oneida.

---

[52]Quoted in Slotkin, "Nostalgia and Progress," 618.
[53]John S. C. Abbot, *A History of the State of Ohio* (Northwestern, 1875), 675, www.google.com/books/edition/The_History_of_the_State_of_Ohio/kJQKdrXTZQkC?hl=en&gbpv=1&printsec=frontcover.

The federal treaty, however, did not prevent the state of New York from pressing hard to purchase Haudenosaunee land, in defiance of federal statutes. The federal government, in fact, turned a blind eye to New York's schemes and even designed a policy that opened reservation land for sale. Faced with relentless pressure, the Oneidas eventually sold most of their land by 1840 and left the state. By 1920, the tribe held only thirty-two acres in New York.

After her review, Ginsburg acknowledges that the sale of the Oneida's reservation lands was illegal and that the nation suffered a "grave, but ancient, wrong." Nevertheless, she writes that the Oneida nation could not "unilaterally revive its ancient sovereignty" over the parcels, because "the Oneidas long ago relinquished the reins of government and cannot regain them through open-market purchases from current titleholders." Ginsburg gives three reasons for the court's decision. First, the present-day population of the area is now "overwhelmingly populated by non-Indians" (99 percent). Second, state, county, and local governments have exercised constant regulatory authority over the land since its sale; and third, the Oneidas had delayed too long in seeking judicial relief.

The court's decision, then, "recognized the impracticability of returning to Indian control land that generations earlier passed into numerous private hands." Any attempt to remedy the present state of affairs, Ginsburg writes, would be unfair and "disruptive" to non-Indian landowners who had bought their property in good faith. Ginsburg also worries that ruling for the Oneida nation would precipitate "a checkerboard of state and tribal jurisdiction" that would "seriously burde[n] the administration of state and local governments" and "adversely affect landowners neighboring the tribal patches." The Oneidas' long delay, and the changes in the land since they sold it, therefore precluded the nation "from gaining the disruptive relief" it sought.[54]

Ginsburg's opinion does not mention that the courts had been closed to the Oneidas until 1974; their delay was the result of having no recourse available to seek the "judicial remedy" the court cited. Ginsburg also does not consider that the non-Indian population was the result of "a systematic

---

[54]City of Sherrill, New York, v. Oneida Indian Nation of New York Et Al., 544 U.S. 197 (2005), www.law.cornell.edu/supct/html/03-855.ZO.html.

program of Iroquois dispossession."⁵⁵ One may ask whose interests are being served by the ruling and who is being shielded from disruption. The decision provides a clear answer: The potential disruption of the non-Indian population and its governing bodies cannot be allowed. Ginsburg argues that what has been done in the past cannot be undone in the present. The rationale for the decision thus reveals a robust settler structure still intent on maintaining settler power, control, and privilege.⁵⁶ It is worth noting, in this regard, that Ginsburg invokes the doctrine of discovery in the first footnote of the opinion.⁵⁷

While not citing the doctrine of discovery, subsequent Supreme Court rulings have continued to assume that the United States has the right to resolve land and treaty claims despite the impact on Indigenous communities. In a 2020 decision involving competing claims of criminal jurisdiction, the court ruled that virtually the entire eastern half of Oklahoma remained Indigenous land (*McGirt v. Oklahoma*). The vast area had been reserved for the Muskogee by treaty in 1856, and Congress had never disestablished the reservation. The ruling affirmed that the federal government, and not states, therefore had the authority to prosecute crimes on the reserved land. In the decision, the court firmly rejected the reasoning that had prevailed in *City of Sherrill*. Writing for the majority, Justice Neal Gorsuch declares, "Many of the arguments before us today follow a sadly familiar pattern. Yes, promises were made, but the price of keeping them has become too great, so now we should just cast a blind eye. We reject such thinking."⁵⁸

The decision generated confusion and appeared to open the door for extensions of tribal authority into the areas of taxation, zoning, and

---

⁵⁵Michael Leroy Oberg, "RBG's Notorious Opinion in the Native American Sovereignty Case Is Also Part of Her Legacy," *The Wire*, September 22, 2020, https://thewire.in/world/ruth-bader-ginsburg-sherrill-v-oneida.

⁵⁶Dana Lloyd, "City of Sherrill v. Oneida Indian Nation of New York," Doctrine of Discovery Project, https://doctrineofdiscovery.org/sherrill-v-oneida-opinion-of-the-court/.

⁵⁷Ginsburg notes that "the lands occupied by Indians when the colonists arrived became vested in the sovereign—first the discovering European nation and later the original States and the United States."

⁵⁸McGirt v. Oklahoma, 591 U.S. __ (2020), Justia, https://supreme.justia.com/cases/federal/us/591/18-9526/; Ian Millhiser, "The Supreme Court's Landmark New Native American Rights Decision, Explained," *Vox*, July 10, 2020, www.vox.com/2020/7/10/21318796/supreme-court-mcgirt-oklahoma-native-american-neil-gorsuch.

regulation.⁵⁹ The state of Oklahoma thus asked the court to reverse its decision and affirm state jurisdiction. In 2022, the court issued another decision, *Oklahoma v. Castro-Huerta*, which ruled that the state and the federal government exercise *concurrent* jurisdiction over criminal prosecution. The ruling thereby undermined the long-standing precedent, established by the Marshall court, that denied state jurisdiction over tribal nations within its boundaries, on the premise that a state has jurisdiction over all land within its borders.⁶⁰

Discovery and Dominion

The doctrine of discovery and the creation mandate evolved over the course of centuries as the circumstances of colonial expansion warranted. By the time the United States was constituted a nation, the two justifications had become unquestioned assumptions, which can be summarized as follows:

1. Christian powers, by virtue of being Christian, have the right to take dominion over any land they discover, provided that it is not already under the dominion of a Christian power.
2. The United States acquired the title to its land legitimately. When the British relinquished their claims to the land, the British title to the land passed to the United States.
3. Christian colonization is a missionary enterprise that is undertaken by the hand of Providence to spread the gospel and to restore creation.
4. Christians have been given a mandate to subdue and take dominion over wilderness land and to render it ordered and productive.
5. Land that is not ordered, settled, and improved belongs to no one and is available for the taking.
6. When improved and transformed into private property, land generates the wealth that is necessary for the prosperity of a market economy. Land as property forms the bedrock of a Christian civilization.

---

⁵⁹See Rachel Monroe, "How Tribal Nations Are Reclaiming Oklahoma," *The New Yorker*, August 5, 2024, www.newyorker.com/magazine/2024/08/12/how-tribal-nations-are-reclaiming-oklahoma.

⁶⁰Castro-Huerta v. Oklahoma, 597 U.S. __ (2022), Justia, https://supreme.justia.com/cases/federal/us/597/21-429/.

Discovering the Indian 49

7. The cultivation of land for the benefit of the nation is a moral imperative.
8. An individual or nation has the right only to as much land as it can cultivate or improve. Indians have far more land than they can use.
9. To the extent that they maintain their traditions and lifestyle, and refuse to improve or sell their land, Indians resist the advance of a Christian civilization that will benefit all of humanity.
10. The United States therefore has the right to take land that it needs and that Indians are not using.

The following chapters will reveal how this thinking played out. Taken together, discovery and dominion justified taking Indigenous land, prosecuting "just" wars against indigenous peoples, and erasing Indigenous identity through civilization programs. Viewing themselves as the rightful sovereigns of the land, the people and government of the United States believed that they had the right to take land and to subdue its Indigenous occupants by any means necessary.

QUESTIONS FOR REFLECTION AND DISCUSSION

1. Do colonization and world evangelism necessarily go together?
2. Do you think that the doctrine of discovery and the creation mandate have shaped the faith and social practice of Christians in the United States? If so, how?
3. What do you think would happen if the United States government repudiated the doctrine of discovery? Do you see that ever happening?
4. Should Christian denominations and communities repudiate the doctrine of discovery? Why or why not?
5. How have the concepts of private property and land development influenced American society and American Christianity?
6. Is Christendom inherently violent and expansionist?

3

EXTORTING THE INDIAN

TREATIES, LEGISLATION, AND EXECUTIVE ORDERS

*It is impossible to destroy men with more respect
for the laws of humanity.*

ALEXIS DE TOCQUEVILLE, *DEMOCRACY IN AMERICA*, 1835

THE SOUTHERN AREA OF ASHLAND COUNTY, Ohio, intersects the line demarcated by the Treaty of Greenville in 1795. Greenville was a landmark treaty between the United States and representatives from twelve Indigenous nations that inhabited lands throughout the Old Northwest.[1] The treaty ended a decade of conflict between the United States and a confederacy of Indigenous nations that resisted American expansion into the Ohio Country.

As the price of peace with the United States, the Indigenous representatives agreed to "indemnify the United States for the injuries and expenses they have sustained during the war" by ceding approximately two-thirds of what would become the state of Ohio. In addition to this cession, the Indigenous signatories agreed to cede smaller tracts of land located at key junctures throughout the Northwest Territory (including the sites of present-day Chicago; Toledo, Ohio; Fort Wayne, Michigan; and Detroit, Michigan) "as evidence of the returning friendship of the said Indian tribes." Finally, the signatories promised to return captives and agreed to allow the United States free transit through all the land that remained in their possession. The United States, for its part, relinquished its claims to all land north and west

---

[1] Treaty of Greenville (1795), https://avalon.law.yale.edu/18th_century/greenvil.asp.

of the treaty line and recognized the right of the Indigenous nations to enjoy, hunt, plant, and dwell on the ceded land "so long as they please, without any molestation from the United States." The United States also promised to "protect all the said Indian tribes in the quiet enjoyment of their lands against all citizens of the United States, and against all other white persons who intrude upon the same." Finally, the United States agreed to send an annual payment of goods to each of the signatory nations.

The seeds of conflict between the United States and the Indigenous confederacy were sown in the aftermath of the Treaty of Paris, when Great Britain relinquished its claims to the land east of the Mississippi and south of the Great Lakes. As noted in the previous chapter, the Continental Congress turned immediately to acquire Indian land in order to address the new nation's crippling debts. Time was of the essence. Squatters and land jobbers (agents representing wealthy clients in the East) were already claiming and settling land in the Ohio Country, complicating plans for organized sale and settlement.[2]

The ink was scarcely dry on the treaty when Congress moved to obtain land cessions and pacify resistant bands in the Ohio Country. In March 1784, it appointed six commissioners to conduct treaty negotiations with the Ohio nations. The treaty commissioners thereupon pushed through a series of sham treaties, with the Six Nations (Haudenosaunee/Iroquois) at Fort Stanwix in New York (1784); the Wyandotte, Lenape, Chippewa (Ojibwe, Anishinaabe), Ottawa (Odawa), and Seneca at Fort McIntosh in Pennsylvania (1785); and the Shawnee at Fort Finney (1785) in the Ohio Country.

The treaty councils followed a common script. American treaty commissioners informed the tribal representatives that the United States and Great Britain had made peace and that they could no longer depend on Britain for aid and assistance against the United States. "Your Fathers the English have made Peace with us for themselves," declared one commissioner, "but forgot you their Children, who Fought with them, and neglected you like Bastards."[3] Tribal representatives soon discovered that the commissioners had not called

---

[2]Congress wanted to avoid the chaotic settlement of Kentucky, which generated considerable violence and resulted in years of litigation to sort out titles to land that squatters occupied but the government claimed for sale.

[3]Quoted in Colin G. Calloway, *First Peoples: A Documentary Survey of American Indian History*, 2nd ed. (Bedford/St. Martin's, 2004), 183.

the treaty council to negotiate a just peace but rather to impose the terms by which the United States would end hostilities. Those terms, above all, called for large cessions of land and recognition of American sovereignty.

Protests from the tribal representatives were met with emphatic rejoinders that they had been defeated and that the United States now owned their land. One commissioner told representatives of the Six Nations at Fort Stanwix that they were a "subdued people," who had been "overcome in a war which you entered into with us, not only without provocation, but in violation of most sacred obligations." In response to Indigenous protests at Fort McIntosh, the commissioners declared, "We claim the country by conquest; and are to give and not to receive. It is of this that it behooves you to have a clear and distinct comprehension."[4]

The commissioners demanded Indigenous land because, they asserted, American warriors "must be provided for. Compensation must be made for the blood and treasures which they expended in the war. The great increase of their people renders more lands essential to their subsistence." By these coercive means, then, the United States "used the procedural forms of treaty negotiations to force unilaterally upon the Indians the demands of the United States . . . most important, land cessions."[5]

To add insult to injury, the commissioners presented the terms of peace as an expression of American magnanimity. The commissioners declared that the United States, as the new sovereign of the land, had the right to occupy the whole country if it chose to. The commissioners presented gifts of goods and permission to hunt in ceded lands as expressions of American largesse. The fact of the matter, however, was that the commissioners were determined to secure a treaty for land cessions and were prepared to employ any means to do so. At Fort McIntosh, the commissioners threatened the tribal representatives and plied them with food and liquor until they procured their signatures. It mattered little that the representatives had no authority to make treaties and cede land on behalf of their people.

Not surprisingly, the Ohio nations scorned and repudiated the treaties. The disrespectful and humiliating treatment that the tribal representatives

---

[4]Quoted in Francis Paul Prucha, *American Indian Treaties: The History of a Political Anomaly* (University of California Press, 1995), 50.
[5]Prucha, *American Indian Treaties*, 43-48.

received stoked resentment and anger. The commissioners' condescending posture and demands strengthened Indigenous resolve to resist American aggression. After Fort Finney, many of the Ohio tribes formed an alliance and prepared for war, encouraged by covert assistance from the British, who had not vacated many of their forts and outposts as agreed in the Treaty of Paris. British agents supplied the confederacy with intelligence and material support, intending to create an Indigenous buffer zone between the United States and British Canada. For their part, the alliance agreed that its members would make decisions in common and would maintain the Ohio River as the boundary between American and Indigenous land, as stipulated by prior treaties.

Congress, on the other hand, shifted from its strong-armed approach and toward a conciliatory posture. In 1787, Congress decided to negotiate new treaties, partly at the urging of Secretary of War Henry Knox. Knox argued for peaceful negotiations and against calls for military action, asserting that the United States was "utterly unable" to wage an Indian war and that doing so would tarnish the honor of the new nation. He urged Congress to follow the "strong principles of humanity which ever forbid a war for an object which may be obtained by peaceable and honorable means."[6] In October of that year, Congress instructed General Arthur St. Clair, the newly appointed governor of the Northwest Territory, to convene a general council to treat with the Ohio nations.

Violence in the Ohio Country, however, was escalating. By the time George Washington assumed the presidency in April 1789, the Ohio Country had erupted into full-blown warfare. The founding of Marietta, at the mouth of the Muskingum River, along with surveys of land in eastern Ohio, signaled the United States' determination to occupy the land ceded by the invalid treaties. Furthermore, the encroachment of squatters on Indian lands precipitated a vicious cycle of reciprocal violence. St. Clair nevertheless succeeded in making two new treaties at Fort Harmar in January of 1789, with representatives of dubious authority. These were as uniformly repudiated as the previous ones. St. Clair did not help matters by reverting to the dictatorial mode of his predecessors and brusquely refusing a compromise proposal.

---

[6]Quoted in Prucha, *American Indian Treaties*, 54.

Knox, the secretary of war in Washington's cabinet, issued a report in June 1789 that addressed the worsening state of affairs in Ohio. He identified only two options: (1) raise an army to extirpate entirely (that is, exterminate) the resistant tribes or (2) "form treaties of peace with them" that would define their rights and that the United States would honor "with the most rigid justice." Knox argued that, although the United States had the right to "proceed to the destruction of expulsion of the savages," the government should follow a humane policy befitting the new nation's ideals. "It is presumable, that a nation solicitous of establishing its character on the broad basis of justice, would not only hesitate at, but reject every proposition to benefit itself, by the injury of any neighboring community, however contemptible and weak it might be." Knox went on to remark that the cost of raising and equipping an army large enough to extirpate the Indian confederacy would require a sum of money "far exceeding the ability of the United States to advance."[7]

Knox advised Washington to take the high road and to recognize the validity of Indian occupancy of the land. He acknowledged that the Treaty of Paris "absolutely invested" the United States with the title to "all Indian lands within the limits of the United States." Yet, he also viewed the Indigenous nations as "the only rightful proprietors of the soil" and believed that their land could best be acquired by purchasing it from them. He therefore concluded that the interests of the nation would be best served by making "the principle of Indian right to the lands they possess" the basis for the "future administration of justice towards the Indian tribes."[8]

Washington, however, decided on the military option. The decision resulted in two catastrophic defeats when US forces invaded Ohio in 1790 and 1791. A third invasion in August 1794, however, crushed Indigenous resistance at Fallen Timbers, near present-day Toledo. The victor, General Anthony Wayne, subsequently called for a treaty council, which met the following August at Fort Greenville.

Unlike many of his predecessors, Wayne honored Indigenous diplomatic protocols and treated tribal leaders with dignity and respect. Nevertheless,

---

[7]Henry Knox, "Enclosure, 15 June 1789," Founders Online, https://founders.archives.gov/documents/Washington/05-02-02-0357-0002.

[8]Knox, "Enclosure, 15 June 1789." See also Francis Paul Prucha, ed., *Documents of American Indian Policy*, 3rd ed. (University of Nebraska Press, 2000), 12-13.

Wayne also negotiated from a position of power and obtained a huge cession of land for what he believed to be a fair price. The façade of treaty making masked the fact that the United States was taking the land and dispossessing its peoples by force—a reality implied ironically by the seemingly benign declaration that the Ohio nations were to acknowledge themselves to be "under the protection of the said United States and no other power whatever."

Beneath the façade was the settler nation's conviction that it would eventually acquire all of the Northwest. The latter expectation was signaled obliquely by a declaration within article 5 of the Treaty of Greenville: "When those tribes, or any of them, shall be disposed to sell their lands, or any part of them, they are to be sold only to the United States; and until such sale, the United States will protect all the said Indian tribes in the quiet enjoyment of their lands against all citizens of the United States, and against all other white persons who intrude upon the same."[9] The statement that the United States had the right of preemption, that is, the exclusive right to purchase Indian land when it became available for sale, implicitly acknowledged US sovereignty over the territory. In particular, the phrase "until such sale" reflects the settler regime's assumption that the Indigenous nations *would* eventually sell their land. It was only a matter of time.

The Treaty of Greenville, in other words, cloaked a huge land grab in the language of fairness and humanitarianism. It satisfied settler aspirations for justice and legitimacy but gave the Indigenous nations little in return beyond annuities, the right to hunt in ceded lands, and a promise of protection against violent settlers. More significantly, it established a precedent by which settler regimes could execute "just and lawful wars" when frontier violence erupted, with the blame laid on those who were defending their homeland.

Legal Thievery

I have begun with the Treaty of Greenville and associated treaties not only because of their association with the Ohio Country but also because these treaties established precedents for subsequent treaties and for the thinking that informed them. Treaty making became the preeminent means of getting Indian land until 1871, when Congress dispensed with the practice. Virtually

---

[9]Treaty of Greeneville.

all treaties the United States made with Indigenous bodies required land cessions as the price necessary to end hostilities or to avert threatened violence. Nevertheless, purchasing land by treaty reinforced the fiction, among settler elites, that the United States acquired the land fairly, honorably, and legally. Adding to the fiction was the settler conviction that the terms the United States dictated were more than generous. The settler nation, after all, already owned the land, having acquired title from Great Britain. The United States, in settler minds, was thus paying the Indians for land that they, the settler nation, already owned.

The perceived generosity of the treaty terms, however, paled in comparison to the magnanimous gift the settler nation believed it gave to the Indigenous peoples, namely, the opportunity to enjoy the benefits of their civilization. In settler thinking, the gift of civilization more than compensated Indians for the loss of their land. If Indians rejected the gift and refused to relinquish their land, the fault for the consequences lay with them. An 1803 letter from President Thomas Jefferson to William Henry Harrison, the governor of the Indiana Territory, makes this clear. In the letter, Jefferson both expresses and belies the belief that the federal government negotiated for land with the best interests of the Indigenous peoples in mind.

> Our system is to live in perpetual peace with the Indians, to cultivate an affectionate attachment from them, by every thing just & liberal which we can do for them within the bounds of reason, and by giving them effectual protection against wrongs from our own people. The decrease of game rendering their subsistence by hunting insufficient, we wish to draw them to agriculture, to spinning & weaving. . . . When they withdraw themselves to the culture of a small piece of land, they will perceive how useless to them are their extensive forests, and will be willing to pare them off from time to time in exchange for necessaries for their farms & families. to promote this disposition to exchange lands which they have to spare & we want, for necessaries, which we have to spare & they want. . . . Our settlements will gradually circumscribe & approach the Indians, & they will in time either incorporate with us as citizens of the US. or remove beyond the Mississippi.

Jefferson goes on to elaborate the government's response to any Indigenous nation that would violently resist American expansion:

It is essential to cultivate their love. As to their fear, we presume that our strength & their weakness is now so visible that they must see we have only to shut our hand to crush them, & that all our liberalities to them proceed from motives of pure humanity only. Should any tribe be fool-hardy enough to take up the hatchet at any time, the seizing the whole country of that tribe & driving them across the Mississippi, as the only condition of peace, would be an example to others, and a furtherance of our final consolidation.[10]

Historian Colin Calloway succinctly summarizes the character and import of the founders' Indian policy:

> Reading the words of Washington, Knox, and Jefferson as they formulated policies to dismantle Indian lands and cultures and justified those policies as serving the Indians' best interests, one cannot help but see hypocrisy, arrogance, and deceit. Certainly Washington, Knox, and Jefferson never doubted they would take away the Indians' lands. However, they also spent much time, energy, and ink devising policies that would give Indian people something in return. The formula they developed—land for civilization—became a strategy for American expansion and a hallmark of US Indian policy for one hundred years. So did the readiness to wage war on Indians who refused the deal.[11]

From the Washington administration on, settler regimes convinced themselves that they acquired Indian land justly, oblivious to the duplicity of their policies.

Between 1778 and 1871, the United States ratified 370 treaties with Indigenous nations. Another forty-five treaties, at least, were negotiated but never ratified.[12] With few exceptions, the treaties centered on land cessions and provided compensation through annuities and incentives for adopting settler civilization. Treaty language typically included declarations of good faith on the part of the Unite States and safeguards against White settler encroachment and violence. Treaties, in short, constituted the primary instrument by which the settler government acquired Indian land and satisfied itself that the it did so honorably.

---

[10] "From Thomas Jefferson to William Henry Harrison, 27 February 1803," Founders Online, https://encyclopediavirginia.org/primary-documents/letter-from-thomas-jefferson-to-william-henry-harrison-february-27-1803/.

[11] Colin G. Calloway, *The Indian World of George Washington* (Oxford University Press, 2018), 329-30.

[12] "Does the United States Still Make Treaties with Indian Tribes?," U.S. Department of the Interior: Indian Affairs, www.bia.gov/faqs/does-united-states-still-make-treaties-indian-tribes.

That this was often *not* the case is demonstrated by the fact that the government often observed or enforced treaty obligations only when doing so served settler ends. At times, the government demanded cessions even from nations who fought alongside the United States in wartime. One example concerns the Oneida nation, which supported the United States during the American Revolution and provided vital intelligence, fighters, and supplies. Oneida shipments of food were crucial for the survival of starving troops at Valley Forge in the winter of 1777–1778. After the Revolution, Congress authorized reparations for damages the Oneidas had suffered at the hands of the British and their allies. Yet, the government responded feebly when the state of New York pressured the Oneidas to agree to a series of treaties that resulted in the loss of millions of acres of their ancestral homeland. Congress even colluded with state authorities to prevent the return of lands that had been taken by New York.

Andrew Jackson's betrayal of Muskogee (Creek) allies in the aftermath of the Creek War of 1813–1814 represents an even more egregious instance of duplicity. Inspired by the Shawnee leader Tecumseh, traditionalist fighters from Muskogee towns in the western part of Muskogee territory (called Red Sticks) launched a war to drive settler colonists from their lands. The war split the nation. Red Sticks towns were situated primarily in the northern part of Muskogee territory (the Upper Creeks), located in present-day Alabama. Prosperous Muskogee towns in the southern part of their lands (Lower Creeks, in present-day Georgia, Florida, and Alabama), however, had developed close economic and social ties with White settler communities and refused to join the campaign against the settlers.

When Tennessee militia led by Andrew Jackson invaded Muskogee territory to exterminate the Red Sticks and destroy the Upper Creek towns, the friendly Lower Creeks gave material support. About one hundred also fought at Horseshoe Bend on March 27, 1814, where US forces crushed the Red Sticks. In recognition of the victory, President James Madison gave Jackson a commission in the regular army at the rank of major general and authorized him to negotiate a peace treaty.

Jackson called for a treaty council in August, but those who attended were primarily Lower Creeks who had been Jackson's allies (the surviving Red Sticks having taken refuge in Florida). At the council, Jackson imposed a treaty on the entire Muskogee nation and demanded that the Muskogees cede twenty-two million acres of their land, to be confiscated from the territories of *both* factions. The demand was nonnegotiable. Seven of the first eight articles of the Treaty of Fort Jackson begin with the phrase, "The United States demand." When Tustunnuggee Thlucco (Big Warrior), Jackson's friend and ally, pleaded with him to relent from punishing the Lower Creeks, Jackson responded that he intended to make a lesson of the whole nation so as to dissuade other Indians from engaging in armed conflict against the United States.

> The United States would have been justified by the Great Spirit, had they taken all the land of the nation. . . . The truth is, the great body of the Creek chiefs and warriors did not respect the power of the United States. They thought we were an insignificant nation, that we would be overpowered by the British. . . . We bleed our enemies in such cases to give them their sense.[13]

THEFT BY TREATY IN THE AMERICAN WEST

Treaties proliferated as the United States expanded across the Mississippi River. From 1843 to 1848, 14,000 settlers traveled the Oregon Trail, bound for the fertile land of the Willamette Valley of the Oregon Territory. Prospectors lured by the discovery of gold in California in 1848 increased the settler population of the California territory from about 1,000 to 100,000 by the end of 1849, and to approximately 300,000 by 1854. To secure lands and rights of transit, US administrations continued to manipulate the treaty process to serve White and economic interests.[14] The settlers who crossed Indigenous land on their way to California and Oregon devastated bison herds and grazing lands, severely disrupting the lives and subsistence of Plains nations. Acknowledging the destruction of buffalo herds and their habitats a few months into the Gold Rush, Commissioner of Indian Affairs William Medill proposed a plan to lessen hostilities by offering the Plains nations "some annual compensation for the right of way through the country, and, in consideration of the destruction of the buffalo therein."[15]

---

[13]Quoted in Roxanne Dunbar-Ortiz, *An Indigenous Peoples' History of the United States* (Beacon, 2014), 100.
[14]Prucha, *American Indian Treaties*, 275.
[15]Quoted in Prucha, *American Indian Treaties*, 237.

Medill's successor, Orlando Brown, implemented the proposal in grand terms. In 1851 he sent commissioners to negotiate a treaty with nine of the Plains nations at Horse Creek, thirty-six miles downriver from Fort Laramie in the Wyoming Territory. Nine to fifteen thousand attended in response. Besides securing the peace, the commissioners hoped the negotiations would "impress the Indians of the Prairies with some just idea of our greatness and power, and to inspire them with a proper degree of respect for the government."[16] The treaty defined and recognized the boundaries and hunting grounds of the signatory nations, allowed the United States to build roads and forts on unceded land, and authorized annuities to compensate the nations for settler depredations.[17]

In the aftermath of the Civil War, and inspired by a renewed sense of national unity and purpose, the federal government stepped up its efforts to take possession of Indian land on what it considered "our soil." The Grant administration implemented a Peace Commission to acquire additional land cessions and to establish a reservation system that the administration believed would provide the means of assisting Indigenous nations in their transformation from a nomadic to an agricultural lifestyle. The treaties therefore commonly contained provisions that promised "the construction of warehouses, mechanics shops, and other buildings; a 'land book' to record individual allotments; compulsory education; agricultural seeds and implements; and a farmer, blacksmith, and physician," along with European-style clothing.[18]

In spring 1868, commissioners negotiated treaties with the Crows, Northern Cheyenne, Northern Arapahos, Lakota, and other nations at Fort Laramie. The government called for the treaty council to open up the Bozeman Trail, which led to the Montana gold fields and which Lakota fighters under Red Cloud had effectively closed. Along with civilizing provisions, the treaty with the Lakota established the Great Sioux Reservation, confirming the boundaries of Lakota land defined by the previous treaty at Laramie in 1851, an area consisting of sixty million acres. The reservation

---

[16]Prucha, *American Indian Treaties*, 238.
[17]"Treaty of Fort Laramie with Sioux, etc. 1851," Tribal Histories Database, https://treaties.okstate.edu/treaties/treaty-of-fort-laramie-with-sioux-etc-1851-0594.
[18]Prucha, *American Indian Treaties*, 281.

included the Black Hills, a region sacred to the Lakota and Cheyenne.[19] Following the treaty-making template, the United States specifically promised that "no white person or persons shall be permitted to settle upon or occupy any portion or the same; or without the consent of the Indians first and obtained, to pass through the same." The Indigenous signatories, in turn, granted the US government permission to survey reservation land and build railroads through it.

Treaty making in the 1860s took place within the context of a vigorous debate about whether the United States should stop making treaties with Indians. Proponents of treaty making raised constitutional concerns and argued that the United States had always recognized the Indigenous peoples as independent, sovereign nations. Their opponents asserted that, while the Indigenous nations had once been great and imposing, their power had diminished significantly, and they were no longer "independent nations with whom we are to treat as our equals."[20] A strong humanitarian impulse guided this argument. Treaties, it was asserted, ignored the reality that Indian nations were no longer capable of dealing with the United States on an equal footing. One prominent advocate for this position was Episcopalian Bishop Henry B. Whipple. Whipple, first of all, believed that it was "impolitic for our Government to treat a heathen community living within our borders as an independent nation, instead of regarding them as our wards." He asserted, furthermore, that treaties were "usually conceived and executed in fraud" and benefited only "Indian agents, traders, and politicians."[21] After years of debate, Congress determined, in the words of one representative, that "we must hereafter deal with the Indians by legislation and not by negotiations, with the proviso that the United States must continue to honor previous treaties."[22] A resolution prohibiting new treaties with Indian nations was attached to an appropriations bill and signed into

---

[19]"Treaty with the Sioux-Brule, Oglala, Miniconjou, Yanktonai, Hunkpapa, Blackfeet, Cuthead, Two Kettle, Sans Arcs, and Santee-and Arapaho, 1868," Tribal Treaties Database, https://treaties.okstate.edu/treaties/treaty-with-the-sioux-brule-oglala-miniconjou-yanktonai-hunkpapa-blackfeet-cuthead-two-kettle-sans-arcs-and-santee-and-arapaho-1868-0998.

[20]US Representative Aaron Sargent, quoted in Mark Hirsch, "1871: The End of Indian Treaty Making," *American Indian Magazine* 15, no. 2 (2014): 4, www.americanindianmagazine.org/story/1871-end-indian-treaty-making.

[21]Quoted in Prucha, *American Indian Treaties*, 290.

[22]Prucha, *American Indian Treaties*, 303.

law by President Ulysses Grant in March 1871. It stipulated, "Henceforth, no Indian nation or tribe . . . shall be acknowledged or recognized as an independent nation, tribe or power with whom the United States may contract by treaty." From this point on, the United States would take Indigenous land unilaterally by more direct means.

The first seizure of land by these means was the Black Hills. In summer 1874, Brigadier General Alfred Terry, commander of the Department of Dakota, sent Lieutenant Colonel George Custer and a large military force into the Black Hills, in direct violation of the Treaty of Fort Laramie, ostensibly to locate a site to build a fort. Rumor had it, however, that the region contained rich deposits of gold. The rumors gained momentum when it was revealed that the expedition included geologists, a scientific corps of engineers, and a large press corps—strange additions for a reconnaissance operation.

A month into the expedition, miners accompanying the force discovered gold. Custer sent a dispatch back to Fort Laramie the next day. Soon after, newspapers across the nation announced a sensational gold strike. The *Chicago Inter-Ocean*, for example, declared, "It would be a sin . . . to permit this region, so rich in treasure, to remain . . . unoccupied, merely to furnish hunting grounds to savages."[23] By the time Custer's force returned to Bismarck, settler communities on the borders of the Black Hills were already organizing companies to encroach into the area. The military tried to curtail gold seekers, but by late 1875, twenty thousand of them had flooded into the region. When the Lakota refused government offers to buy the Black Hills for six million dollars, President Grant ordered them onto their reservations by January 31, 1876, with a warning that all who refused to do so would be considered hostile. Congress also threatened to cut off rations, promised by treaty, until the Lakota ceded the land. After a combined force of Lakota, Arapahos, and Cheyennes wiped out Custer's command the following June, Congress passed legislation that confiscated the Black Hills.[24]

---

[23]Quoted in William C. Patric, "Custer's Black Hills Campaign," *American History* (June 2003): 39.

[24]The Supreme Court later ruled, in the case of *Lone Wolf v. Hitchcock* (1903), that Congress's plenary power gives it the authority to stop making treaties with Indigenous nations and to void obligations to honor the commitments made in previous treaties.

Theft by Legislation

The US government laid the foundation for the congressional theft of Indigenous land with the passage of two landmark laws that were designed to stimulate the settlement and economic development of western land. The first was the Homestead Act, which President Abraham Lincoln signed into law in 1862. The law granted 160 acres of surveyed public land to any citizen or aspiring citizen who occupied and improved the allotment over five years, or who did so in six months after paying $1.25 an acre for the land. Although the legislation was intended to benefit farmers, much of the land was snapped up by land speculators.[25]

The second piece of legislation, the Pacific Railway Act, was signed into law by Lincoln the same year. The legislation authorized the construction of a transcontinental railroad and telegraph line, designated two railroad companies to build it, and established the means for financing the operation. The act also awarded huge grants of public land for rights of way, which the railroad companies could sell to subsidize the project. The legislation was the first in a series of acts that facilitated the development of a western railway infrastructure through land grants awarded to railroad interests, eventually totaling 174 million acres. A significant amount of the land granted to the railroads was located on unceded land.[26]

The government took even more land through the General Allotment Act, also known as the Dawes Act. Enacted in 1887, the legislation was the brainchild of reform-minded philanthropists and politicians who had been moved by reports of the dire conditions endured by Indians residing on reservations. Poverty was endemic, and corruption and mismanagement were rife among the Indian agents who represented the government on the reservations. The core of the problem, the reformers concluded, was that Indigenous people did not embrace the idea of private property and thought of themselves in corporate terms rather than as individuals. The communal orientation of Indigenous communities, in the reformers' view, prevented them from

---

[25]"The Homestead Act (1862)," Milestone Documents, www.archives.gov/milestone-documents/homestead-act.

[26]"Pacific Railway Act (1862)," Milestone Documents, www.archives.gov/milestone-documents/pacific-railway-act?_ga=2.262402252.1973260317.1683641608-312252762.1669824443. See also "Dawes Act and Commission," Library of Congress Research Guides, https://guides.loc.gov/chronicling-america-dawes-act-commission/selected-articles.

participating in the market economy and enjoying the benefits of a society based on enlightened self-interest, the possession and improvement of property, and the spirit of enterprise. Senator Henry Dawes, who wrote the bill, put the problem with reservation Indians in the following terms: "There is no enterprise to make your home any better than that of your neighbors. There is no selfishness, which is at the bottom of civilization. Till this people will consent to give up their land, and divide among their citizens so that each can own the land he cultivates they will not make much progress."[27]

Congress intended for the General Allotment Act to help Indigenous communities make progress toward civilization. The legislation broke up reservations into private plots of real estate and allotted the plots to families and individuals. Heads of families received 160-acre allotments of farmland or 320 acres of grazing land; smaller allotments were granted to orphans and single adults. The legislation required tribal members to be numbered in Dawes rolls in order to confirm their eligibility to receive an allotment. Even then, Indigenous recipients did not own the plots. Instead, the government held allotments in trust.[28] Implementation was compulsory, even though no Indigenous people were consulted. Tribes did not have the liberty of refusing allotment, nor could any family refuse to receive one.[29]

The allotment of reservation land opened up large amounts of surplus land, which the government bought at a reduced rate and sold to White settlers at a fixed price. The funds from the sale of those lands went into a government trust fund, with a percentage earmarked for developing the infrastructure that would facilitate Indigenous assimilation into American civilization. By the time Congress stopped the allotment program in 1934, the Indigenous land base had been reduced to a third of what it had been in 1887, declining from 138 to 48 million acres.

The disastrous impact of the Allotment Act, and the subsequent legislation that extended and revised it, reached beyond the enormous loss of land. It did little to improve life on the reservations, and it did not prevent the corruption and greed that motivated many Indian agents. Agents

---

[27]Quoted in Dunbar-Ortiz, *Indigenous Peoples' History*, 158.
[28]"Dawes Act (1887)," Milestone Documents, www.archives.gov/milestone-documents/dawes-act?_ga=2.137543152.1973260317.1683641608-312252762.1669824443.
[29]Alan L. Neville and Alyssa K. Anderson, "The Diminishment of the Great Sioux Reservation," *Great Plains Quarterly* 33, no. 4 (2013): 241.

assigned to distribute allotments often reserved the best parcels for their supporters or sold them at a profit to White homesteaders. The sale of surplus land to White settlers resulted in checkerboards of Indigenous and White parcels within reservation boundaries. In the process, the Great Sioux reservation was broken up into six separate reservations. Local and state governments taxed allotted land and foreclosed on it when its Indigenous occupants—to whom taxation was often a foreign concept—could not pay. Many allotments consisted of land that was virtually unusable for farming or grazing. Determining the heirs of allotted lands also created a raft of complications. In the end, legislation that reformers championed to improve the lives of Indians resulted instead in "poverty, disenfranchisement, and the breakdown of Indian families."[30]

Government attempts to assimilate Indigenous people and take more of their land base, however, did not end with the Dawes Act. In the years following World War II, Congress embarked on yet another project to mainstream Indigenous nations and to get Indigenous land. Simply put, the plan sought to terminate federal recognition of Indigenous nations and to end federal trusteeship over their land, thereby putting Indigenous rights and obligations on a par with those of all other US citizens. Termination meant, in effect, that terminated nations and tribes no longer existed in the eyes of the government.

The termination project began when Congress passed House Concurrent Resolution 108 in 1953. Titled the Act to Free Indians from Federal Supervision, but also known as the Termination Act, the legislation sought to end the "government to government" relationship by which the United States recognized Indigenous nations as self-governing entities, with jurisdiction over their territory and with specified rights and benefits; these included federal protections of the land base, assistance in health care and education, and the exemption of Indigenous land from taxation.

The Termination Act immediately ended federal recognition of all tribes within four states, along with a number of additional, specified nations. The consequences were dire. With the dissolution of the trust relationship, reservation land became real estate, which was appraised and then sold to the

---

[30]David Treuer, *The Heartbeat of Wounded Knee: Native America from 1890 to the Present* (Riverhead, 2019), 150. My summary of termination relies largely on Treuer's account.

federal government, tribal members, and non-Indians.[31] In addition, the federal government stepped out of the business of managing land and natural resources for tribes and lifted federal protections relative to the sale of land.

Tribal lands also lost their tax-exempt status, generating an immediate and heavy tax burden. In all, more than three million acres were lost. Members of the Klamath nation, one of a small number of nations specifically targeted by the initial legislation, were forced to sell six hundred thousand acres of reservation land. By the time that Congress halted the termination program, 110 tribes and bands had been terminated, and the amount of land occupied by Indigenous nations had been depleted by more than 3 percent.[32] The program was not officially halted until the Richard Nixon administration, which implemented a new policy of "self-determination without termination."[33]

Theft by Eminent Domain

The practice of taking land for development continued into the twentieth century, mainly through the confiscation of Indigenous land for public works and infrastructure projects. I have already cited President Theodore Roosevelt's confiscation of eighty-six million acres of Indigenous land for the National Parks system. Federal projects that dammed rivers for flood control, water storage, or generating hydroelectric power also brought about a loss of significant land, not to mention the relocation of hundreds of families.

One such project, the Kinzua Dam in Pennsylvania, was completed in 1965. The dam created a reservoir that submerged almost ten thousand acres of Seneca land. Nine communities were flooded, and six hundred people were relocated. The project directly violated the Treaty of Canandaigua, between the Haudenosaunee and the Washington administration in 1794. Article 3 of that treaty defined the boundaries of the Seneca reservation, acknowledged the land to be Seneca property, and promised that the United States would "never claim the same, nor disturb the Seneka nation . . . in the

---

[31]Michael C. Walch, "Terminating the Indian Termination Policy," *Stanford Law Review* 35, no. 6 (1982): 1123. Some of the land was transferred to trusts or tribal corporations that were maintained for the benefit the tribal members.
[32]Charles F. Wilkinson and Eric R. Biggs, "The Evolution of the Termination Policy," *American Indian Law Review* 5, no. 4 (1977): 139.
[33]Walch, "Terminating the Indian Termination Policy," 1191.

free use and enjoyment thereof."³⁴ Despite vigorous opposition from the Seneca nation, a federal judge affirmed the government's authority to take the land by eminent domain, ruling that a treaty "cannot rise above the power to legislate."³⁵

The most devastating project of this kind, however, was the Pick-Sloan Missouri Basin Program, which was authorized by the Flood Control Act of 1944. The program resulted in the construction of twelve dams, in two phases, along the Missouri River Valley. By the time it was completed, the project had forced the abandonment of twelve towns and displaced more than thirty-five hundred people on twenty-three reservations. The dams flooded more than five hundred thousand acres of Sioux land in seven reservations, destroying 90 percent of the timber and arable farmland on the Standing Rock and Cheyenne River reservations.³⁶

The plan began through the efforts of a coalition of political and business interests (the Missouri River Basin Committee), which pushed for the development of the vast area. The heart of the plan called for the construction of four multipurpose dams and massive reservoirs, the purpose of which would be to provide flood control, irrigation, hydroelectric power, and enhanced navigation. No representative of any of the twenty-three affected Indigenous nations was invited to participate in the Missouri River Basin Committee, and none of the forums held to inform the public were convened on the land of the twenty-three nations that would be affected by the plan. The government sought input only from tax-paying citizens, because Indigenous land along the Missouri was "underutilized."³⁷

The Army Corps of Engineers subsequently situated the dams on or near reservations so that the reservoirs would flood Indigenous land rather than

---

[34] "Treaty with the Six Nations, 1794," Tribal Treaties Database, https://treaties.okstate.edu/treaties/treaty-with-the-six-nations-1794-0034.

[35] Maria Diaz-Gonzalez, "The Complicated History of the Kinzua Dam and How It Changed Life for the Seneca People," *Environmental Health News,* January 30, 2020, https://www.alleghenyfront.org/the-complicated-history-of-the-kinzua-dam-and-how-it-changed-life-for-the-seneca-people/.

[36] Christina Rose, "Echoes of Oak Flat: 4 Pick Sloan Dams That Submerged Native Lands," *Indian Country Today,* September 23, 2018, https://ictnews.org/archive/echoes-of-oak-flat-4-pick-sloan-dams-that-submerged-native-lands. See also "Dam Indians: The Missouri River," Native American Roots, March 10, 2010, http://nativeamericannetroots.net/diary/405.

[37] Robert Kelley Schneiders, "Flooding the Missouri Valley: The Politics of Dam Site Selection and Design," *Great Plains Quarterly* 17, no. 3/4 (1997): 237-49, https://digitalcommons.unl.edu/greatplainsquarterly/1954.

settler towns. Again, fiscal responsibility provided the ostensible rationale. The cost of purchasing developed real estate and prime farmland, and of relocating urban populations, was considered prohibitive.

The Three Affiliated Tribes: A Case Study

The settler government's seizure of land on the Fort Berthold reservation in North Dakota demonstrates the range of land-theft mechanisms practiced by the federal government. The Treaty of Fort Laramie of 1851, to which the Affiliated Tribes were signatories, preserved over twelve million acres of the tribes' ancestral homeland. After the treaty was ratified, the US military garrisoned a trading post named Fort Berthold. A significant influx of settlers into the area led to a second treaty in 1866, in which tribes ceded territory by purchase, granted the United States the right to build roads and telegraphs on their lands, and agreed to submit to US laws and authority.[38] The Senate never ratified the treaty, but the federal government proceeded as if it had. Four years later, President Grant seized the land specified in the agreement.

An additional, larger reduction took place in 1880, when President Rutherford Hayes confiscated more land and awarded it in the form of land grants to the Northern Pacific Railroad. The land left to the Three Tribes was poor and lightly timbered, and it contained very little water. It was virtually unusable for cultivation.[39] The cumulative effect of these executive orders reduced the reservation to a little over a million acres, about 10 percent of the land reserved for the tribes thirty years before by the Treaty of Laramie.

In 1891, Congress passed another law that mandated the allotment of the Fort Berthold reservation to tribal members, thus opening surplus land for settlement. The legislation justified the allotments and White settlement with familiar arguments. It began by declaring, "It is the policy of the Government to reduce to proper size existing reservations when entirely out of proportion to the number of Indians existing thereon." To stimulate a work ethic, article VIII dictated, "Hereafter no subsistence shall be furnished any adult male Indian (the aged, sick, and infirm excepted) who does not

---

[38]"Agreement at Fort Berthold, 1866," Tribal Treaties Database, https://treaties.okstate.edu/treaties/agreementatfortberthold1866.

[39]"President Hayes's Executive Order, 1880," University of North Dakota, US Government Documents Related to Indigenous Nations, https://commons.und.edu/indigenous-gov-docs/160.

endeavor by honest labor to support himself, nor to children between the ages of eight and fifteen years (the sick and infirm excepted), unless such children shall regularly attend school."[40] None of the tribal members received any of the promised compensation of $800,000 from the sale of the surplus land. That money instead was directed toward the support of the Indian agency, a Christian mission, and reservation schools.[41]

This was not the end of the matter. The Affiliated Tribes suffered another drastic land loss when the Corps of Engineers decided to divert a proposed location for the Garrison Dam and Reservoir from the town of Williston, North Dakota, to the Fort Berthold Reservation for the fiscal rationale mentioned above. The Affiliated Tribes were not informed that their lands were to be flooded until government representatives approached them to negotiate a price for the sale of the 152,360 acres the government intended to confiscate. The tribes protested to Congress and bought some time to negotiate by invoking the Fort Laramie Treaty of 1851. General Lewis Pick was subsequently sent to settle with the Fort Berthold nations. The negotiations did not go well. In a particularly contentious session, tribal members attended in full regalia and an elder declared, "You have come to destroy us!" Pick closed down the negotiations and revoked previous agreements, arguing that the tribes had become belligerently uncooperative.[42] Facing the imposition of eminent domain, the tribes ended up selling the land for much less than its fair market value, approximately $33 an acre. Work on the Garrison Dam began in 1947 and was completed in 1953.

The land confiscated by the government contained vast stands of timber and prime range land, as well as wild herbs and plants that were used for

---

[40]Indian Department Appropriations Act of the 51st Congress, second session, 1891: Indian Department Appropriations, section 23, chapter 543.

[41]This summary primarily follows "Lesson 1: Changing Landscapes; Topic 4: Reservation Boundaries," State Historical Society of North Dakota, www.ndstudies.gov/gr8/content/unit-iii-waves-development-1861-1920/lesson-1-changing-landscapes/topic-4-reservation-boundaries/section-4-creating-fort-berthold-reservation. The article contains a number of primary sources. The summary also draws on "MHA Nation History," Mandan, Hidatsa and Arikara Nation, www.mhanation.com/history.

[42]Meteor Blades, "How the Garrison Dam on the Missouri River Ruined a Way of Life for the Mandan, Hidatsa, and Arikara," *Daily Kos*, December 15, 2018, www.dailykos.com/stories/2018/12/26/1820327/-How-the-Garrison-Dam-on-the-Missouri-River-ruined-a-way-of-life-for-the-Mandan-Hidatsa-and-Arikara. See also Lisa Jones, "A Dam Brings a Flood of Diabetes to Three Tribes," *Indian Country Today*, July 6, 2011, updated September 13, 2018, https://ictnews.org/archive/a-dam-brings-a-flood-of-diabetes-to-three-tribes?redir=1.

traditional foods and ceremonies. In addition, the government prohibited the Mandan, Hidatsa, and Arikara from fishing in the reservoir and from hunting, harvesting timber, and grazing their livestock along the shoreline. The loss of land destroyed the tribes' economic base. Many ranchers had to liquidate or severely reduce their herds. The government relocated approximately one thousand people, 90 percent of the reservation population. One writer described the impact. "The community life for these people, who relied heavily on kinship groups and other primary groups was destroyed. Some people moved to urban areas where they lived a life of despair. Among these previously successful ranchers and farmers, unemployment rose to 79 percent."[43]

In December 2016, the Department of the Interior announced the transfer of approximately twenty-five thousand acres of reservation land back to the Three Affiliated Tribes. At a ceremony marking the transfer, Mark Fox, chairman of the Three Affiliated Tribes, remarked, "The return of these lands is an important step toward mending a historic injustice.... Half of our adult men were fighting for their country and their homes in World War II when the federal government began making plans to take our lands for the Garrison Dam. The flood caused by the Dam ... literally destroyed our heartland."[44]

The flooding and expropriation of tribal lands by eminent domain, as experienced by the Three Affiliated Tribes, underscores the calculus of settler thinking. In the settler mind, Indigenous land can be taken because it affects fewer people, is less valuable real estate, and is undeveloped. The government's decision comes down to money; taking Indigenous land makes fiscal sense. Yet, one must question the morality of this thinking. What of the solemn promises that the United States has made by treaty? Are they void because the settler government determines that too many settler people will be affected? Since Indigenous nations are often a minority population in affected lands, is it right that they persistently bear most of the consequences when the government wants to confiscate or develop their land?

The seizure of indigenous land by treaty, legislation, and executive action rests on the unquestioned assumption that the United States possesses the

---

[43] Karen M. Griffin, "Reservoirs and Reservations," *Nebraska Anthropologist* 94 (1996): 23-30, https://digitalcommons.unl.edu/nebanthro/94.
[44] "Transfer Restores Nearly 25,000 Acres of Tribal Homelands Lost to the Garrison Dam Project," US Department of the Interior, Indian Affairs, December 20, 2016, www.bia.gov/as-ia/opa/online-press-release/interior-department-and-army-corps-announce-restoration-tribal-lands.

land within its borders via the doctrine of discovery. Early federal administrations considered cessions by treaty to be honorable and magnanimous, as settler regimes maintained the fiction that they were purchasing land freely and fairly from the occupants of the soil.

As the nation expanded westward, the United States assumed the right, as sovereign, to enter, explore, and eventually to take outright the land it wanted. The United States continued to acquire land through treaties after the Civil War. When it met with fierce resistance from the Indigenous peoples, however, settler regimes dispensed with treaty making altogether, subjugated resistant nations, and moved them on to reservations. Since then, the theft of Indigenous land has continued by other legal means, through acts of Congress, executive order, and eminent domain.

QUESTIONS FOR REFLECTION AND DISCUSSION

1. How does what you have read in this chapter challenge or confirm your understanding of US treaty making?
2. How did the United States acquire the land in which you now live? And from whom?
3. US administrations consistently believed that they negotiated treaties of cession with good faith. Does what you have read bear that out?
4. Were settler administrative regimes right in seeing the benefits of Christian civilization as a fair compensation for Indigenous land?
5. What does this overview reveal about the way the settler legal system works for minority populations?
6. Is it accurate to assert that the United States stole its land from the Indigenous peoples?
7. In hindsight, do you think the United States could have acquired land in any other way than how it did?
8. What story from this chapter sticks with you? Take a few moments to imagine yourself in the experience of those whose land has been taken and justified by the means elaborated in this chapter. What do you see? How do you feel?

4

EXTERMINATING THE INDIAN

Frontier Violence and Military Conquest

Aborigines, *n. Persons of little worth found cumbering the soil of a newly discovered country. They soon cease to cumber; they fertilize.*

Ambrose Bierce, *The Cynic's Word Book*, 1906

On the morning of March 7, 1782, a force of over one hundred militia from western Pennsylvania arrived at the town of Gnadenhutten, which was located along the Tuscawaras River in the Ohio Country. The residents of the village were Christian Lenapes who had been converted through the ministry of Moravian missionaries. The town was the second of three founded by the Moravians in 1772, after tensions with settlers and colonial authorities pushed their leader, David Zeisberger, and his congregation out of Pennsylvania. The Moravians found refuge with Lenapes in Ohio, who granted the congregation permission to settle with them in the Tuscawaras River Valley.

With the onset of the American Revolution, however, the Ohio Country became a war zone. Conflict erupted between the British and their tribal surrogates on the one hand, and colonial militias and a small military force stationed at Pittsburgh on the other. The Lenapes attempted to maintain neutrality but found themselves increasingly harassed by the colonial militia and by settlers who were moving into Ohio. The tipping point came in 1781, when a colonial force from Pittsburgh launched an unprovoked attack against Lenape towns in Ohio. The militia devastated several towns, including Lichtenau, another Moravian settlement. The attacks pushed the

Lenapes to the British side. Most left the region and moved to British-controlled territory along the Sandusky River.

The Moravians, however, chose to remain. They soon found themselves caught in the middle as the conflict intensified. Although the Christian Lenapes were pacifists and remained staunchly neutral, the British suspected Zeisberger and his associate John Heckewelder of spying for the colonists. The settler population, on the other hand, believed that the Moravians were aiding the parties of Wyandottes, Senecas, and Shawnees who were raiding White settlements.

In summer 1781, the British ordered the Moravians to be relocated to makeshift quarters on the Sandusky River, at place called Captives Town. A contingent of Wyandottes was dispatched to relocate them. Once the Moravians arrived at Captive Town, however, they were marginalized by the other Lenapes, who disdained their Christianity and distrusted their favorable inclination toward the colonial cause. They were given little food and lived constantly on the brink of starvation during a difficult winter. After repeated appeals, a group of about 150 were finally given permission to return to their three towns on the Tuscarawas River to gather the unharvested corn they that was left in the fields when they were removed. The group left in March and divided into three groups, bound for Gnadenhutten, Salem, and New Schoenbrunn. Shortly after the main group arrived in Gnadenhutten, a Shawnee raiding party passed through with news that a militia force was in hot pursuit. The Moravians decided to stay, as they believed they had nothing to fear.

The militia that approached Gnadenhutten on March 7 was made up of a mob of settlers from Washington County, Pennsylvania, who were intent on destroying the Lenape towns they believed were still located in the Tuscawaras River valley. The Pennsylvanians were particularly incensed by the murder of a young woman and her child, whose bodies had been impaled by the Shawnees. When Colonel John Gibson, the colonial commander at Pittsburgh, learned of the militia's plans, he sent word to the Moravian towns. The warning came too late.

The settlers were out for blood. While some distance from the town, they encountered a young man, who welcomed the party and introduced himself as a Christian Indian. He was shot dead and scalped. When the militia reached the cornfields, they hailed the harvesters and told them they had come to take them to Fort Pitt. The Moravians received the news with joy, as Lenapes had been treated well there. The militiamen took them back to the town. Once there, they confiscated their firearms and any other implements they thought could be used as weapons. A search of their camp revealed fine cookware and farming utensils, which convinced the militiamen that the people had participated in or sheltered raiding parties. Indians, they reasoned, did not use pewter pots and bowls and did not brand their horses. "That they were found in the hands of Indians could only mean theft. Indians, as they said, used wooden bowls and spoons."[1]

A detachment was sent to apprehend the people harvesting at Salem. The remaining militiamen then imprisoned the men in one building and the women and children in another. Then they conducted a sham trial, which found the Moravians guilty of complicity in settler deaths. A vote was taken to determine whether to execute a few or all of the group. The vote to execute the entire community received overwhelming support; only eighteen voted no. The group deliberated on the mode of execution next. The settlers rejected setting fire to the buildings with the people inside as too barbarous. They eventually decided to smash the Moravians' skulls with cooper's mallets in order to stun them and then to finish them off with fatal scalping wounds. The mode of execution—binding, stunning, and slitting—resembled the way that colonists slaughtered cattle, "a way of saying that the Indians there were like dumb beasts."[2]

When informed of their fate, the Moravians pled for mercy, but to no avail. They then made a single request, namely that the executions be delayed until the next morning so that they could prepare their souls for death. That granted, the groups in both buildings spent the night praying and singing hymns.

On the morning of March 8, the executioners brought members of the community in twos and threes into two buildings, where the members of the militia smashed their skulls as they knelt in prayer. None resisted. As the

---

[1] Richard White, *The Middle Ground: Indians, Empires, and Republics in the Great Lakes Region, 1650–1815* (Cambridge University Press, 1991), 390.
[2] Peter Silver, *Our Savage Neighbors: How Indian War Transformed Early America* (Norton, 2008), 271.

killing was going on, the group from Salem arrived. They had also been disarmed and now were confronted with the horror that awaited them. The militiamen ordered them to strip off their clothing, presumably to save the garments. Then they were "fetch'd . . . two or three at a time with Ropes about their Necks and dragged . . . into the Slaughter houses where they knocked them down."[3] The Pennsylvanians did not stop until they had killed everyone: twenty-eight men, twenty-nine women, thirty-nine children. Then they plundered the houses and set fire to the town. Finally, they burned the bodies and put the ashes in a heap.

Two boys escaped to tell the tale. One had hidden in a cellar. The other survived, covered in blood, under a pile of bodies and somehow remained motionless as he was scalped. When the work was done, the militia force departed for Pittsburgh with "'a huge amount of plunder—especially furs and skins but also household pewter, tea things, honeycombs, clothes, and everything else a farming settlement held—amounting to at least eighty horseback loads of goods."[4]

On their return to Pittsburgh, the militia attacked a contingent of Continental soldiers who were guarding a small group of allied Indians. The garrison kept the group "cooped up in a miserable hut" in sight of the fort. The militia killed two of the soldiers and a number of the captives. Then they sent a message to Colonel John Gibson, acting commander of the post, threatening to scalp him for "ha[ving] an attachment to Indians in general." Brigadier General William Irvine, the post's commander, returned shortly thereafter and later summarized the precarious situation he encountered. "No reasoning," he wrote, "can persuade the people of this country, but that an officer who will protect an Indians at all, on any account or pretense, must be a bad man."[5]

Irvine could do little. Settlers in the region were unruly, uncontrollable, and defiant toward colonial authorities. In frontier settlements, the news of the massacre was "highly gratifying to many."[6] A visitor to Pittsburgh later

---

[3]Charles Burleigh, *History of Ohio* (American Historical Society, 1925), 1:146.
[4]Burleigh, *History of Ohio*, 273.
[5]Burleigh, *History of Ohio*, 273-74.
[6]Eric Sterner, "Moravians in the Middle: The Gnadenhutten Massacre," *Journal of the American Revolution* (February 6, 2018), https://allthingsliberty.com/2018/02/moravians-middle-gnadenhutten-massacre/.

that year reported that "the Country talks of Nothing but killing Indians, & taking possession of their lands."[7] Irvine himself reported to George Washington that "the country people were to all appearances, in a fit of frenzy."[8] One settler boasted of killing a Lenape man with an axe and said he "would kill every Man that was blacker than a white man."[9]

Irvine was appalled that the militia had killed Christian Indians "in cold blood" and "fell on them while they were singing hymns and killed the whole. Many children were killed in their wretched mothers' arms." He went on to report, however, "Whether this was right or wrong, I do not presume to determine."[10] The massacre also horrified colonial elites on the East Coast. Washington expressed outrage. Benjamin Franklin wrote to an English friend that the "account of the abominable Murders committed by some of the frontier People on the poor Moravian Indians, has given me infinite Pain and Vexation."[11]

Congress demanded that Virginia and Pennsylvania conduct inquiries into the atrocity. Virginia demurred, arguing that only one Virginian had been part of the militia and that he had died. Pennsylvania also refused, asserting that an inquiry would only produce confusion. In the end, neither Williamson nor any of his men were ever called to account for the heinous murders. To the contrary, Williamson became a local hero. His fellow citizens elected him to several terms as sheriff of Washington County. And within a year after receiving news of the massacre, General Irvine had modified his views. In a letter to Washington, he wrote that he was "almost persuaded" that violence with the Ohio nations would continue "till the western tribes are driven over the Mississippi and the lakes, entirely beyond the American lines."[12]

The village of Gnadenhutten is a ninety-minute drive from my home in Ashland. The park where the Moravian settlement was located is bordered

---

[7] Colin G. Calloway, *The Indian World of George Washington* (Oxford University Press, 2018), 275.
[8] "IX—Irvine to Washington, April 20, 1782," in *Washington-Irvine Correspondence* (Madison, WI, 1882), 99, www.google.com/books/edition/Washington_Irvine_Correspondence/eEgSAAAAYAAJ?hl=en&gbpv=0&bshm=bshwcqp/1.
[9] Quoted in Patrick Griffin, *American Leviathan: Empire, Nation, and Revolutionary Frontier* (Hill and Wang, 2008), 175.
[10] Quoted in Calloway, *Indian World of George Washington*, 275.
[11] "From Benjamin Franklin to James Hutton, 7 July 1782," Founders Online, https://founders.archives.gov/documents/Franklin/01-37-02-0377.
[12] Silver, *Our Savage Neighbors*, 275.

on two sides by the village cemetery. The cooper's building and a cabin have been reconstructed on the site, and a small museum and gift shop are located at the southwest corner, not far from the Tuscarawas River. Across a narrow path and next to the parking lot stands a burial mound that contains the ashes of those murdered by the militiamen. A thirty-seven-foot marble obelisk stands at the center of the original settlement and dominates the site. Erected and dedicated by the Gnadenhutten Monument Fund in 1872, it bears an inscription that reads, "Here triumphed in death ninety Christian Indians, March 8, 1782."

The monument unsettles me. In both size and shape, it seems an unbefitting memorial. One of my visits to the site occurred after some kind of commemorative event. Plywood standups of smiling Lenape Christians in colonial dress stood at various locations around the park. Someone wanted to honor the people by remembering their life in the village. Both commemorations—the monument and the cutouts—remember the event by putting a positive spin on the brutality of what happened there. They celebrate the Christian martyrs who triumphed. They commemorate Gnadenhutten as the first Christian town in Ohio. The burial mound, however, testifies to the unspeakable murders perpetrated by White settlers.

Squatters, Settlers, and Scalps

Few icons in the American settler narrative embody America's sense of self more than the gritty and enterprising pioneers: the trappers and backwoodsmen who opened the way west, and the settlers in flatboats and wagon trains who traveled westward with their families, seeking a better life in a new land that promised freedom and prosperity for those who possessed the courage, perseverance, and work ethic required to transform a boundless wilderness into a new nation. Pioneers personified the attributes of the nation and celebrated settler triumphs throughout the nineteenth and twentieth centuries. Some, such as Daniel Boone, became larger than life.

Looking more closely into the settler narrative, however, reveals a less noble truth. Settler mythology celebrates Boone for initiating western expansion by leading a group of Virginia settlers through the Cumberland Gap and into Kentucky in 1772. Rarely mentioned in the myth is the fact that the Virginians were trespassing on Cherokee land and were repelled. A second attempt in 1775 succeeded, in large part because the Transylvania Land Company, a syndicate of wealthy land speculators, negotiated the purchase of twenty million acres from a group of Cherokee leaders who had no authority to sell them. Boone's forays into Kentucky explicitly violated the Proclamation of 1763, which the British Crown established in part to honor its treaties with Indigenous nations. The proclamation explicitly prohibited settlement of the land west of the Appalachian Mountains. It therefore infuriated colonial governments bent on westward expansion and so elicited one of the grievances that ignited the American Revolution.[13]

Savage violence accompanied the expansion of the frontier throughout the period of settlement. Although inflicted by Indigenous fighters and White colonists alike, the violence perpetrated by White settlers and soldiers far exceeded the violence inflicted by Indigenous peoples in its scale and frequency. Settler violence often constituted the primary means by which settler America implemented the logic of elimination as it gobbled up Indigenous land. Settlers along the frontier committed countless unprovoked acts of murder, violence, and intimidation. Violence imposed by organized military force did much the same.

The settler sentiments that celebrated the Gnadenhutten massacre were by no means limited to Pittsburgh. Rather, they constituted attitudes and perspectives that characterized settler attitudes and practices throughout US colonial expansion. Patrick Wolfe remarks on the role of frontier settlers in the colonial project in ways that illumine the attitudes and practices of the Pennsylvania militia and the settler population of Pittsburgh.

> Rather than something separate from or running counter to the colonial state, the murderous activities of the frontier rabble constitute its principal means of expansion. These have occurred "behind the screen of the frontier," in the wake of which, once the dust has settled, the irregular acts that took place have been regularized and the boundaries of White settlement extended. Characteristically, officials express regret at the lawlessness of this process while resigning themselves to its inevitability.[14]

---

[13]The Declaration of Independence concludes the list of grievances against the king with the accusation that he "has endeavoured to bring on the inhabitants of our frontiers, the merciless Indian Savages, whose known rule of warfare, is an undistinguished destruction of all ages, sexes and conditions."

[14]Patrick Wolfe, *Settler Colonialism and the Transformation of Anthropology* (Cassell, 1999), 392.

Squatting on unceded or newly acquired land proved alluring to thousands of destitute immigrants. Many of the early settlers had experienced violence and oppression at the hands of tyrannical monarchies. The Scots-Irish in particular brought with them the trauma of colonial violence at the hands of the British monarchy and exercised a strident defiance of any form of political authority.[15] Most settlers simply wanted to establish a farm and to be left alone. Squatting allowed indigent immigrants a way around the costly and laborious process of purchasing land, which required extinguishing Indigenous title, surveying the land, and dealing with the often-complicated processes for purchasing it. An exasperated agent for the Pennsylvania colony expressed the chaotic conditions on the frontier in a lament about the flood of "So many Idle worthless people flocking" to the wilderness, "Who Coming full of Expectation to have Land for nothing Are Unwilling to be Disappointed."[16]

Many settlers justified their illegal occupation of Indigenous land with the same rationale that the elites give for confiscating the same. That is, they saw the land as unoccupied and unused and thus available for settling. One group of settlers chastised the Pennsylvania colonial authorities for tying up vast lands for later sale, asserting that it was "against the Laws of God & Nature that so much land should lie idle, while so many Christians wanted it to labour on and [to] raise their Bread."[17] Daniel Boone rejoiced to see Kentucky, "lately a howling wilderness, the habitation of savages and wild beasts, become a fruitful field; this region, so favourably distinguished by nature, now becomes the habitation of civilization."[18] An editorial in the influential *Freeman's Journal* of Philadelphia, written toward the end of the Revolution, expresses the justification in familiar terms:

> Valuable lands of immense extent are now lying in a wild state of nature, possessed by indolent Indian savages, who without all doubt, ought upon the plainest principles of reason, either to be expelled from thence as soon as it shall be in our power, or be obliged to conform to a life of agriculture, the

---

[15]Dunbar-Ortiz calls the Scots-Irish the "shock troops" of westward expansion. See Roxanne Dunbar-Ortiz, *An Indigenous Peoples' History of the United States* (Beacon, 2014), 52.
[16]Silver, *Our Savage Neighbors*, 8.
[17]Alan Taylor, *American Colonies: The Settling of North America* (Penguin, 2001), 222.
[18]Griffin, *American Leviathan*, 179.

natural cause of civilization, and without which there appears little or no hopes of their ever becoming *men*, much less christians."[19]

Frontier settlers often formed themselves into loosely organized groups for the defense of their settlements and, in the case of government land, from attempts to evict them. They tended to be a law unto themselves. A French diplomat to the Washington administration wrote to his superiors, "It is generally agreed here that the American emigrants established on the frontiers are the scum of mankind and infinitely more ferocious, more perfidious and more intractable than the savages themselves."[20] Frontier Whites contested colonial and federal forces and sometimes fought with soldiers who tried to maintain order. The imposition of token force by a chronically overstretched military rarely accomplished anything. Military campaigns to burn settler houses and crops in the Ohio Country, for example, had little success; the settlers often fled into the forest before the military arrived and rebuilt their homes after it left.[21] Military campaigns to expel settlers, moreover, were infrequent and generally halfhearted, as federal authorities were reluctant to antagonize people who might one day become voters.

As at Gnadenhutten, settler vigilante groups often cared little about distinguishing peaceful Indians from hostile ones. In December 1763, one such mob, who called themselves the Paxton Boys, crept into Conestoga Town, near present-day Lancaster County, Pennsylvania, under cover of night. The town was home to the last few members of the once-powerful Susquehannock confederacy. The twenty residents had been living among the Pennsylvanian colonists for generations and were well regarded by most of them.

The Paxton Boys, however, wanted the land cleansed of Indians and were frustrated by what they considered the colonial government's lax policy. They killed and scalped six residents and set the village on fire while the rest of the people were away. Colonial authorities subsequently brought the remaining Conestogas, a group of only six adults and eight children, into protective custody. They housed them in a jail and set about identifying the perpetrators. Thirteen days later, however, the Paxton Boys broke into the

---

[19]Silver, *Our Savage Neighbors*, 280-81.
[20]Calloway, *Indian World of George Washington*, 334.
[21]R. Douglas Hurt, *The Ohio Frontier: Crucible of the Old Northwest, 1729–1830* (Indiana University Press, 1998), 140-48.

jail and killed, scalped, and mutilated the entire group. Then they marched to Philadelphia, where they had heard more Indians had taken refuge. By the time they reached the city, their numbers had swelled to a mob of six hundred settlers. The mob threatened to plunder Philadelphia unless their demands were met. A tense standoff ensued. It was resolved only after Benjamin Franklin and a delegation of city leaders assured the mob that the colony's legislature would give their demands a thorough hearing.

The colonial authorities were outraged by the brutal massacres. Franklin published a tract a year later that lamented the atrocity and distanced the good people of Philadelphia from the frontier rabble. "The universal concern of the neighboring white people on hearing of this event, and the lamentations of the younger Indians when they returned and saw the desolation and the butchered, half-burned bodies of their murdered parents and other relations cannot well be expressed."[22] The Paxton Boys, however, were staunch Presbyterians and justified the killing in biblical terms.

> Now, Sirs, I ween it is but right,
> That we upon these Cananites,
> Without delay should Vengeance take,
> Both for our own, and the K—k's sake [sic]:
> Destroy them quite frae out the Land;—
> And for it we have God's Command.[23]

The Bible, the Paxton Boys believed, clearly directed what they should do to the nations that inhabited the land God had given to them. From this perspective, then, the affront to God did not lie in the massacre but in the colonial authorities' refusal to exterminate the Indians. In the end, the settler response followed the script of Gnadenhutten and virtually all settler massacres throughout the period of western expansion: outrage, an official review, and no action taken against the perpetrators.

Among the demands that the Pennsylvania legislature granted the Paxton Boys was the restoration of a scalp bounty. Where and how scalping

---

[22]Benjamin Franklin, "A Narrative of the Late Massacres [30 January? 1764]," Founders Online, https://founders.archives.gov/documents/Franklin/01-11-02-0012.

[23]Quoted in Andrew Kirk, "Desperation, Zeal, and Murder: The Paxton Boys," Pennsylvania Center for the Book, 2009, https://pabook.libraries.psu.edu/literary-cultural-heritage-map-pa/feature-articles/desperation-zeal-and-murder-paxton-boys.

originated is the subject of considerable debate. Whatever the origins, colonial governments issued payment for scalps in times of conflict as a way of inducing settlers to extirpate (that is, exterminate) Indigenous groups they considered to be hostile. During the eighteenth century, all colonies issued bounties at one time or another. Some offered huge financial incentives. In 1756, Lieutenant Governor Robert Hunt Morris of Pennsylvania offered a bounty of 130 pieces of eight for the scalp of Lenape males over twelve and 50 pieces of eight for Lenape women (although the bounty faced strenuous opposition and appears to have expired within a few months).[24] In 1723, Massachusetts issued a bounty of £100 for the scalps of male Indians and £10 for those of women.

The impact of scalp bounties, however, extended beyond the number of Indigenous people who were slain. The bounties in essence dissolved the boundaries between military and noncombatants and, in some cases, between allied and enemy nations. A scalp did not announce its tribal identity, nor often its gender. The bounties thus incentivized killing and intensified the level of frontier violence. "Scalp hunting," writes John Grenier, "offered American frontiersmen acting as *entrepreneurs de guerre* the potential for an economic windfall.... By embracing scalp hunting, American society, besides commercializing war, had made the killing of noncombatants a legitimate act of war" and a "permanent feature of both the colonial frontier economy and Americans' way of war."[25]

The uncontrollable violence of frontier Whites, along with the authorities' inability to prevent it, often undercut the colonists' credibility with Indigenous nations. Wanton violence complicated the settler government's plans to purchase more Indian land through treaties. Squatting interfered with the orderly sale and settlement of land, tying up land sales in countless legal disputes to determine a clean title.

Yet, settlers and authorities, despite their divergent interests and perspectives, often worked in concert to generate violence. Settler depredations destabilized Indigenous societies, and settler hunting on Indigenous land

---

[24]Henry J. Young, "A Note on Scalp Bounties in Pennsylvania," *Pennsylvania History* 24, no. 3 (1957): 207-18.

[25]John Grenier, *The First Way of War: American War Making on the Frontier, 1607-1814* (Cambridge University Press, 2005), 42, 43.

typically brought about a precipitous decline in game animals. Settler harassment could become intolerable, as illustrated in the case of the Seneca of Sandusky, sometimes forcing the Indigenous inhabitants to give up more land. "Frontiersmen," in short, "did much of the dirty work of expansion. The federal government deplored their actions as contrary to its declared policies but did little to stop them. Even imposing what little control it could on the frontier risked losing westerners' loyalties and votes."[26]

Over time, a pattern emerged. Settlers would encroach on Indian land and eventually provoke an Indian war, with the expectation that the government would intervene on their side. War, or the threat of war, would then lead to a new treaty for the land they had settled, thus securing their claims and possession. John Heckewelder, one of the Moravian missionaries who established the Ohio towns, expressed the scenario in stark terms:

> [The Indians] will tell you, that there is not a single instance in which the whites have not violated the engagements that they had made at treaties. They say that when they had ceded lands to the white people, and boundary lines had been established—"firmly established!" beyond which no whites were to settle; scarcely was the treaty signed, when white intruders again were settling and hunting on their lands! It is true that when they referred their complaints to the government, the government gave them many fair promises, and assured them that men would be sent to remove the intruders by force from the usurped lands. The men, indeed, came, but with chain and compass in their hands, taking surveys of the tracts of good land, which the intruders, from their knowledge of the country, had pointed out to them! What was then to be done, when those intruders would not go off from the land, but on the contrary, increased in numbers?? "Oh!" said those people, (and I have myself frequently heard this language in the Western country,) "a new treaty will soon give us all this land; nothing is now wanting but a pretence to pick a quarrel with them!"[27]

Throughout the colonial and revolutionary eras, then, "race and violence went hand in hand, one feeding the other."[28]

---

[26]Calloway, *Indian World of George Washington*, 335.
[27]Anthony J. C. Wallace, *Jefferson and the Indians: The Tragic Fate of the First Americans* (Belknap, 1999), 195.
[28]Griffin, *American Leviathan*, 171.

Settler violence continued unabated during the nineteenth century. In 1869, an act of Congress established the Board of Indian Commissioners, for the purpose of advising the president, secretary of the interior, and Congress on Indian affairs. The board's first report, issued in 1869, included a scathing indictment of "the actual treatment" that Indians had received from the US government. After marking the government's "shameful record of broken treaties and unfulfilled promises," the board addressed the problem of settler violence. "The history of the border white man's connection with the Indians is a sickening record of murder, outrage, robbery, and wrongs committed by the former as the rule, and occasional savage outbreaks and unspeakably barbarous deeds of retaliation by the latter as the exception." At a later point in the report, the board reinforced its assessment by citing military leaders, who reported:

> In our Indian wars, almost without exception, the first aggressions have been made by the white man. . . . In addition to the class of robbers and outlaws who find impunity in their nefarious pursuits upon the frontiers, there is a large class of professedly reputable men who use every means in their power to bring on Indian wars, for the sake of the profit to be realized from the presence of troops and the expenditure of government funds in their midst. They proclaim death to Indians at all times, in words and publications, making no distinction between the innocent and the guilty.[29]

A pair of editorials in the *Aberdeen* (South Dakota) *Saturday Pioneer*, published on December 20, 1890, and January 3, 1891, reveal that the genocidal impulse of frontier Whites remained alive and well even after the Indigenous peoples in an area had been "subdued." In the first editorial, the editor comments on the recent assassination of Sitting Bull, admitting that "his conquerors were marked in their dealings with his people by selfishness, falsehood and treachery." Nevertheless, the writer exclaims, "the Whites, by law of conquest, by justice of civilization, are masters of the American continent, and the best safety of the frontier settlements will be secured by the total annihilation of the few remaining Indians. . . . We cannot honestly regret their extermination." The editor expanded on these sentiments two weeks later, after the Seventh US Calvary killed 250–300 Lakota men, women,

---

[29]"Report of the Board of Indian Commissioners, November 23, 1969," in *Documents of American Indian Policy*, 3rd ed., ed. Francis Paul Prucha (University of Nebraska Press, 2000), 130-31. Transcript at https://digitalcommons.law.ou.edu/indianserialset/5614/.

Exterminating the Indian 85

and children at Wounded Knee. "Our only safety depends upon the total extirmination [*sic*] of the Indians. Having wronged them for centuries we had better, in order to protect our civilization, follow it up by one more wrong and wipe these untamed and untamable creatures from the face of the earth."[30] The author of these words was L. Frank Baum, who, ten years later, would publish a children's book titled *The Wonderful Wizard of Oz*.

JUST WARS

Military campaigns against Indigenous nations were often as vicious and indiscriminate as settler violence, differing only in the scale of the body counts. Colonial, state, and federal military forces launched preemptive strikes against Indigenous towns and camps, sometimes against people who were at peace with the settler authorities or who had been guaranteed safety in return for putting themselves under the protection of the authorities. Military attacks against Indigenous people, furthermore, generally made no distinction between combatants and noncombatants, even targeting women, children, and the elderly while the warriors were away.[31]

Preemptive strikes and indiscriminate killing occurred in all regions within the boundaries of the United States. The violence constituted an integral part of settler America's efforts to eliminate the Indigenous people from land it craved. This will be demonstrated by well-known scenarios in the settler narrative: colonial New England in the seventeenth century and the Plains during the 1860s and 1870s.[32]

NEW ENGLAND

Plymouth Colony experienced hardship and starvation in the years following its founding in 1620. Because the colonists struggled to subsist in their new

---

[30] "L. Frank Baum's Editorials on the Sioux Nation," https://warwick.ac.uk/fac/arts/english/current students/undergraduate/modules/fulllist/second/en213/term1/l_frank_baum.pdf.

[31] Historical accounts of massacres often differ from each other; written reports and oral traditions often conflict. And no more so than in the body counts. Many accounts of settler violence deny the scale of the killing or spin the incident to serve settler ends. So, for example, settler accounts often label the murders of hundreds of Indigenous people "battles," while the murders of settlers, however few, are commemorated as "massacres."

[32] In many cases, the numbers of those killed and injured vary significantly, often because of the size of the killing field and sometimes because settler forces reduced the body count in order to diminish the outrage.

environs, they had little time to make a sufficient return on the investment made by the syndicate of English merchants who underwrote funding for the colony. In 1622, the syndicate's leader, Thomas Weston, sent sixty-seven men to establish a trading post and stockade at Wessagussett, about thirty miles northwest of Plymouth. Weston hoped to gain a large profit by trading for firs, timber, and fish. The group, made up of "rude fellows" who were "not fit for an honest man's company," did not ask permission for the enterprise from the Massachusetts tribe and were woefully unprepared for the undertaking.[33] Many considered manual labor beneath their dignity.

When winter came, the Englishmen had no food. At first, they were able to trade for food with the Massachusetts. When their surplus was exhausted, however, the Massachusetts stopped supplying the colonists with corn. The colonists thereupon began stealing it. After repeated robberies, a tribal representative named Pecksuot arrived at Wessagussett with an armed escort and asked what wrong his people had done to deserve this treatment. "I have sent you word times without number," he said, "& yet our Corn is stole."[34]

When the colonists received a report, of questionable veracity, that the Massachusetts were preparing to attack them, they took action. Miles Standish, Plymouth's military leader, traveled to Wessagussett with a small force of soldiers. Standish invited a visiting Massachusetts delegation into the settlement's blockhouse, where his men stabbed all seven to death, including the sachem (principal leader). Standish carried the sachem's head back to Plymouth, where he was received with a hero's welcome. Then he impaled the head on a spike, along with a blood-soaked cloth. All this occurred just two years after the Pilgrims landed at Plymouth Rock.

Tensions with the surrounding nations intensified during the 1630s, when twenty thousand to thirty thousand English colonists arrived at the Massachusetts Bay Colony. The crush of immigrants pressed colonial authorities to get more land and to extend colonial jurisdiction over Indigenous land. As the colonists grew more numerous, they began to demand tribute in the form of wampum (intricate beaded belts that, among other things, recorded significant events, facilitated exchange, and defined social relationships).

---

[33]Quoted in Bernard Bailyn, *The Barbarous Years* (Knopf, 2021), 339.
[34]Quoted in Ana Schwartz, "Ethics and Epistemology at Plymouth Plantation," *Early American Literature* 57, no. 2 (2002): 404, https://doi.org/10.1353/eal.2022.0033.

The colonists traded the wampum to other tribes in exchange for furs. When the colonial authorities tried to levy taxes on the Pequots, whose lands encompassed most of present-day Connecticut, the Pequot tribal council refused. Relations worsened. The flashpoint came in 1636, when a well-respected trader named John Oldham was murdered. Although members of another tribe, the Narragansetts, probably killed Oldham, the colonial authorities blamed the Pequots and demanded that they surrender the suspects, pay tribute, and hand over hostages. When the Pequots refused, the Massachusetts colonies raised a volunteer force to take the fight to the enemy.

The conflict began badly for the colonists. A first strike by the Massachusetts militia, against Narranssetts on Block Island, failed miserably. The Pequots subsequently laid siege to a settler farm at Saybrook Fort and attacked the town of Wethersfield in Connecticut, killing nine people. Connecticut then raised a force of ninety soldiers under the command of John Mason, a mercenary hardened by Europe's religious wars. Joined by another twenty colonists under the command of John Underhill, as well as about two hundred Narragansett and Mohegan allies, the colonists set out against the Pequots in May 1637.

Mason's objective was a palisaded town of about five hundred people, located by the Mystic River in Connecticut. Women, children, and elders populated the town, as the fighting force was encamped at another location. At the first light of dawn, the colonial soldiers burst into the village. When they encountered a stiffer resistance than expected, they retreated back through the entrance. As they did, Mason shouted, "We must burn them!" and set fire to the village. The New Englanders stationed themselves at the two entrances, with the Narragansetts behind them, and killed everyone trying to escape. The conflagration, fueled by a stiff northeastern wind, consumed the village in about half an hour. According to Underhill, "many were burnt in the Fort, both men, women, and children, others forced out, and came in troops to the Indians, twenty, and thirty at a time, which our soldiers received and entertained with the point of the sword; down fell men, women, and children, those that escaped us, fell into the hands of the Indians, that were in the rear of us."[35] The Narragansetts were horrified by the carnage and shouted, "Too much! Too much!"

---

[35] "Being Bereaved of Pity," in *Puritans, Indians and Manifest Destiny*, ed. Charles M. Segal and David C. Stineback (G. P. Putnam's Sons, 1977), 136.

Before the attack, many soldiers appeared to have had misgivings about what they were about to do. To reassure them, "the reverend ministers" preached sermons that presented the attack as a just war. Underhill summarizes their message: "You need not question your authority to execute those whom God, the righteous Judge of all the world, hath condemned for blaspheming His sacred majesty and murdering His servants."[36]

After the massacre, Mason was exultant. He proclaimed that God "laughed his enemies and the enemies of his people to scorn, making them a fiery oven. . . . Thus did the Lord judge among the heathen, filling the place with dead bodies."[37] William Bradford, governor of the Plymouth Colony (who did not participate in the massacre), later wrote about what he had been told about the slaughter. "It was a fearful sight to see them thus frying in the fire and the streams of blood quenching the same, and horrible was the stink thereof. But the victory seemed a sweet sacrifice, and they gave praise thereof to God, who had wrought so wonderfully for them."[38]

Mason attacked another town two weeks later and slaughtered all of its inhabitants as well. The remaining Pequots mounted a series of counterattacks but were eventually defeated in battle at Munnacommuck Swamp. Colonial militia ranged widely, burning Pequot towns and capturing or killing surviving groups. The war ended with a treaty at Hartford in September 1638, which was imposed by the settlers and their Narragansett and Mohegan allies. The treaty confiscated all Pequot land, forbade Pequots from returning to it, and even outlawed the use of their name.

The colonists enslaved some of the surviving Pequots and sold others into slavery in the Caribbean. Recent research has revealed that the timing of the Pequot War coincided with a looming crisis for the colonial economy, which relied heavily on the labor of indentured servants. The terms of a sizable number of these individuals were set to expire in 1635–1638, and the colonists had discussed taking slaves as they prepared for an impending conflict with the Pequots. Slaves captured during the Pequot War increased the colonial labor force by a third and thus covered the

---

[36]"Every Faithful Soldier of Jesus Christ," in Segal and Stineback, *Puritans, Indians and Manifest Destiny*, 132.
[37]Quoted in Segal and Stineback, *Puritans, Indians and Manifest Destiny*, 111.
[38]Segal and Stineback, *Puritans, Indians and Manifest Destiny*, 111.

anticipated loss of indentured labor. Working out the status and ownership of these slaves led Massachusetts to become the first English colony to publish a slave code.[39]

Over the course of the next three decades, the English colonists continued to take the lands of the surrounding peoples, including those of erstwhile allies. Settlers disrupted Indigenous towns and mistreated the residents. Colonial authorities violated existing treaties and agreements and increasingly extended their claims to jurisdiction over Indian people and land. Escalating tensions reached the breaking point when colonial authorities blamed three Wampanoags for the death of a Christian Indian who, it was rumored, had been murdered because he was going to inform the colonies of an impending attack. The colonists apprehended the three and then tried, convicted, and executed them by hanging in January 1675.

The Wampanoags, under the leadership of Massasoit, had befriended the Plymouth Colony and given the colonists the protection, food, and teaching they needed to survive its first few years. His son, Metacom (known to the colonists as King Philip), was now sachem and had been subject to a very different relationship with the colonists. The following June, Metacom launched a series of attacks against the Swansea Colony in present-day Massachusetts, with the intention of driving the colonists from Wampanoag land. The war that followed resulted in the deaths of twenty-five hundred colonists—about 30 percent of the settler population—and more than double that number of Indigenous people, about 50 to 70 percent of the remaining population. The New Englanders' eventual victory effectively ended Indigenous resistance in New England. It also put the settlers in possession of the remaining Indigenous land, as the Narragansetts, Nipmucs, and other tribes had rallied to the Wampanoags by the war's end.

The Puritan forces employed the tactic of preemptive strike and massacre they had used to subdue the Pequots. On a frigid December morning in 1675, about one thousand colonial soldiers attacked a Narragansett fort in the Great Swamp near West Kingston, Rhode Island. The Narragansetts were neutral; Rhode Island leader Roger Williams and three Narragansett

---

[39]Margaret Ellen Newell, *Brethren by Nature* (Cornell University Press, 2016), 17-42.

emissaries had earlier made a nonaggression pact with the Puritans. The colonial force attacked anyway. When the Narragansetts inflicted heavy casualties, the colonists set fire to the fort, killing three to six hundred of the town's occupants, half of whom were women, children, and elderly.

The colonists struck again the following May, this time launching a surprise attack on a large encampment of Wampanoag, Narragansett, Nipmuc, and Pocumtuc families. The families had gathered, as they had for centuries, for a traditional fish run at the falls of the Connecticut River. The warriors were some distance downriver, in a separate camp. The colonial force, under the command of Captain William Turner, attacked the family camp early in the morning. When the warriors heard the commotion, they rushed to the encampment and drove off the attackers, but not before the colonists had killed more than one hundred from the defenseless families. The warriors gave chase and killed some of the attackers, including Captain Turner. The colonists later named the site Turner Falls in his honor.[40]

The Puritans described the conflicts as defensive wars and therefore just wars. They maintained that the lands they took through the wars were also justly acquired, and they saw their victories as signs of divine favor. Increase Mather, an influential clergyman of the time, began a history of King Philip's War by declaring, "The heathen people amongst whom we live, and whose Land the Lord God of our Fathers hath given to us for a rightful Possession, have at sundry times been plotting" against "the English Israel"—only for God to "lay the fear of the *English* and the dread of them upon all the *Indians*."[41] Even Roger Williams, who had labored hard to cultivate respectful relations with the Narragansetts, eventually saw the colonists' victories as a sign of God's Providence. "God had prospered *us* so that we had driven the Wampanoags with Philip out of his Country and the Nahigonsiks out of their Country, and had destroyed Multitudes of them in Fighting and Flying, in Hunger and Cold, etc.: and that God would help us to Consume them."[42]

---

[40] See "Basic Context and Timeline of Contextual Events of the Falls Fight of May 19, 1676," compiled by D. Brule, Montague Historical Commission, n.d.

[41] Increase Mather, *A Brief History of the War with the Indians in New-England, 1676*, National Humanities Center, https://founders.archives.gov/?q=%22a%20narrative%20of%20the%20late%20massacres%22&s=1111311111&sa=&r=1&sr=.

[42] Quoted in Taylor, *American Colonies*, 200.

Pacifying the Plains

After the end of the Civil War in 1865, the US government turned its attention to expanding settlement in the West and building the railroads and telegraph lines that would facilitate it. The most pressing matter entailed the completion of the Transcontinental Railroad, which began construction in 1862. The project required obtaining land and rights of way for those parts of the planned route that traversed Indigenous land and hunting grounds that were protected by treaties. The question of how to get this land occupied the postwar administrations.

The frontier was ablaze. Settlers were encroaching on unceded land, generating cycles of reciprocal violence. Between 1864 and 1866, thirty-five hundred miners traveled the Bozeman Trail, which had opened access to gold fields in Montana. Decades of transit and settlement were destroying the grazing lands that sustained the buffalo, threatening the well-being of Plains nations. To protect settlers, the US government built three forts on the Platte and Powder Rivers, provoking outrage among the Lakota, Cheyenne, and Arapaho, who launched raids that shut the trail down.

The decade saw atrocious massacres. Following the strategy that settler forces had employed since the colonial era, federal military forces responded to Indian raiding with surprise attacks on Indigenous towns and camps. Many of the officers who led the attacks were dissatisfied with their assignment to Indian Country and were looking for victories that would get them a post back east. Military authorities often held an entire village responsible for raiding parties that killed settlers or stole their horses and cattle. Sometimes they did not bother to find out whether the villages they attacked were at peace with the United States.

In January 1863, a force of three hundred infantry and cavalry under the command of Colonel Patrick Connor attacked a camp of Shoshones along the Bear River in present-day Idaho. The Shoshones had assisted Lewis and Clark's expedition but now found themselves beset by hostile miners and settlers. When a settler was killed in a dispute over cattle, a judge called for the arrest of Shoshone suspects and ordered Connor to apprehend them. Connor, who had made no secret of the fact that he wanted to kill Indians, surrounded the village accused of sheltering the suspects. When Sagwitch, one of the leaders, came out to meet Connor, the troops killed him and rushed into the village, firing into the lodges and at those who attempted to flee. The villagers had few guns and little ammunition. Many were driven to the banks of the river, where they faced either being shot or jumping into the frigid water. Another leader, Bear Hunter, was tortured and then killed with a red-hot bayonet that was thrust through his head from ear to ear. When the shooting ended, 250 to 350 men, women, and children lay dead. Some of the soldiers finished off those who were seriously wounded. The attackers retrieved their dead but left Shoshone bodies where they lay, "to be scattered by wolves and magpies."[43] *The New York Times*, reporting on "the extermination of the Bannock and Shoshone Army," declared, "Though Col. Connor cannot say 'I came, I saw, I conquered,' he may report 'I went, I fought, I conquered, I exterminated,' for such, indeed, was the fact."[44]

In September of the same year, US forces launched a punitive campaign against Dakota bands in present-day North Dakota, having put down a Dakota "uprising" in Minnesota the previous year. A force of four thousand troops under the command of General Alfred Sully went in search of hostile Indians. His troops encircled a large encampment, made up primarily of Yanktonai, at Whitestone Hill. When tribal leaders sought to avoid bloodshed through negotiation, the troops refused. At sunset, the main column of Sully's troops charged into the village, killing more than three hundred men, women, and children. After the slaughter, the force destroyed the lodges, property, and food, including four hundred thousand to five hundred thousand pounds of dried buffalo meat, leaving the survivors unprepared to face the winter. An interpreter for Sully's command later called the attack "a perfect massacre" and declared that Sully had done "what no decent man would have done, he pitched into their camp and just slaughtered them. . . . He killed very few men and took no hostile ones prisoners. . . . If he had killed men instead of women & children, then it would have been a success, and the worse of it, they had no hostile intention

---

[43] Brigham D. Madsen, "Bear River Massacre," *Utah History Encyclopedia*, 1994, https://historytogo.utah.gov/bear-river-massacre/.

[44] Quoted in John Barnes, "The Struggle to Control the Past: Commemoration, Memory, and the Bear River Massacre of 1863," *The Public Historian* 30, no. 1 (2008): 89-90. See also Dana Hedgpeth, "This Was the Worst Slaughter of Native Americans in U.S. History. Few Remember It," *Washington Post*, September 26, 2021, www.washingtonpost.com/history/2021/09/26/bear-river-massacre-native-americans-shoshone/.

whatever."[45] Sulley, however, boasted that he had delivered "one of the most severe punishments that the Indians have ever received."[46]

In November 1864, Colonel John Chivington, a Methodist minister, led a force of 675 troops in an attack on a peaceful encampment of 750 Cheyenne and Arapahos at Sand Creek, in the Colorado Territory. Black Kettle, the community's principal leader, had been an advocate for peace with the settlers and had accepted the settler government's invitation to place himself under the protection of the United States. As directed, he encamped at a location about thirty miles from Fort Lyon and flew an American flag with a white flag from his lodge. The day of the attack, the encampment consisted primarily of women, children, and elderly, as most of the young men were away on a hunt.

At dawn, Chivington ordered his men to charge the encampment, shouting, "Kill and scalp all, big and little; nits make lice!" while howitzers fired canister at those who fled. After the initial charge, the Coloradans spent the next seven hours hunting down and killing every person they could find. An estimated 230 people died, two-thirds of them women and children, and including most of the leaders who had advocated for peace.

A number of junior officers refused to order their units to participate in the massacre. An interpreter for the troops described what happened:

> All manner of depredations were inflicted on their persons, they were scalped, their brains knocked out; the men used their knives, ripped open women, clubbed little children, knocked them in the head with their guns, beat their brains out, mutilated their bodies in every sense of the word.... Worse mutilated than any I ever saw before, the women all cut to pieces.... Children two or three months old; all ages lying there, from sucking infants up to warriors.[47]

Soldiers caught off the genitalia of the slain and paraded them as trophies when they returned to Denver. Outrage at the massacre prompted Congress

---

[45]"Punitive Expeditions," Minnesota Historical Society, www.usdakotawar.org/history/aftermath/punitive-expeditions; Clay Jenkinson, "The Forgotten Battle of Whitestone Hill, North Dakota," *Listening to America*, July 31, 2023, https://ltamerica.org/the-forgotten-battle-of-whitestone-hill-north-dakota-2/.

[46]Eric Ringham, "Massacre Clouds Story of the Soldier on Minnesota's Pedestal," *MPRNews*, September 27, 2018, www.mprnews.org/story/2018/09/27/iconic-minnesota-soldier-part-of-atrocity.

[47]"Sand Creek Massacre Witness Accounts," The Sand Creek Massacre, https://sandcreekmassacre.net/witness-accounts/.

to launch an investigation. Yet, no charges ensued. Neither Chivington nor any of his men were ever called to account.

Sand Creek infuriated many of the Plains nations. The massacres, unrelenting encroachment, and settler violence invalidated White promises of peace, order, and protection. After the Civil War, the federal government developed a strategy for securing safe passage for settlers moving west and getting lands along the uncompleted route of the Transcontinental Railroad. The western Indians would be removed from lands along the paths of railroads and onto two large reservations, one south of Kansas and the other north of Nebraska. In these territories, the government assumed, the nations of the Plains would be insulated from the deleterious influence of frontier Whites. There, the US government would feed and clothe them, and provide them with livestock, agricultural implements, schools, and missionaries, so that they could advance toward civilization.

To begin the process of pacifying the 360,000 Indigenous people who stood in settler America's way, General Ulysses S. Grant appointed William Tecumseh Sherman in 1865 as the commander of US military forces in the West. Sherman was celebrated in the north for his execution of "total war" against the civilian population of Georgia during his march from Atlanta to the Atlantic Ocean. The tactic took the fight to civilians, with the aim of destroying their crops and possessions and thus breaking their will to resist.

Sherman harbored a deep antipathy for Indians. General Philip Sheridan, who commanded the army in the Division of the Missouri, despised them as well. When a Comanche leader introduced himself to Sheridan by saying he was "a good Indian," Sheridan reportedly answered, "The only good Indians I ever saw were dead."[48] Sherman and Sheridan were among those who believed that Indians could never be civilized and would eventually die out, expedited by military force if necessary. Both opposed making treaties and advocated the exertion of military force. After a couple of years in his position, Sherman wrote, "The more we can kill this year the less will have to be killed the next war, for the more I see of these Indians the more convinced I am that all have to be killed or maintained as a species or pauper. Their attempts at civilization are simply ridiculous."[49] When, in December 1866, a

---

[48] Sheridan denied he had ever said this. The association stuck nonetheless.
[49] Quoted in Stewart Russell, "Villainous Heroes," *History Today* 44, no. 2 (1994): 6.

Lakota force led by Crazy Horse wiped out Captain William Fetterman's command of eighty soldiers in an ambush, Sherman declared, "We must act with vindictive earnestness against the Sioux, even to the point of their extermination, men, women, and children."[50]

Sherman, however, kept his opinions to himself when President Grant appointed him, along with six other military and civilian leaders, to serve on an Indian Peace Commission, which Congress established in 1867 to secure peace and get more Indian land. The commissioners fanned out across the West with promises and proposals. Most were rebuffed, but in two instances, commissioners succeeded in making peace, recognizing Indigenous claims, and securing land cessions. One was a second treaty at Fort Laramie in 1868, with the Dakota, Lakota, Nakota, and Arapaho. The treaty established the Great Sioux Reservation, which encompassed western South Dakota and specifically designated the Black Hills as "unceded Indian territory."[51] The other was the Medicine Lodge Treaty, which was negotiated with a grand council of five thousand. The treaty set aside 2.9 million acres for the Comanches and Kiowas and 4.3 million acres for the Cheyenne and Arapaho.[52]

The treaties, however, did not secure a lasting peace. First, settler encroachment into unceded land broke treaty provisions within weeks. Second, cultural differences and mistranslation resulted in different understandings of the terms of the treaties and how they would be implemented. An officer who kept a record of the proceedings remarked, "They have no idea that they are giving up, or that they have ever given up the country which they claim as their own. . . . The treaty amounts to nothing, and we will certainly have another war sooner or later with the Cheyenne, at least, and probably with the other Indians."[53] Finally, the United States continued the practice of negotiating with tribal leaders as if they represented their entire nations, thus

---

[50] "People & Events: Native Americans and the Transcontinental Railroad," The American Experience, n.d., www.pbs.org/wgbh/americanexperience/features/tcrr-native-americans-and-transcontinental-railroad/. See also Sam Vong, "The Impact of the Transcontinental Railroad on Native Americans," National Museum of American History, June 3, 2019, https://americanhistory.si.edu/explore/stories/TRR.

[51] "Treaty of Fort Laramie (1868)," Milestone Documents, www.archives.gov/milestone-documents/fort-laramie-treaty.

[52] "Treaty with the Kiowa, Comanche, and Apache, 1867," Tribal Treaties Database, https://treaties.okstate.edu/treaties/treaty-with-the-kiowa-comanche-and-apache-1867-0982.

[53] "Medicine Lodge Treaty," Fort Larned National Historic Site, Kansas, www.nps.gov/fols/learn/historyculture/medicine-lodge-treaty.htm.

holding all members of the nation to the treaty terms, whether they had agreed to them or not. The Indigenous groups that repudiated the treaties did not regard themselves bound by the treaties and did not observe the terms.

The Medicine Lodge and Fort Laramie treaties therefore did not prevent continuing attacks. The need to protect the railroads and to clear railroad lands required a more effective strategy. Facing continued resistance, the Grant administration concluded that moving the Plains nations onto reservations was the best course of action for all concerned. Reservations would allow the government to move forward with the development of its rail network, while helping Indigenous nations to advance toward civilization.

Sherman believed that the most effective means toward this end was to exterminate the buffalo herds that provided food, hides, and other necessities for the Plains nations. Annihilating the buffalo, he reasoned, would drive Indians to starvation, leaving them no choice but to move to reservations and dependence on the US government. The treaties guaranteed hunting rights on ceded lands, but those rights would mean little if the buffalo were gone. In a letter to Sheridan in May 1868, Sherman floated the idea. "I think to would be wise to invite all the sportsmen of England and America there this fall for a Grand Buffalo hunt, and make one grand sweep of them all. Until the Buffalo and consequent[ly] Indians are out [from between] the Roads we will have collisions and trouble."[54] Sheridan, who believed that guaranteeing hunting rights by treaty had been a great mistake, shared Sherman's sentiments. In October 1868, he told Sherman that the best way to subjugate the nations was to "make them poor by the destruction of their stock, and then settle them on the lands allotted to them."[55]

The plan to exterminate the buffalo was too outrageous to be adopted as policy. Sherman, however, began to implement the plan informally, sending Sheridan on a campaign to reduce buffalo herds in 1868–1869. When newly inaugurated President Grant put Sherman in command of the US Army,

---

[54] "Sherman to Sheridan, 10 May 1868," in *The Papers of Philip H. Sheridan*, quoted in David D. Smits, "The Frontier Army and the Destruction of the Buffalo: 1865–1883," All About Bison, n.d., https://allaboutbison.com/articles-publications/frontier-army-and-the-destruction-of-the-buffalo/.

[55] J. Weston Phippen, "'Kill Every Buffalo You Can! Every Buffalo Dead Is an Indian Gone,'" *The Atlantic*, May 13, 2016, www.theatlantic.com/national/archive/2016/05/the-buffalo-killers/482349/.

Sheridan assumed Sherman's former post as commander of the Division of the Missouri. In this post, he continued to use the army both directly and indirectly to slaughter the buffalo.

Sherman and Sheridan furnished wealthy citizens and foreigners with letters that funded hunting parties and authorized expenditures necessary to acquire supplies, scouts, and military escorts. Officials encouraged members of these parties to slaughter buffalo with abandon and cut the tongues and choice cuts from the carcasses to confirm the kills. Contests awarded prizes to hunters who killed the highest numbers of buffalo. "Buffalo Bill" Cody got his name by slaughtering 4,280 buffalo in eighteen months. Officers gave seasoned soldiers hunting passes, and entire units pursued and killed as many buffalo as they could, often holding contests that, like those of civilian hunting parties, gave awards to who killed the most buffalo. Later, "hide hunters" joined the killing, taking buffalo skins to supply a burgeoning trade in buffalo leather. When the buffalo became scarce on federal lands, civilian hunters were encouraged to hunt in lands that had been reserved for the Indigenous nations.[56]

The scope and wantonness of the killing astonished many who witnessed it. An estimated thirty to sixty million bison roamed the plains when Jefferson sent the Corps of Discovery across the Mississippi. By 1873, the buffalo herds had been decimated. Lieutenant Colonel Richard Irving Dodge, who had taken civilians on hunts, described the aftermath of an expedition of hide hunters in Kansas: "Where there were myriads of buffalo the year before, there were now myriads of carcasses. The air was foul with a sickening stench, and the vast plain, which only a short twelvemonth before teemed with animal life, was a dead, solitary, putrid desert."[57] By the turn of the century, only 325 buffalo were left.[58]

Subjugating Indigenous enemies by destroying their food, homes, and livelihoods was not a new strategy. During the American Revolution, George Washington sent troops into Haudenosaunee land on a scorched-earth campaign; Washington intended to take the Six Nations out of the war and

---

[56]Smits, "Frontier Army."
[57]Smits, "Frontier Army."
[58]Erin Blakemore, "Native Americans Have General Sherman to Thank for Their Exile to Reservations," History, October 29, 2018, www.history.com/news/shermans-war-on-native-americans?cmpid.

precipitate a refugee crisis for the British. This was despite the fact that only the Senecas and Mohawks actively fought for the British. In early 1779, Washington directed Major General Philip Schuyler to strike the principle town of the Onondagas, most of whom were neutral. The force "put to death all the Women and Children, excepting some of the Young Women, whom they carried away for the use of their Soldiers & were afterwards put to death in a more shameful manner." That summer Schuyler sent another force of Continental troops, under the command of Major General John Sullivan, to invade Haudenosaunee lands, declaring, "The immediate objects are the total destruction and devastation of their settlements and the capture of as many prisoners of every age and sex as possible. It will be essential to ruin their crops now in the ground and prevent their planting more."[59]

Sullivan launched an invasion from the south on August 9, 1779, in concert with another force invading from the west and a third that invaded the Ohio Country. As Sherman's forces would do during the Civil War, Sullivan's troops destroyed everything in their path. They burned houses, plundered their contents, destroyed corn in the fields and storehouses, and girdled the bark of fruit trees so that they would die. By the time Sullivan finished his work almost two months later, his troops had destroyed forty towns, along with 160,000 bushels of corn and vast orchards and vegetable fields. The campaign achieved the desired effect, thoroughly demoralizing many of the Haudenosaunee and driving thousands of refugees to Canada.

WINTER WAR

A second element of Sherman's frontier strategy called for attacks on Indian villages and encampments. The US military had long avoided pitched battles with Indigenous forces, favoring preemptive strikes on villages instead. Sheridan adopted preemptive strikes as military policy. He proposed to launch surprise attacks on Indigenous encampments in the dead of winter, when most of the men of fighting age would be away on winter hunts. The goal of the attacks would be to inflict as much damage as possible: killing and wounding those in the camps, burning lodges, destroying food and possessions, and slaughtering or taking horses. Sheridan justified the

---
[59]Calloway, *Indian World of George Washington*, 249-50.

strategy by asserting, "I have to select that season when I can catch the fiends; and if a village is attacked and women and children killed, the responsibility is not with the soldiers but with the people whose crimes necessitated the attack. . . . Did we cease to throw shells into Vicksburg or Atlanta because women and children were there?"[60]

In late November 1868, Sheridan sent Lieutenant George Armstrong Custer and the Seventh Cavalry to locate and destroy Cheyennes and Arapahos who were raiding across the southern plains. Sheridan ordered Custer "to destroy villages and ponies, to kill or hang all warriors, and to bring back all women and children survivors," so as to make "all segments of Indian society to experience the horrors of war as fully as the warriors."[61] Trekking through deep snow, Custer's scouts discovered a trail that led to an encampment of about 250 Cheyenne located on the Washita River, in present-day Oklahoma. Custer surrounded the camp and prepared to attack at dawn.

The group encamped by the Washita was led by Black Kettle, whose people Chivington's cavalry had massacred at Sand Creek. Despite the massacre, the band remained at peace with the United States, although some of the young men had participated in raids against Black Kettle's wishes. Having been warned of the military offensive against the Cheyenne, Black Kettle led his people to Fort Cobb, where he was informed that they must surrender to Sheridan and return to their reservation. He made ready to comply.

Custer did not bother to learn anything about the camp before he attacked. At daybreak on a bitterly cold morning, he commanded his troops to charge into the village from all sides, while the regimental band played "Garry Owens," a popular tune at the time. The killing lasted about two hours, leaving about one hundred Cheyenne dead, including Black Kettle and his wife, who were shot in the back while trying to cross the Washita. As per Sheridan's orders, the troops slaughtered the band's ponies and mules after culling about a quarter of the herd. They burned the lodges and food supply

---

[60]Quoted in Paul Andrew Hutton, *Phil Sheridan and His Army* (University of Oklahoma Press, 1999), 185.
[61]Quoted in Martin Hannan, "General Custer and the Massacre of Washita River," *The National*, November 27, 2018, www.thenational.scot/news/17257248.general-custer-massacre-washita-river/.

and took fifty-three women and children captive. Calvary losses numbered about twenty.

Sheridan later employed the strategy in the northern plains, with similar effects, to subdue the Piikuni band of the Blackfoot (Siksikaitsitapi) confederacy. Following an 1865 treaty that had been negotiated but not ratified, settlers began trespassing on land reserved for the Blackfeet by the treaty. Within a few years, White ruffians began to attack and murder Blackfeet throughout the region. The Blackfeet appealed to the United States to remove the instigators but received no response. Then, in August 1869, a Blackfoot man named Peter Owl Child killed a prominent rancher who had whipped him for allegedly stealing his horses. He took refuge with a Blackfeet band led by Mountain Chief. When a second settler was killed in October, the frontier Whites demanded that the military chastise the Blackfeet, asserting without evidence that "predatory bands of Indians" had killed many settlers. A grand jury subsequently issued a warrant for the arrest of Owl Child and four others.

Sheridan saw the settlers' appeal as an opportunity to subjugate the Piikuni (Piegan). In late October, he asked Sherman to "let me find out exactly where these Indians are going to spend the Winter; and about the time of a good heavy Snow I will send out a party and try and strike them," when "they will be very helpless." He justified the plan by asserting that "we must occasionally strike where it hurts."[62] Sherman approved the plan in November. Shortly thereafter, Sheridan ordered Major Eugene Baker and the Second US Cavalry to attack the Blackfeet, with orders to "strike them hard." In January 1870, the Second Cavalry departed Fort Shaw in search of the Piegan camp, augmented by 138 infantry. Scouts led the force north to the Marias River, where they found a large encampment and surrounded it.

The camp was not Mountain Chief's but a group of peaceful Piegans. Many in the camp were recovering from an outbreak of smallpox. All the able-bodied men had departed the camp a couple of days earlier on a hunt. At daybreak, on a morning in which the temperature dropped well below zero, one of the scouts realized that the encampment was not Mountain

---

[62]Quoted in Rodger C. Henderson, "The Piikuni and the U.S. Army's Piegan Expedition: Competing Narratives of the 1870 Massacre on the Marias River," *Montana: The Magazine of Western History* (Spring 2018): 55, https://mhs.mt.gov/education/IEFA/HendersonMMWHSpr2018.pdf?ver=2020-01-16-091410-447.

Chief's and informed Baker. Baker replied, "That makes no difference, one band or another of them; they are all Piegans and we will attack them." Shortly thereafter, Heavy Runner, the group's leader, approached Baker, shouting that he had papers that verified that he was on friendly terms with the United States. The soldiers shot him to pieces and began firing into the lodges from nearby bluffs. After a while, the troops rushed into the camp, killing most in their lodges and leaving few survivors. The scout later reported, "Those who were killed were the Chief and such Indians as could not hunt, being the old men, women and children. . . . Only one shot was fired by any of the Indians."[63] Counts of the dead numbered from 173 to 327. Baker's troops destroyed food stores, burned the lodges, and captured four hundred to five hundred horses.

Baker reported that his troops had killed a far smaller number and identified most of the dead as warriors. He also claimed that he had taken a large number of captives but released them when he discovered that some were infected with smallpox. Baker cited smallpox as the reason he burned the lodges and their contents.

William B. Pease, an Indian agent for the Blackfeet, sent a very different report to the Board of Indian Commissioners. The report was subsequently published by *The New York Times* and provoked an outcry against Baker and Sheridan. In response, the army attempted to take control of the narrative by justifying and minimizing the slaughter. A flurry of explanations ensued. Quarter had been given to noncombatants. Captives had been taken but released unhurt. Warriors killed their wives so they wouldn't be tortured. The Piegans deserved chastisement. Pease's report was slanderous. The soldiers found themselves in a ferocious firefight and fought nobly. The casualty figures also shifted back and forth. Sherman defended the two commanders, endorsed the military's version of the massacre, and described it as a battle against a determined foe.

The White settlers of Montana did not share the outrage voiced in eastern papers. *The Helena Daily Herald* crowed, "General Sheridan ordered men to

---

[63] Quoted in Gail Schontzler, "Blackfeet Remember Montana's Greatest Indian Massacre," *Bozeman Daily Chronicle*, January 25, 2012, www.bozemandailychronicle.com/news/sunday/blackfeet-remember-montana-s-greatest-indian-massacre/article_daca1094-4484-11e1-918e-001871e3ce6c.html.

hunt them down, just as we hunt down wolves. When caught in camp, they were slaughtered, very much as we slaughter other wild beasts, when we get the chance."[64] No one was ever called to account for the atrocity. In the end, the public response to the report followed the coverup–outrage–investigation–no action pattern.

THE EXTERMINATION SCRIPT

As the above accounts demonstrate, the best-known of all Indigenous massacres, at Wounded Knee in 1890, was not an anomaly but an exclamation mark. The massacre on the Pine Ridge Reservation was the grim finale of a centuries-long effort to exterminate Indigenous people, which began with the brutal killing of four hundred Pequots at Mystic River, at the hands of settler Christian forces in 1637. Wounded Knee followed a patterned and practiced script that was honed by innumerable killings in every location in settler America and that was replicated during the entire course of settler expansion. The elements of the script can be exemplified in a summary of the Wounded Knee massacre.

1. *Fear or hatred of Indians leads to an unprovoked massacre.* The massacre at Wounded Knee was rooted in settler alarm at the spread of the Ghost Dance, and particularly the misplaced fear that the Ghost Dance would precipitate an uprising among Plains nations. Ghost Dancers followed the teaching of a prophet named Wovoka, who urged Indigenous peoples to keep the peace and return to traditional ways. He proclaimed that, if they did so, the Creator would remove the Whites, revive the buffalo, and restore the Indigenous nations and lands. US troops, however, were told that the Ghost Dance was a ritual preparation for battle. In December 1890, a Lakota Indian agent named Daniel Royer sent a frantic telegram to the Bureau of Indian Affairs, which read, "Indians are dancing in the snow and are wild and crazy. We need protection, and we need it now."[65] The military banned the Ghost Dance, sent additional troops, and made plans to arrest Sitting Bull, whom it believed was promoting the Ghost Dance.

---

[64]Schontzler, "Blackfeet Remember."
[65]"Wounded Knee: United States Versus the Plains Indians," Charles Phillips, HistoryNet, June 12, 2006, www.historynet.com/wounded-knee-massacre-united-states-versus-the-plains-indians/.

2. *The settler military prepares for a preemptive strike, with force, against perceived but relatively defenseless Indigenous enemies.* When Sitting Bull was murdered while being arrested, many Lakota feared that the military intended to exterminate the entire nation. One group of Miniconjou Lakota, led by Sitanka (Big Foot), traveled to the Pine Ridge reservation for protection but was intercepted on December 28, 1890, by US cavalry. The commander, Colonel James Forsyth, told the band to camp at Wounded Knee Creek. He then directed the five-hundred-strong cavalry force to surround the camp and stationed Hotchkiss guns (an early form of machine gun) on a hill.

3. *The settler force engages in an indiscriminate slaughter of the Indigenous group.* The next morning, Forsyth commanded the Lakotas to give up their firearms. They complied, but when Forsyth informed them that they would be taken to a location off Lakota territory, some began the sing the Ghost Dance. Some accounts say that a firearm misfired while being taken from a deaf Miniconjou, while others report that a Ghost Dancer alarmed the soldiers by throwing a handful of dirt into the air. Whatever the case, the cavalry immediately began firing from all quarters, pursuing and killing those who fled for a distance of up to three miles. Current scholarship estimates the number slain at 250 to 300, half of whom were women and children. Cavalry losses amounted to twenty-five, most of whom were probably slain by friendly fire (as most of the band had been disarmed).

4. *The settler military spins the massacre as a battle and justifies it as a necessary military engagement.* When word of the massacre got out, Major General Nelson Miles relieved Forsyth of his command and launched an investigation. The investigation exonerated Forsyth, and Miles restored him to command. Twenty members of the Seventh Cavalry subsequently received the Congressional Medal of Honor, the nation's highest military award, for heroism at Wounded Knee. No one was ever brought to account.

Settler Violence and the Myth of Innocence

Nothing exemplifies more clearly the denial mechanisms that configure the American settler narrative than its determination to suppress the violence that White settlers perpetrated. Instead of acknowledging and addressing countless atrocities, the settler narrative constructs a myth of innocence that covers over innumerable acts of violence and casts massacres as battles against hostile Indians. In so doing, the myth covers over deliberate, determined, and calculated efforts to exterminate the peoples of the land, by both informal and formal means, throughout the entirety of the colonial program.

The myth would have us believe that White settlers had a right to the land by virtue of discovery and followed a divine mandate to transform a disordered wilderness into an ordered, replenished Eden. The people of the land were savage, heathenish, and lawless nations, who had the right only to occupy the land. When Indigenous nations resisted colonial expansion, as they almost always did, settler pioneers and regimes defended themselves and the nation's destiny through just wars and violence. By this move, then, the myth could place blame for the violence suffered by Indigenous peoples squarely on their own shoulders.

QUESTIONS FOR REFLECTION AND DISCUSSION

1. Did settlers execute violence against the Indigenous people in your location and state? Against which nations or tribes?
2. What happened?
3. Where did the violence occur? Are there memorials at the sites of violence? How does your local settler narrative present the events?
4. How does the overview of settler violence shape your image of the American pioneers?
5. Can any of the military actions elaborated in this chapter be considered just?
6. What story from this chapter sticks with you? Spend a few moments to imagine yourself in the experience of the affected people. What do you see? How do you feel?

5

EXPELLING THE INDIAN

Removal and Relocation

Rightly considered, the policy of the General Government toward the red man is not only liberal, but generous. He is unwilling to submit to the laws of the States and mingle with their population. To save him from this alternative, or perhaps utter annihilation, the General Government kindly offers him a new home, and proposes to pay the whole expense of his removal and settlement.

Andrew Jackson, message to Congress,
"On Indian Removal," 1830

On July 12, 1843, the Wyandottes departed from their Grand Reserve in Upper Sandusky, Ohio, and began a journey to newly purchased land west of the Mississippi River. The first leg of their journey took them overland to Cincinnati, where they were to board two steamboats bound for the mouth of the Kansas River. During the weeklong journey, crowds of White settlers gathered to ogle the somber procession of 664 individuals, over one hundred wagons, and approximately three hundred horses as they passed by. The Wyandottes were the last of the Indigenous nations that the federal government expelled from their homelands in Ohio. Their departure provoked a sense of nostalgia and sympathy in the onlookers. Many believed that the Indians were a dying race and viewed their removal from Ohio as the inevitable consequence of the advance of civilization. An account of their journey in the *Xenia Torch-light* captures the wistful tone of many newspaper reports.

> The remains of this once flourishing tribe of Indians passed through our town on Sunday last. . . . Our citizens seemed to look upon the scene of their departure from among us with feelings of melancholy interest. To reflect that the last remnant of a powerful people, once the proud possessors of the soil we now occupy, were just leaving their beloved hunting grounds and the graves of their ancestors—that their council fires had gone out and their wigwams were deserted—was well calculated to awaken the liveliest sympathies of the human heart. No one, we are sure, who felt such emotions, could refrain from breathing a devout aspiration to the "Great Spirit," that he would guide and protect them on their journey.[1]

The nostalgic tone, however, stood in stark contrast to the harsh treatment the Wyandottes had received from White settlers and to the duplicity of the government's dealings with them. Both the settlers and the government wanted the Wyandottes' land, and now that they had it, their attitude shifted from meanness to nostalgia.

The Wyandottes migrated into Ohio in the early 1700s and established towns along the Sandusky River. They fought alongside the British during the Revolutionary War and played a leading role in the Indian wars that followed when US forces invaded the Ohio Country. They observed the peace since that time and fought for the United States against the British in the War of 1812.

During that war, settlers began squatting on Wyandotte land. By summer 1814, approximately eighty settler cabins had been erected in the Wyandotte's principal village at Lower Sandusky. When the war ended, the squatters petitioned the federal government to allow them to stay, in the hope that they would be able to purchase the land they had taken and improved. Others began surveying for a new settler town. The federal government, for its part, was preparing to build a road through Wyandotte territory. The Wyandottes protested these encroachments and elicited a sympathetic response, but no action, from President James Madison.[2] Instead, the United States pressed for the cession of their land and all Indigenous land remaining within the bounds of the state. Treaty commissioners exploited every

---

[1] "The Last Good-Bye: The *Xenia Torch-light* Notes the Departure of the Wyandots, 1843," in *The Ohio Frontier: An Anthology of Early Writings*, ed. Emily Foster (University of Kentucky Press, 1996), 214.

[2] Bowes, *Land Too Good for Indians*, 117-23.

advantage and succeeded in gaining cessions. In 1817, the Ohio nations ceded their remaining territory, about 4.6 million acres, at the Treaty of the Maumee Rapids.[3] The treaty established two reserves for the Wyandottes along the Sandusky, a Grand Reserve of 114,000 acres and a smaller reserve of 39,200 acres at Big Springs.

In 1830, President Andrew Jackson signed the Indian Removal Act into law. The legislation authorized the United States to grant land west of the Mississippi River to tribes in the east that relinquished and departed from their land. Upon passage, the Jackson administration immediately embarked on a program to take the remaining reservation lands and deport their occupants across the Mississippi. By the end of the next year, all Ohio nations except for the Wyandottes had departed.

The Wyandottes rebuffed all efforts to negotiate a cession treaty. They had embraced much of the US civilization program and had grown prosperous, with well-built houses, copious fields and livestock, and several improvements. About half of the nation had converted to Methodist Christianity, under the ministry of John Stewart, an African American lay preacher, and Methodist pastor James Finley. The settlements on the Wyandotte reservations, in short, looked little different from the White settlements that were springing up throughout Ohio.

Nevertheless, the United States wanted the Wyandottes off the land. President Jackson appointed James Gardiner, an alcoholic with an inflated ego, to oversee the removal of the Ohio Indians. Gardiner, as we have seen, supervised the removal of the Senecas in 1831. In the same year, he persuaded the Wyandottes to send a delegation across the Mississippi River to assess land the United States offered in exchange for their Ohio reservations. Confident that they would find the land suitable, Gardiner wrote to Secretary of War Lewis Cass, "I flatter myself that I shall be able, in four or five weeks, to present you with a definitive treaty with this sagacious, intelligent and crafty tribe of Indians."[4] Upon its return, however, the delegation reported the

---

[3] "Treaty with the Wyandot, 1832," Tribal Treaties Database, https://treaties.okstate.edu/treaties/treaty-with-the-wyandot-1832-0339.

[4] J. Orin Oliphant, ed., "The Report of the Wyandot Exploring Delegation, 1831," *Kansas History* 14, no. 3 (1947): 248-62, www.kshs.org/p/the-report-of-the-wyandot-exploring-delegation/13064.

land was completely inadequate and emphatically advised against selling their land.

Undeterred, Gardiner turned to a divide-and-conquer approach. He initiated negotiations with a minority faction at the Big Springs reservation that wanted to sell the smaller reservation. Gardiner assured Cass that "they have Chiefs and Headmen among them who they recognize and obey" and that he was working with them."[5] The "chiefs and headmen" in fact did not have the stature or authority Gardiner claimed. Nevertheless, the faction signed a treaty with the United States in which they sold the Big Springs reservation. Having heard of the hardships suffered by the Senecas and the other Ohio tribes, members of the group migrated to Michigan or Canada instead.

The Wyandottes at the Grand Reserve repudiated the treaty but had no ability to void it. The national council henceforth enacted a law "prohibiting any individual from attempting to conclude a Treaty with a view of extinguishing their title to the whole or part of their Reservation or remove to the West."[6] In response, the settler regime intensified its efforts to remove the remaining Wyandottes. In a message to the Ohio Legislature in 1834, Governor Robert Lucas proposed extending Ohio's jurisdiction over the Grand Reserve, thus making the Wyandottes subject to state law. If adopted, the legislation would effectively eliminate Wyandotte self-governance and further erode the tribe's ability to safeguard its well-being and property. Then, in 1835, the legislature attached the reserve to Crawford County. The Wyandottes responded by requesting that treaty negotiations be reopened. In 1836, they agreed to sell approximately thirty-eight thousand acres on the eastern side of the reserve. They then used proceeds of the sale to further improve the land, thus enhancing their bargaining position with the federal government over against the state of Ohio.

By 1837, however, a group of Wyandottes favoring cession and removal had arisen. Agents Henry Brish and Joseph McCutcheon exploited the division by presenting a removal treaty modeled on the 1831 Seneca removal treaty. Ignoring protocol, they invited any individual Wyandotte who wanted to sell their land to sign it and depart. The measure created significant

---

[5]Oliphant, "Report of the Wyandot."
[6]Bowes, *Land Too Good*, 141.

dissension, prompting an appeal by the national council and an agreement to send a new delegation to visit western land.

Then, in December 1840, settlers murdered a highly esteemed leader of the Christian group, along with his sister and brother-in-law, while they were hunting off-reservation. The three had welcomed and fed a couple of settlers. The settlers, in turn, waited until their hosts fell asleep and then killed them. A joint group of Whites and Wyandottes soon identified the perpetrators, who had plundered some of the victims' possessions. Local authorities jailed the two perpetrators, but they escaped a few weeks later. Local authorities made no attempt to apprehend them.

It was too much. The murders accentuated the hard truth that the settlers surrounding their Grand Reserve would never consent to live in peace with the Wyandottes. Members of the tribe were harassed when they left the reserve. The local authorities did not provide protection or bring perpetrators to justice, claiming that they lacked the resources to do so. About four hundred White squatters and renters resided on the reserve with impunity. Liquor merchants constantly badgered Wyandotte men to buy whiskey.

On March 17, 1842, seven authorized leaders ceded the 114,000 acres of the Grand Reserve in exchange for 148,000 acres of land granted by the United States west of the Mississippi. The negotiations that led up to the treaty were prolonged by the fact that the Wyandottes had learned from the perfidy, ineptitude, and corruption that marked the government's earlier deportations of the Shawnees, Delawares, and Senecas. They held out for the sale of their lands at a price close to market value. They also set the timetable and conditions for their departure. Receiving full compensation for the land's improvements, however, dragged on for years; the improvements were valued at $126,000 by Wyandotte estimates, but the deportees received only $20,000. They were therefore not entirely able to escape the fraudulent schemes of dishonest land speculators and corrupt bureaucrats.[7]

The Wyandottes departed according to plan and in good weather. They contracted for provisions and transportation and arrived at their destination after a couple of weeks. They could not, however, entirely avoid the racist hostility of White settlers and the suffering the other Ohio nations had

---

[7]James H. O'Donnell III, *Ohio's First Peoples* (Ohio University Press, 2000), 124-26.

endured. The captain of the *Nodaway*, one of two steamboats the Wyandottes contracted, removed the carpets that decorated the cabin floors. When they reached their destination, he forced them to sleep on the dew-soaked riverbank rather than on the boat. The groups disembarked with the location of their land yet to be determined. A small delegation had scouted the area the previous May and had agreed to purchase thirty thousand acres, between the Kansas and Missouri Rivers, from the Delawares. The US government, however, had yet to approve the purchase. The Wyandottes were forced to adopt temporary quarters near Westport, Missouri, where they endured harsh conditions. Measles broke out, leaving about one hundred dead in its wake within the year.[8]

The Road to Removal

The departure of the Wyandottes manifests two of the operations of the logic of elimination that Patrick Wolfe has identified in settler colonial programs, namely, legal and political marginalization and displacement. As in the case of the Senecas, the government employed treaties as a means of getting Indigenous land and then removed Indigenous people from the land. Treaties and removal are thus intertwined, so that it is difficult to describe one operation without speaking of the other. I have nevertheless followed Wolfe's lead in discussing them as separate operations, as each was motivated by a different set of intentions and objectives. The employment of legal means, discussed in chapter three, manifests the settler society's determination to get Indigenous land and to do so in a way that ostensibly confirms that it acted fairly and honorably. The removal of Indigenous peoples, on the other hand, expresses a racist aversion to the Indian that refused to allow even one to remain in the newly acquired settler homeland.

The question of what to do with the Indigenous people who had relinquished their lands affected American Indian policy from the Washington administration onward. Many settler elites believed that the Indians were human beings, who could and should be assimilated into the new civilization the United States was establishing in the land. Thomas Jefferson, one of the most ardent proponents of this view, wrote, "I believe the Indian then

---

[8]Bowes, *Land Too Good*, 147-48.

Expelling the Indian

to be in body and mind equal to the white man."⁹ Those sharing Jefferson's views believed that Indian savagery was a consequence of environment and climate. They believed that Indians would adopt civilization once they realized its benefits. If some tribes were slow to arrive at this realization, the depletion of the game on which they depended would eventually require them to abandon the hunt and adopt European-style agriculture and settlements. Many agreed with George Washington that the bestowal of civilization to the Indians more than compensated them for the sale of their lands. With this in mind, settler elites could imagine a humane and benevolent program that lifted Indians from savagery to civility, while at the same time allowing settlers to reap the benefits of lands Indians no longer used.

Jefferson expressed this view in 1808, when as president he wrote to "my children, the Delawares, Mohicans, and Munsees," after another in a long series of land cessions required them to move west to the Indiana Territory. Noting that subsistence from hunting often left them with a scarcity of food, Jefferson observed that White settlers always had food in abundance and doubled their numbers every twenty years. The remedy for the Indians' scarcity was therefore in their hands:

> You see then My Children, that it depends on yourselves alone to become a numerous and great people. Let me entreat you therefore on the lands now given you, to begin to give every man a farm, let him enclose it, cultivate it, build a warm House on it, and when he dies let it belong to his wife and children after him. Nothing is so easy as to learn to cultivate the earth.

Jefferson concluded with an idealistic vision of a future that foresaw the mixing of settler and Indigenous into one nation: "You will unite yourselves with us, join in our great Councils & form one people with us and we shall all be Americans, you will mix with us by marriage, your blood will run in our veins, & will spread with us over this great Island."¹⁰

By 1814, however, Jefferson's vision no longer held traction with most Whites. The quixotic idea that Indigenous nations would readily embrace

---
⁹Quoted in "Thomas Jefferson's Enlightenment and American Indians," Thomas Jefferson Foundation, www.monticello.org/thomas-jefferson/louisiana-lewis-clark/origins-of-the-expedition/jefferson-and-american-indians/jefferson-s-enlightenment-and-american-indians/.
¹⁰"From Thomas Jefferson to Hendrick Aupaumut, 21 December 1808," Founders Online, https://founders.archives.gov/documents/Jefferson/99-01-02-9358.

American civilization foundered on the hard reality that most did not want to be civilized, preferred their "heathenish" ways, and maintained a vigorous determination to keep their lands. There was also the fact that most of the Indigenous nations had rebuffed the Americans and fought for the British during the war. Indigenous refusal to make decisions that Whites believed were in their best interests had by this time convinced most settler minds that Indians were incapable of rising from savagery to civilization. White society explained this perceived incapacity in terms of an emerging racial consciousness.

Many among the founding generation believed Providence was guiding the United States to establish a new nation of liberty, achievement, and civilization. In the words of John Adams, the United States was "destined beyond a doubt to be the greatest power on earth."[11] In the early decades of the nineteenth century, this conviction received support from a belief that the Anglo-Saxon race was superior to all others, uniquely gifted, and destined to advance human progress, liberty, and humane values. It was a small step from this belief to the conviction that other races, namely, Africans and Indigenous peoples, were incapable of advancing toward civilization; at best, they could rise no higher than menial laborers for the White empire. Other European races, perhaps, could be civilized. Non-European races could not.

The developing racial hierarchy thus explained, in settler eyes, the Indians' baffling resistance to American civilization. That is, Indians were an inferior race, genetically predisposed to lawlessness, indolence, wastefulness, and violence. Indians thus constituted an impediment to human progress and the fulfillment of Anglo-Saxon destiny. They therefore had to be removed from the land. Many who held this view believed that the Indians would gradually die out, as had happened throughout history when a superior people overcame an inferior one. Destiny dictated, and history confirmed, that Anglo-Saxon civilization would thrive and expand, while Indigenous peoples would dwindle and die.

This perspective is epitomized by the views of Henry Clay, who served as John Quincy Adams's secretary of state. Adams summarized Clay's views as follows:

---

[11]Quoted in Reginald Horsman, *Race and Manifest Destiny* (Harvard University Press, 1981), 86.

It was impossible to civilize Indians; that there never was a full-blooded Indian who took to civilization. It was not in their nature. . . . They were destined to extinction, and although he would never use or countenance inhumanity towards them, he did not think of them, as a race, worth preserving. He considered them as essentially inferior to the Angle-Saxon race, which were now taking their place on this continent. They were not an improvable breed, and their disappearance from the human family will be no great loss to the world. In point of fact they were rapidly disappearing, and he did not believe that in fifty years from this time there would be any of them left.[12]

Another writer expresses the perspective more succinctly: "That they should become extinct is inevitable."[13]

An honorable solution to the Indian problem presented itself with the Louisiana Purchase in 1803. Most settler Americans viewed the vast lands west of the Mississippi River as virtually empty, even though many of the peoples throughout the West lived in settlements sustained by agriculture. The Louisiana Purchase provided President Jefferson with an opportunity to resolve White settlers' insatiable greed for Indian land on the one hand and to ensure the preservation of Indian nations on the other. Jefferson believed that the interests of both parties would therefore best be served if the Indigenous nations east of the Mississippi River would exchange their land for land of comparable or greater value west of the Mississippi. The plan would allow Indigenous people to live as they pleased, free from harassment by White settlers, and would relieve settler pressure by opening the West for sale and settlement.

In his second inaugural address on March 4, 1805, Jefferson declared that, since Indians had been "reduced within the limits too narrow for the hunter's state, humanity enjoins us to teach them agriculture and the domestic arts."[14] Three days later, he floated his plan for land exchange to a delegation of Chickasaws. Jefferson informed the delegation that the United States had recently obtained, beyond the Mississippi, "a great deal of land unoccupied by red men." He elaborated by telling them, "We would prefer giving you lands there, or money and goods, as you like best, for such parts of your land

---

[12]Quoted in Horsman, *Race and Manifest Destiny*, 198.
[13]Quoted in Dippie, *Vanishing American*, 11.
[14]"Thomas Jefferson Second Inaugural Address," March 4, 1805, The Avalon Project, https://avalon.law.yale.edu/19th_century/jefinau2.asp.

on this side of the Mississippi as you are disposed to part with."[15] Jefferson even drafted a constitutional amendment to implement the plan. Although he did not submit it, he continued to advocate for the plan as an honorable means of facilitating colonial expansion, protecting Indian people, and allowing them to advance toward civilization at their own speed.

Jefferson's proposed solution prompted the United States to negotiate thirty treaties with more than a dozen nations, which yielded cessions totaling two hundred thousand square miles. After the War of 1812, public sentiment increasingly inclined toward expelling nations east of the Mississippi once and for all. Under increasing pressure, the Monroe administration worked with Congress on a plan for what was euphemistically called Indian removal.

Just before Monroe's inauguration in 1817, the Senate Committee on Public Lands endorsed Jefferson's plan for the exchange of land, and commissioners fanned out to acquire cessions. The commissioners, however, met with limited success, leading to a more vigorous policy of removal. Toward the end of his second term in 1825, Monroe proposed to Congress that the eastern nations should be removed "from the lands which they now inhabit." Employing an argument that was now generally accepted, he declared that removal "would not only shield them from impending ruin, but promote their welfare and happiness." In addition, Monroe asserted, "Experience has clearly demonstrated that in their present state it is impossible to incorporate them in such masses, in any form whatever, into our system."[16]

The Road to Removal

Georgia in particular pressed hard for removal. In 1802, President Jefferson secretly promised the state that the federal government would expel the Cherokees from its borders as soon as it could be done "peaceably and on reasonable terms." In exchange, Georgia agreed to relinquish its claims to land west of its current border. The Cherokees, however, had no intention

---

[15]Quoted in Richard Drinnon, *Facing West: The Metaphysics of Indian-Hating and Empire-Building* (University of Oklahoma Press, 1997), 83-84.
[16]Quoted in "Manifest Destiny and Indian Removal," Smithsonian American Art Museum, https://americanexperience.si.edu/wp-content/uploads/2015/02/Manifest-Destiny-and-Indian-Removal.pdf.

of parting with any more of their land. They enjoyed widespread support from those in settler America who promoted the civilization program and pointed to the Cherokees as proof that Indians could be civilized. The Cherokees had adopted European farming practices, wore European-style clothing, and welcomed Christian missionaries. Furthermore, they developed a written script of their language and established a centralized government under a national council. "The great difficulty" in removing the Cherokees, observed John C. Calhoun, "arises from the progress of the Cherokees in civilization. They are now, within the limits of Georgia, about fifteen thousand, and increasing in equal proportion with the whites; all cultivators, with a representative government, judicial courts, Lancaster schools, and permanent property."[17]

The Georgians demanded that the federal government remove the Cherokees, by force if necessary. The prospect of their removal, however, was vigorously opposed in Congress and the settler society at large. Opponents of removal argued that the United States must not renege on treaty obligations to a nation that exemplified the viability of the civilization program. Settler elites outside the South, furthermore, insisted that all land cessions must be voluntary. All the while, government agents continued to purchase lands from Indigenous peoples in the northwest and southeast, acquiring approximately six hundred thousand square miles of land during the first two decades of the nineteenth century.[18] The Cherokees, however, still refused to sell.

Georgia's frustration intensified when, in 1827, the Cherokees adopted a national constitution modeled on the US Constitution. Infuriated Georgia politicians declared that the action created a separate state within Georgia's borders and challenged Georgia's sovereignty. The following year, Elias Boudinot founded a newspaper called *The Cherokee Phoenix*, published in both English and Cherokee, which advocated the Cherokee cause. Then, later that same year, gold was discovered on Cherokee land in the Appalachian foothills near present-day Dahlonega, Georgia. Within a year, fifteen thousand miners descended on Cherokee land.

---

[17] Quoted in Horsman, *Race and Manifest Destiny*, 196-97.
[18] Claudio Saunt, *Unworthy Republic: The Dispossession of Native Americans and the Road to Indian Territory* (Norton, 2020), 7.

In December 1827, the Georgia legislature proclaimed that it possessed the authority to extend its laws over the Cherokees and "to coerce obedience" from "all descriptions of people," be they "white, red, or black."[19] The resolution, among other things, constituted a forceful assertion of states' rights, as only the federal government was authorized to regulate trade and negotiate treaties with Indigenous peoples. In blatant defiance of federal jurisdiction, Georgia passed a series of laws over the next few years that aimed to dissolve Cherokee Nation. The state shut down the Cherokee National Council and tribal courts. It prohibited Cherokees from selling their land or its gold. It classified them as "free persons of color," a status that took away their right to own land. Finally, the state annexed Cherokee lands to counties in the northwest area of the state, exerted its laws over the annexed land, and nullified Cherokee jurisdiction. The recently admitted states of Alabama and Mississippi followed suit with similarly restrictive laws against resistant Indigenous groups. "One great argument for removal of the Indians," wrote Secretary of War James Barbour, "is that they *cannot remain where they are*, on account of the determination of the States of Georgia, Alabama, and Mississippi that they shall *not*."[20]

Voluntary Removal

In 1828, the people of the United States elected Andrew Jackson to the presidency on a platform that advocated Indian removal. On taking office, Jackson immediately got to work on a bill that would authorize the president to implement an exchange of Indian land. The bill precipitated a year of fiery debate in Congress and in the news media, letter writing and petitions from those opposing removal, and a full-court press from Southern politicians. Northerners, most of whom opposed removal, pointed to the success of the civilization program and asserted that Indians should be treated with dignity. They pointed to the nation's moral and legal obligation to honor treaties and decried the immorality and injustice of coercing Indigenous nations to leave their ancestral homelands.

Southerners retorted that whatever level of advancement the Indians attained was due to the White blood that coursed through the veins of many

---

[19]Saunt, *Unworthy Republic*, 86.
[20]Horsman, *Race and Manifest Destiny*, 200.

of their leaders. They questioned the validity of making treaties with Indian nations as equals. They pointed to the deceitful character of federal treaty making in general. And they accused Northerners of hypocrisy, since Northerners too inhabited land taken from Indian nations. After months of impassioned debate, Congress passed the Indian Removal Act in April 1830, by a vote of 28 to 19 in the Senate and 103 to 97 in the House of Representatives. Jackson signed the bill into law on May 28.

The election of Jackson and the passage of the Indian Removal Act emboldened the Georgia elites, who recognized that they had a friend in the president. The state government thereupon took additional measures to dissolve Cherokee sovereignty and force the nation off its Georgia lands. Later in the year, Georgia expelled federal troops that were stationed on Cherokee land to protect Cherokee property. In place of the federal garrison, the state established a paramilitary force of sixty men, called the Georgia Guard, to patrol Cherokee land. The Georgia Guard replaced the Cherokee Light Guard, which Cherokee Nation established in 1827 to expel the thousands of squatters and miners encroaching on Cherokee land. The Georgia Guard ostensibly was to conduct the same mission. The force was far too small, however, to stem a settler tide that reached four thousand by mid-1831 and over seven thousand by year's end. The guard's mission was undercut by the fact that it had no authority to levy fines or penalties against the few individuals it arrested. The Cherokees were therefore left without effective recourse against squatting and harassment.

In 1831, Cherokee Nation sought an injunction against Georgia's effort to drive it off its land, citing the treaties in force. The litigation reached the Supreme Court in the case of *Cherokee Nation v. Georgia*. The Court ruled for the Cherokees, declaring that they were a separate nation and that the treaties and laws of the United States had always recognized them as such. Yet, Chief Justice John Marshall also declared that the Cherokees were not a foreign nation but rather a "domestic dependent nation," whose relation to the United States "resembles that of a ward to his guardian." Because the Cherokees constituted a separate nation, the court concluded, they had no legal standing in US courts. For that reason, the court dismissed the suit.[21]

---

[21]Cherokee Nation v. The State of Georgia, Legal Information Institute, www.law.cornell.edu/supremecourt/text/30/1.

The Cherokees were party to another case a year later. The case challenged a Georgia law that required Whites who resided in Cherokee territory to obtain a license from the governor and swear allegiance to the state. Two missionaries, Samuel A. Worcester and Elizur Butler, refused to obey the law and were tried and convicted in a Georgia court. Worcester was sentenced to four years of hard labor.

Worcester's case attracted the attention of William Wirt, who had served as attorney general under Monroe and Adams and had represented the Cherokees in *Cherokee Nation v. Georgia*. Wirt brought Worcester's case before the Supreme Court with the intent of resolving the issue of Georgia's claims and actions against the Cherokees. In March 1832, the court again ruled against Georgia in the case of *Worcester v. Georgia* and affirmed the Cherokees' rights. Justice Marshall declared that the United States was bound by its treaty commitments and reaffirmed that authority over Indian affairs resided with the federal government and not with the states. The Cherokees, he wrote, did not surrender their independence or right to self-government when they placed themselves under the protection of the United States. "The laws of Georgia," he asserted, "can have no force," and "the citizens of Georgia have no right to enter but with the assent of the Cherokees themselves or in conformity with treaties and with acts of Congress." In a striking summation, Marshall declared, "The acts of Georgia are repugnant to the Constitution, laws, and treaties of the United States."[22]

The decision encouraged the Cherokees. Georgia, however, refused to recognize it and dared the federal government to enforce it. It did not, and Georgia tightened the noose. Just two months after the *Worcester* ruling, Georgia passed legislation that declared all Cherokee laws null and void. Then, in fall 1832, Georgia held a lottery for the Cherokee land that the state had annexed the previous December. The lottery sold land to fifty-three thousand winners, who rushed into Cherokee territory to claim their new property and force the Cherokee occupants off it. *The Cherokee Phoenix* decried the "atrocious injustice" in which a lottery winner entered his newly purchased plot and "drove the innocent Indian from his well cultivated

---

[22]Worcester v. The State of Georgia, 31 U.S. 515 (1832), Justia, https://supreme.justia.com/cases/federal/us/31/515/.

field."²³ Georgia, however, continued to press. In 1833, the legislature passed legislation that prohibited members of Cherokee Nation from bringing lawsuits against White citizens. As the testimony of a Cherokee was now inadmissible in court, Cherokee property owners were left with no means of protecting or recovering confiscated land.

The measures that settler regimes enacted in Georgia, Alabama, and Mississippi were designed to preserve the fiction that the Indigenous nations agreed voluntarily to exchange their homelands for western land. The states believed that they owned the land and that their actions were legitimate extensions of their sovereignty. On its face, the choice they gave the Cherokees—stay and be subject to our laws or resettle in another land—appeared equitable. Yet, as the states' actions demonstrated, there was nothing voluntary in the way the Cherokees were dispossessed. The Georgia state legislature stripped the Cherokees of their rights, removed protection from harassing settlers, confiscated their lands, and sold them by lottery. And it did so with impunity. Faced with a relentless settler tide, threats from the states, and no federal protection, the nations of the Southeast were going to lose their land one way or another. The states gave them the illusion of choice but effectively coerced them into ceding their land.²⁴

The Chickasaws, Choctaws, and Muskogees experienced similar pressure from state and federal authorities as the Cherokees experienced from Georgia. Shortly after the passage of the Indian Removal Act, President Jackson called for a meeting with delegates from the southeastern nations to orchestrate their removal. Only the Chickasaws sent a full delegation. They were nonetheless adamant that they would not exchange land. The two treaty commissioners, John Eaton and John Coffee, pressed hard on the intolerable situation the Chickasaws would face if they chose to live under the jurisdiction of the state of Mississippi. "Mississippi or happiness," they declared, "must and will follow on the decision you shall make."²⁵ Under extraordinary duress, the Chickasaws signed a removal treaty.

---

²³Sarah H. Hill, "Cherokee Removal Scenes: Ellijay, Georgia, 1838." *Southern Spaces*, August 23, 2012, https://southernspaces.org/2012/cherokee-removal-scenes-ellijay-georgia-1838/.

²⁴For a detailed account of Georgia's measures to dispossess the Cherokees, see Steve Innskeep, *Jacksonland: President Andrew Jackson, Cherokee Chief John Ross, and a Great American Land Grab* (Penguin, 2015); Saunt, *Unworthy Republic*.

²⁵Saunt, *Unworthy Republic*, 88.

Two weeks later, at Dancing Rabbit Creek, the commissioners met with Choctaw leaders and presented them with the same choice: to stay and endure the "attendant train of evils" they would experience or to undergo "the privations and sufferings of a reluctant removal."[26] Recognizing the commissioners' end game, Choctaw leaders argued for compensation in addition to the exchange of land: representation in Congress, funding for schools, and a national endowment. The commissioners, however, were not there to bargain. Faced with what appeared to be the prospect of losing their land by removing west or seeing their lands allotted by the states, the Choctaws also signed a treaty of removal.

The Muskogees lost what remained of their Georgia land in 1825, when a leader named William McIntosh was bribed into secretly ceding it by treaty. Although the federal government rejected the fraudulent treaty, Georgia acted as though it were in force. In 1832, Muskogee leaders proposed a plan for ceding their lands in Alabama without being required to move. In return for ceding all their lands in the state, the Muskogees proposed that families who chose to remain would receive individual allotments grouped into reservations, which they could either sell or gain title after occupying their plot for five years. The United States agreed to a compromise. In the Treaty of Cusseta, the United States approved the allotment of land and agreed on a payment of $100,000 at signing, annual payments for the next fifteen years, and compensation for improvements on Muskogee land. The United States, however, also declared its desire that "the Creeks should remove to the country west of the Mississippi" and "as fast as the Creeks are prepared to emigrate, they shall be removed at the expense of the United States," although they would not be compelled to do so. The United States also promised to remove "all intruders" from Muskogee land.[27]

Implementing the treaty turned into a fiasco. A census was required to determine allotments, but taking it was fraught with complications and errors. White settlers continued to encroach on unceded land. They forced Muskogee families from their homes, fenced in and plowed their property,

---

[26]Saunt, *Unworthy Republic*, 90.
[27]"Treaty with the Creeks, 1832," Tribal Treaties Database, https://treaties.okstate.edu/treaties/treaty-with-the-creeks-1832-0341; "Creek Indians," *New Georgia Encyclopedia*, last edited August 25, 2020, www.georgiaencyclopedia.org/articles/history-archaeology/creek-indians/.

Expelling the Indian 121

and stole their livestock. Francis Scott Key, whom President Jackson sent to investigate Muskogee appeals, reported the presence of numerous White towns on Muskogee land. The federal government, however, refused to evict the settlers as it had promised. To make matters worse, unscrupulous land speculators took advantage of the fact that the processes of land certification and title were foreign to most Muskogees. Countless numbers were swindled out of their allotments. As one historian notes, "White behavior was so wanton that even government officials were shocked by the fraud and violence."[28] A contemporary account describes the chaos at a land office:

> The land stealers were crowding into the [land] office by droves, and certifying contracts very fast, and it appeared as though they would steal all the Indians' land; they seemed to carry on the business in sport; that a toast was given in a crowd by one of those concerned in these nefarious practices, "Here's to the man that can steal the most land to-morrow without getting caught at it."[29]

By 1835, most of those who had taken allotments had lost them. Many were reduced to eating bark and animal carcasses to survive. The dire situation and unrelenting loss of land led some of the Muskogee bands to strike back against the settlers, igniting a brief but bloody war. President Jackson dispatched fourteen companies of Army regulars under the command of General Winfield Scott. The force defeated the Muskogee fighters and rounded up their families into concentration camps. Then it forced fifteen thousand of them to walk to Oklahoma, with little more than the clothes they wore. Thirty-five hundred died along the way. When the survivors reached their destination at Fort Gibson, the Army gave each family a blanket and then abandoned them.[30]

The Cherokees held out tenaciously in the face of Georgia's efforts to remove them but eventually fractured. One party (the Treaty Party), led by John Ridge, Major Ridge, Andrew Ross, and Elias Boudinot, saw no viable alternative but to negotiate a removal treaty on the best terms possible. The opposing party, led by principal leader John Ross and the Cherokee

---

[28] David S. Heidler and Jeanne T. Heidler, *Indian Removal* (Norton, 2007), 37.
[29] "Stealing Land from the Creeks, 1835," in Heidler and Heidler, *Indian Removal*, 169.
[30] "Second Creek War," *Encyclopedia of Alabama*, October 5, 2016, https://encyclopediaofalabama .org/article/second-creek-war/; "Forced Removal of the Creeks," ExploreSouthernHistory.com, www.exploresouthernhistory.com/creektrail.html.

government, refused to cede Cherokee land and believed the settler state could be persuaded to stop Georgia's land grab and honor its treaty obligations. In 1834, John Ross led a delegation to Washington, DC, to enlist federal support for the Cherokee cause.

Eager to exploit the division, Jackson sent John Schermerhorn and a group of commissioners to Georgia in 1835 to extract a removal treaty by hook or by crook. Ross was still in Washington when Schermerhorn ordered the Georgia Guard to shut down *The Cherokee Phoenix* and seize Ross's house and land for inclusion in the land lottery. The Guard then briefly imprisoned Ross and a friend on their return.

In December, Schermerhorn called members of the Treaty Party to a meeting at New Echota, a former principal city of Cherokee Nation. Those who attended had no formal authority to represent the Cherokee national government and represented a significant minority of the nation. Nevertheless, twenty of them signed a treaty ceding all seven million acres of Cherokee land east of the Mississippi River for $5 million, the price that the Senate had offered Ross for the land, less expenses to cover the cost of Cherokee expulsion. The Cherokee national council repudiated the treaty and instead sent a petition to the US government, with 3,352 Cherokee signatures. The petition read, in part:

> By the stipulations of this instrument, we are despoiled of our private possessions, the indefeasible property of individuals. We are stripped of every attribute of freedom and eligibility for legal self-defence. Our property may be plundered before our eyes; violence may be committed on our persons, even our lives may be taken away, and there is none to regard our complaints. We are denationalized; we are disfranchised. We are deprived of membership in the human family![31]

Additional petitions from White allies inundated the Senate. Nevertheless, the Senate ratified the treaty by a single vote on March 1, 1836. The federal government immediately began to make plans for the deportation of the entire nation by the end of 1838.

---

[31] "1836 Protest Petition Excerpt: Transcription," Native Knowledge 360°, https://americanindian.si.edu/nk360/removal-cherokee//transcripts/pdf/petition-original.pdf.

THE OPERATIONS OF REMOVAL

The deportations of Indigenous peoples from the Southeast and the Old Northwest inflicted unimaginable suffering. Despite the enormous windfall the United States received from the sale and settlement of Indigenous land, the federal government conducted the deportations on the cheap, employing an administrative system that had never before managed and provisioned the migration of tens of thousands of people at a time. It was, in the words of Massachusetts congressman Edward Everett, "an experiment on human life and human happiness of perilous novelty."[32]

An army of bureaucrats and accountants coordinated the provisioning of these massive undertakings. Their budget estimates and dispersals typically reflected best-case scenarios and assumed the competence and honesty of merchants and contractors. Budgeting normally left little room for unplanned contingencies of climate, human error, and the myriad unforeseen situations that arose from the forced migration of thousands of human beings. The chaos was exacerbated by the fact that planners sometimes had to work with maps that were inaccurate or incomplete. Nevertheless, the government officials overseeing deportation insisted on the strict application of regulations, which generally meant "saving money, even at the expense of the families who were being expelled from their homes."[33]

The Choctaws were the first to depart. When the time came, thousands decided instead to accept land allotments and remain in Mississippi, a number far more than the government had anticipated. The agent appointed to register the names for the allotments, one William Ward, was a mean-tempered drunk who did all he could to prevent applicants from enrolling, including destroying tribal records and registry books. By the federal government's accounting, 1,585 families were to receive allotments, encompassing one to two million acres. Only 143 families actually acquired them, for a total of 140,241 acres.[34] The Treaty of Dancing Rabbit Creek promised compensation for the land, livestock, and improvements left behind by

---

[32]Quoted in Saunt, *Unworthy Republic*, 111. The following summary follows Saunt's accounts of the Choctaw, Chickasaw, and Creek expulsions.
[33]Saunt, *Unworthy Republic*, 121.
[34]Saunt, *Unworthy Republic*, 202.

those who departed for the West. Yet, only 5 percent of this group ever received money from the sale of their lands.

The removal plan called for the transport of most of the Choctaws via steamboats from Vicksburg or Memphis, thence to Arkansas Post, near the mouth of the Arkansas River, and from there to Little Rock. From that point, they would walk the final 230 miles on foot to their destination. The journey did not begin until November, when the deportees were packed onto steamboats and sent south into one of the most severe winter storms in fifty years—the same storm that slammed into the Senecas of Sandusky as they trekked westward. When twenty-five hundred who reached Arkansas Post in late November and early December arrived without shoes and coats, they were forced to take shelter in about one hundred tents. Another group traveled on a route that required them to walk in frigid conditions, leading to the deaths of thirty-four along the way. Cholera struck a second wave of deportees who set out in October 1832, killing many of the four thousand who traveled by steamboat. Because of the outbreak, another one thousand refused to board the boats and struck out on their own through icy swamps.[35]

The United States deported the Chickasaws in 1837. As with the Choctaws and Muskogees, land speculators swindled individual Chickasaws. The federal government, for its part, paid for the land purchases with paper money, which lost much of its value when the markets crashed later that year. The loss of value, however, did not deter the United States from billing the Chickasaws for every expense associated with the deportation, from the census taking and surveys required for land sales to office furniture and supplies. Embezzlement and inflated charges siphoned off more of the proceeds. When all was said and done, 95 percent of the Chickasaws received no actual compensation for the purchase of their land. "The United States," writes Claudio Saunt, "made Chickasaws finance their own dispossession and pay for their own deportation."[36]

The federal government conducted Cherokee removal through the exertion of overwhelming military force. The government's ratification of the fraudulent Treaty of New Echota generated a groundswell of opposition in the northern states and, as the deadline for removal approached, provoked

---

[35]Saunt, *Unworthy Republic*, 124-55.
[36]Saunt, *Unworthy Republic*, 217.

Expelling the Indian

significant opposition in Congress. John Ross continued his tireless efforts to plead the Cherokee's cause. By May 1838, the deadline stipulated by the treaty, only about two thousand Cherokees had departed for the West. Based on the fraudulent Treaty of New Echota, the settler government now considered the remaining Cherokees to be illegal occupants, subject to arrest and expulsion.

President Martin Van Buren, Jackson's successor, ordered General Winfield Scott to supervise the forcible eviction of those Cherokees who remained. To ensure success, he gave Scott the authority to muster up to three thousand militia into federal service, which would supplement a force of twenty-two hundred army regulars. On May 26, Scott ordered the troops to arrest all the Indians they could find and herd them under guard to the nearest fort, and from there to eleven concentration camps in Alabama and Tennessee. The soldiers went from house to house at all hours of the day and night, sometimes taking families from their homes during mealtimes and from their beds, often leaving them no opportunity to prepare or pack belongings. About a thousand fled to the mountains of North Carolina ahead of the soldiers. By the end of June, the military had gathered fifteen thousand Cherokees into the concentration camps. Scott announced that the mission was accomplished by reporting, "Georgia has been entirely cleared of red population."[37]

The US government cared little about learning from the errors of past deportations. The Cherokee deportation was plagued with the same mismanagement, underfunding, fraud, lack of provisions, and unsanitary conditions that characterized the earlier deportations. Dysentery, measles, and other diseases ravaged the camps. In June, the Army crowded about three thousand deportees onto steamboats for a twelve-hundred-mile journey. The boats foundered when the water in the Arkansas River dropped so low that they could no longer proceed; many deportees were forced to complete the journey on foot during one of the hottest and driest summers in memory. The remainder of the Cherokees embarked by land in October via three overland routes. They encountered torrential rains and vicious cold. Typhus, dysentery, measles, pleurisy, and other fevers took a toll, especially on the very young and the very old.

---

[37]Saunt, *Unworthy Republic*, 279.

More than three thousand people died on the journey to Oklahoma. Another sixteen hundred died in the camps. Eight hundred more died shortly after arriving at their destination; the total number of deaths constituted approximately one out of every four persons who walked what the Cherokees called the Trail of Tears. An army private by the name of John Burnett, assigned to the last departing group headed by John Ross, recalled:

> Men working in the fields were arrested and driven to the stockades. Women were dragged from their homes by soldiers whose language they could not understand. Children were often separated from their parents and driven into the stockades with the sky for a blanket and the earth for a pillow. And often the old and infirm were prodded with bayonets to hasten them to the stockades.[38]

Burnett recalled that when the Cherokee departed in October, "many of these helpless people did not have blankets and many of them had been driven from home barefooted." When the deportees were hit by fierce winter storms, they "had to sleep in the wagons and on the ground without fire." During a particularly fierce storm, Burnett saw the wife of John Ross give her blanket to a sick child and ride "thinly clad through a blinding sleet and snowstorm." She later died of pneumonia, and "her unconfined body was buried in a shallow grave by the roadside." Burnett later remarked, "I fought through the civil war and have seen men shot to pieces and slaughtered by thousands, but the Cherokee removal was the cruelest work I ever knew."[39]

Cherokee Nation never received the $5 million that Congress promised to pay for their lands in the Treaty of New Echota.

The Long Walk

The ineptitude, chicanery, and cruelty that characterized the removals of the 1830s were replicated throughout the nineteenth century as the settler nation expanded westward. While the deportation of the Southeastern nations was accomplished only after a long period of struggle and resistance, subsequent deportations typically followed a more direct trajectory and involved the

---

[38] "Primary Source: A Soldier Recalls the Trail of Tears," Anchor: North Carolina History Online Resource, 2009, www.ncpedia.org/anchor/primary-source-soldier-0.

[39] "Primary Source: A Soldier Recalls." See also James Mooney, "The Removal—1838–39," in *Myths of the Cherokee* (Government Printing Office, 1902), 130-35.

military at the earliest stage of the process. In many instances, advocates justified the removal of Indigenous populations as a measure necessary to protect White settlers.

Such was the case with the removal of the Navajo nation (Diné), which the Navajo call the Long Walk. Conflict between the US military and the Navajo began according to the typical script; settlers encroached on Navajo land that the United States claimed, provoking raids by the Navajo. To put an end to raiding, the US military established a fort deep in Navajo territory in September 1851. The army named it Fort Defiance and stationed four companies of US cavalry there. Federal authorities used the fort as a base for negotiating a series of peace treaties. None of them stopped Navajo raiding, because the United States stubbornly continued to treat with leaders of small bands as if they represented the nation as a whole.

At the outbreak of the Civil War in 1861, the army abandoned the fort in order to secure New Mexico for the Union. When that was accomplished, the military turned its attention to subjugating the Navajo and the Mescalero Apaches, with the intention of removing them to a reservation and teaching them how to farm. Brigadier General James H. Carleton was appointed military commander of the newly created Department of New Mexico for that purpose. Carleton rebuilt Fort Defiance as the center of operations against the Navajos and Mescaleros. He built another, Fort Sumner, almost two hundred miles east of the Navajo homeland, where subdued Navajos and Mescaleros would be exiled. Carleton also established a camp in the vicinity (Bosque Redondo), encompassing about forty square miles, for the "concentration and maintenance of all captive Indians from the New Mexico territory."[40] For reasons known only to him, Carleton believed the remote, desolate territory would promote a rapid transition to an agricultural economy.

Carleton then ordered Colonel Kit Carson and a company of New Mexico Volunteers to hunt down the Mescaleros, with the following orders: "There is to be no council with the Indians nor any talks. . . . The men are to be slain whenever and wherever they can be found. The women and children may

---

[40]Denis Foster Johnston, *An Analysis of Sources of Information on the Population of the Navaho* (U.S. Government Printing Office, 1966), 23.

be taken as prisoners, but, of course, they are not to be killed."[41] Carson prosecuted a brief campaign that resulted in the surrender and relocation of four hundred Mescaleros by the end of the year. He refused, however, to follow Carleton's order to kill all the men.

After imprisoning the Mescaleros at Bosque Redondo, Carleton gave the Navajos until July 20, 1863, to assemble at the camp, after which time they would be considered "hostiles." As the deadline approached, Carleton sent a message to the Navajos through Carson. "You have deceived us too often, and robbed and murdered our people too long, to trust you again at large in your own country. This war shall be pursued against you if it takes years, now that we have begun, until you cease to exist or move."[42] When the deadline passed without response, Carleton ordered Carson to devastate Navajo land and starve the Navajos into submission. On July 7, Carson's troops, accompanied by allied Utes, set out to apprehend the Navajos, destroy Navajo villages, slaughter sheep and cattle, burn cornfields, and destroy thousands of peach trees.

The campaign lasted into January, when Carson's troops trapped a large number of Navajos who had taken refuge in Canyon de Chelly. The Navajos were able to hold out for some time on stockpiled provisions, but when these ran out, those in the canyon had little choice but to accept a promise by Carson that any Navajos who surrendered would not be harmed. Within a few weeks, twenty-four hundred starving Navajos had given themselves up at Fort Defiance. By mid-March the number reached approximately six thousand. And by the time the last group left Fort Defiance in 1866, the total count hovered around ten thousand. Most had walked 300–450 miles via various routes to Fort Sumner.

The deportation to Bosque Redondo occurred in waves. The first group left Fort Defiance on March 6, 1864, for a three-hundred-mile journey by foot through desolate desert country. The soldiers who escorted the group left only vague accounts of the journeys. Navajo tradition, however, remembers that the troops harassed the people along the way and shot stragglers, mainly pregnant women and the elderly, who could not keep up in the

---

[41] Quoted in Mike Phifer, "The Legendary Kit Carson: Scout and Soldier," *Warfare History Network*, July 2016, https://warfarehistorynetwork.com/article/the-legendary-kit-carson-scout-and-soldier/.

[42] "Kit Carson," *New World Encyclopedia*, revised April 19, 2018, www.newworldencyclopedia.org/p/index.php?title=Kit_Carson&oldid=1010825.

searing heat and heavy snows the deportees endured during their forced marches. About two hundred perished on the way.

The military was ill-prepared to receive the massive influx of deportees who arrived at Bosque Redondo. There was not enough food, and much of it was unfit for human consumption. There were not enough tents to shelter the deportees from the sun, nor enough blankets for the chilly nights. There was no wood for cooking. The water was heavily alkaline and caused severe intestinal irritation. There was too little forage for the few sheep the Navajo brought with them. And the soil turned out to be very poor for corn and other crops.

The military authorities imposed a harsh regimen on the detainees. They organized Navajo men into companies of six hundred, each with a head man who represented the group to the post commander. A count was taken every day. Behavior was regulated, and soldiers policed the grounds. A Catholic school was built to Christianize and civilize the captives. Measles, dysentery, and pneumonia afflicted the malnourished residents. Then, in 1865, smallpox broke out, killing more than twenty-three hundred and prompting the Mescaleros to elude the guards and escape from the reservation.

After three years of crop failures, reports of corruption and mistreatment, and appeals by the Navajo, General Sherman and a delegation from the Peace Commission visited Bosque Redondo. The commission quickly recognized that the project was a failure. Sherman offered to move the Navajos to fertile land in Oklahoma. They refused and asked instead that they be allowed to return to their homeland. Negotiations ensued, and in a treaty signed at Bosque Redondo on June 1, 1868, the United States released the Navajos to return to an area that encompassed about one-fourth of their original land. The treaty included what had become typical incentives for encouraging civilization: schools, agricultural implements and seeds, and individual allotments of 160 acres to anyone who wanted. In addition, the government agreed to provide fifteen thousand sheep and goats to rebuild the Navajo herds and to provide rations for a ten-year period. The Navajos, for their part, agreed to stop raiding, to allow railroads through the reservation, to stay on their reservation, and to "compel their children, male and female, between the ages of six and sixteen, to attend school."[43]

---

[43]"Article 6, Treaty with the Navajo, 1868," https://treaties.okstate.edu/treaties/treaty-with-the-navaho-1868-1015. For a detailed account of the Long Walk, see Dee Brown, *Bury My Heart at Wounded Knee: An Indian History of the American West* (Holt, Rinehart & Winston, 1970), 13-36.

The removals of Indigenous nations belied the settler fiction that US policy toward the Indian demonstrated humane convictions, honesty, and fair dealing. Although settler elites voiced concern for the survival and well-being of Indigenous peoples, removals revealed a deep racial antipathy toward them. Settler minds concocted many ways of denying and masking Indian hating. One denial mechanism projected settler violence and treachery on to Indigenous adversaries, as illustrated by Carleton's declaration to the Mescaleros that "you have deceived us too often, and robbed and murdered our people too long, to trust you again at large in your own country." Indian attacks, in settler eyes, confirmed Indigenous savagery and necessitated the removal of the population. In cases such as the Southeastern nations, settler elites justified removal by presenting it as a legal and equitable process. Indian removal, in short, "was a rejection of Indians as Indians, not simply a rejection of unassimilated Indians who would not accept the American life-style."[44] Settler America wanted all the land, and it wanted the land all for itself.

QUESTIONS FOR REFLECTION AND DISCUSSION

1. How do you think an attachment to land is related to a sense of identity?
2. Why do you think morally minded Whites accepted the explanations that justified removing Indigenous people from their homelands?
3. What do the accounts of removals in this chapter reveal about settler attitudes toward Indigenous people?
4. Do you think these attitudes persist today? Are there Americans who still think of Indigenous societies as primitive and undeveloped?
5. What story from this chapter sticks with you? Spend a few moments to imagine yourself in the experience of the affected people. What do you see? How do you feel?
6. How could things have been different?

---

[44] Horsman, *Race and Manifest Destiny*, 192.

6

ERASING THE INDIAN

THE CIVILIZATION PROJECT

Gradually, with the divine blessing, to make the whole tribe English in their language, civilized in their habits, and Christian in their religion; this is the present plan.

AMERICAN BOARD OF COMMISSIONERS
FOR FOREIGN MISSIONS, 1815

It costs less to civilize than to kill.

INDIAN PEACE COMMISSION, 1868

ON SEPTEMBER 20, 1957, the front page of *The Cleveland Plain Dealer* included an article titled, "Real Indians Soon to Call City Home." The article reported that Clevelanders could soon expect an influx of Indians who "will be brought to Cleveland direct from reservations in the west," under the auspices of the federal government's Urban Relocation Program. The program offered transportation, assistance, and vocational training for Indigenous Americans who agreed to move from their reservations to a designated relocation city. Cleveland, the farthest east of the relocation centers, promised good-paying jobs, particularly in industry and construction. The *Plain Dealer* article informed readers that the Bureau of Indian Affairs had established a relocation office in the city and that the transit board had approved a five-year lease for the location. It also provided a short biography of Verdon C. Christiansen, who had been appointed the relocation officer for Cleveland, after serving in the Denver office and, prior to that, on the Rosebud Sioux reservation.[1]

The article peppered the account with Indian stereotypes and tropes. "Honest Injun, these will be real Indians," the writer exclaimed. The arrival of Indians in Cleveland would begin "before another moon goes by." The "headquarters tepee" had already been set up at the CTS Building. The "first smoke signals telling of Indians on a peace path to Cleveland were sent up at a transit board meeting yesterday morning," which resulted in a "treaty." The article went on to introduce Christiansen as the "Great White Father" in Cleveland.

The reporter's colorful language was likely informed by more than an attempt at humor. A public-relations campaign typically accompanied the launch of a relocation center. Pamphlets and news reports encouraged citizens to aid the newcomers' transition to urban life and sought to defuse racial animus against them. Christiansen himself explained the goal of the relocation succinctly. "If we have done our job properly," he was quoted as saying, "after 12 months a family will be fully assimilated into the community."[2]

The voluntary relocation program, launched in 1952, constituted a final, aggressive effort to erase Indian identity by enticing Indigenous Americans to leave their reservations and move to urban centers. The program worked in conjunction with the termination policy discussed in chapter three. As with termination, Indian relocation employed the language of beneficence to mask the erasure of Indigenous identity and the confiscation of Indigenous land. The government marketed relocation to people living on western reservations, where the unemployment rate often approached 80 percent. Most reservations were impoverished and had no electricity or indoor plumbing. Schools were substandard. Business investment was scant or absent altogether. Alcoholism, lack of access to health care, and other

---

[1] A Bureau of Indian Affairs press release on July 17, 1958, however, reported that the relocation office would open on September 1 of that year and that it would be headed by Kurt Dreifuss, former chief of the Chicago relocation service. See "Indian Bureau Expanding Program to Develop Industrial Jobs Around Reservations," US Department of the Interior: Indian Affairs, July 17, 1958, www.bia.gov/as-ia/opa/online-press-release/indian-bureau-expanding-program-develop-industrial-jobs-around.

[2] Quoted in James Workman, "American Indians in Cleveland," Cleveland Museum of Art, 2010, www.clevelandart.org/articles/american-indians-cleveland.

maladies manifested in a median life expectancy in the forties (at a time when overall US life expectancy was seventy years).

The relocation program promised government assistance to those who chose to leave the dismal living conditions on the reservations and to start a new life in the city. It thereby aspired to give Indigenous Americans the opportunity to participate in the post–World War II economic boom and to take their places among America's growing middle class. Advocates believed that, if successful, the program would not only assimilate Indigenous people into mainstream America but would so depopulate reservations that those who remained on them would eventually have to abandon them. The government appears not to have considered the obvious alternative, namely, to invest the resources and expertise necessary to alleviate the dire conditions on many reservations and to empower residents to pursue economic and community development. Once again, the prospect of getting more Indigenous land proved to be the principal driver of settler policy.

The termination and relocation programs originated in an effort to streamline the federal bureaucracy, cut costs, and eliminate fraud and inefficiency. The effort was stimulated by the need to pay down the debt incurred by World War II and to fund the expansion of the industrial economy. In 1949, a blue-ribbon committee chaired by former President Herbert Hoover published recommendations that targeted the Bureau of Indian Affairs and the federal government's attempts to solve the "Indian problem." The committee advocated "progressive measures to integrate the Indians into the rest of the population."[3] Acknowledging the government's repeated failure to assimilate the Indian, the commission recommended abolishing the Bureau of Indian Affairs, dissolving tribal governments and reservations, and assimilating Indians as rapidly as possible. Proponents touted these "progressive measures" as a fitting way to honor the 150,000 Native Americans who served in military and support capacities during World War II. The proposal also mitigated concerns about the dual allegiance of Indigenous citizens (to their nations and to the United States) in the early days of the Cold War. In short, the commission envisioned a time when there would

---

[3]*Hoover Commission on Indian Affairs* (Government Printing Office, 1949), 63.

be "no more BIA, no more tribal governments, no more reservations, and no more Native Americans."[4]

Relocation was primarily the brainchild of Dillon S. Myer, whom President Harry Truman appointed commissioner of Indian Affairs in 1950. As director of the War Relocation Authority during World War II, Myer had overseen the relocation of 119,000 Japanese American citizens to internment camps. He viewed Indian reservations as internment camps of a different order. In Myer's view, Indians could never assimilate as long as they remained on reservations and dependent on the federal government. The sooner Indians could be relocated, he believed, the better their chances of integrating into mainstream America.

Myer thus conceived of a large-scale relocation of Indigenous citizens modeled on the War Relocation Authority, with the addition of job training and placement services. In 1951, he created a new Branch of Placement and Relocation and set up relocation offices in Los Angeles, Salt Lake City, Denver, and Chicago. From this office, he dispatched a cadre of relocation officers to Indian reservations to enlist participants in a trial program. The program promised funds for transportation and an allowance of three weeks' living expenses to anyone leaving their reservation to pursue employment in the cities. Many, particularly veterans and war-industry workers, welcomed the initiative. During 1952, 1,785 Indigenous citizens relocated to cities to pursue the promise of a better life.

In 1953, President Dwight Eisenhower appointed banker Glenn Emmons to succeed Myer as Bureau of Indian Affairs commissioner. Emmons shared Myer's views and expanded the relocation program, moving the main office from Washington, DC, to Denver and opening relocation offices in St. Louis, San Francisco, San Jose, Dallas, Cincinnati, Cleveland, and Joliet and Waukegan, Illinois. Relocation officers, who "resembled army recruiters trying to fill quotas," traveled to reservations to sign citizens up for the program.[5]

The officers extolled the opportunities relocation would bring. They passed out posters, pamphlets, and other promotional material that

---

[4]Max Nesterak, "Uprooted: The 1950s Plan to Erase Indian Country," *MPR News Podcasts*, November 4, 2019, www.mprnews.org/story/2019/11/04/uprooted-the-1950s-plan-to-erase-indian-country.

[5]Kenneth R. Philp, "Stride Toward Freedom: The Relocation of Indians to Cities, 1952–1960," *Western Historical Quarterly* 16, no. 2 (1985): 175-90.

portrayed a satisfying life in America's cities. Pictures showed well-dressed, smiling families living in attractive housing, with refrigerators, television sets, and other modern appliances. They also portrayed Indian mothers pushing baby strollers along manicured urban streets, Indian men working factory jobs, and Indian children studying in well-resourced classrooms. Boarding schools aided the recruitment efforts by encouraging graduates to relocate. The Veterans Administration also played a supportive role; Indigenous veterans seeking benefits through the GI Bill were frequently steered toward the Bureau of Indian Affairs and into vocational training programs and prelocation job training.

Under Emmons, the Bureau of Indian Affairs covered the cost of one-way tickets to a relocation city, provided a modest stipend for living expenses for a period of three to four weeks, and offered assistance in making the transition to urban life. The program generated a flood of applicants. Sixty-two hundred Indigenous Americans relocated in just the first two years. The Bureau of Indian Affairs, however, was ill-equipped to deal with the unexpectedly high interest, as Emmons had reorganized the Bureau of Indian Affairs and made deep cuts in its budget. As a result, overworked and understaffed relocation offices usually offered only a bare minimum of assistance.

Recruitment officers on the reservations were to screen applicants in order to assess their readiness to adjust to urban living. The process, however, was often cursory and haphazard. Upon arriving in a city, the newcomers typically had to wait long hours for an appointment with a relocation officer. The assistance frequently consisted of little more than a map (and instructions on how to read it) and directions on how to shop at grocery and department stores, how to use a telephone, and how to use a checking account and manage finances. The officer typically secured temporary housing in low-cost hotels and tenements. A follow-up interview focused on how to secure employment.[6]

After that, relocation officers largely left their charges to fend for themselves in a world that for most of them was completely alien. The pace and competitiveness of urban life, the crowded living spaces, the foreign landscape, the fixation on time, clocks, and schedules, and a sense of isolation—all

---

[6]Philip, "Stride Toward Freedom," 183-84.

constituted a jarring change from the slower-paced and community-oriented life on reservations. Those who relocated rarely found others from their tribes in the same cities. Many did not speak English well, if at all. Children who spoke only their tribal language had to adapt quickly to classroom instruction in English. And for the most part, the only employment available to Indians were menial, low-paying jobs. The immediacy and immensity of the culture shock was underscored by one relocation officer, who wrote of the daunting task that faced someone who "has never been permanently employed, has never looked at a clock, and is expected with a week's counseling or three weeks' counseling to go out and face the world."[7]

Relocated Indigenous Americans also had to deal with discrimination. Many employers refused to hire Indians. Redlining made it difficult to escape the slums and get loans for good housing. Neighborhoods signed petitions to keep Indians out. For many who relocated, the dream of a bright future in urban America turned out to be a nightmare world of poverty, isolation, and discouragement. Relocation, in short, constituted "an underfunded, ill-conceived program . . . essentially a one-way ticket from rural to urban poverty."[8]

Russell Means, a Lakota man who relocated with his family to Cleveland, later called relocation "a horrible experience." Means related that the Bureau of Indian Affairs gave him $88 to drive his family of four from South Dakota to Cleveland, where, upon arrival, the officer placed them "in a sleazy hotel where a society of degenerates lived. There were prostitutes, drug dealers, people making love in the hallways." Means went back to the office the next day to demand better housing but was denied. After persisting for weeks, the officer finally assigned his family housing in a nice suburb. Recalling his first night in Cleveland, Means reported, "A Choctaw family had already been living in that same hotel for a year and half. . . . Three years later they were still living there. The wife couldn't speak English and the husband spoke broken English. They had laborer jobs."[9]

---

[7]Larry W. Burt, "Roots of the Native American Urban Experience: Relocation Policy in the 1950s," *American Indian Quarterly* 10, no. 2 (1986): 91.
[8]Nesterak, "Uprooted."
[9]Laura Putre, "Trail of Broken Dreams," *Cleveland Scene*, November 23, 2000, www.clevescene.com/news/trail-of-broken-dreams-1475696. Means later founded the American Indian Center in Cleveland and became a founding member of the American Indian Movement.

In March 1956, two articles in prominent journals pulled the veil back on the relocation program. In an article titled "The Raid on the Reservations," published in *Harper's Magazine*, Dorothy Van de Mark identified the unstated goal of the relocation policy, namely, the seizure of more Indian land and its transference to the federal government.[10] The second article, written by Ruth Mulvey Harmer, appeared in *The Atlantic Monthly*. Mulvey Harmer exposed the dreadful conditions that relocated Indigenous Americans endured in the urban slums. The article questioned the success of the program and reported that up to 60 percent of the participants returned to their reservations. Harmer called for the program to live up to its promise by providing better counseling, more robust assistance, better educational opportunities, and more access to health care. "For every success story," she wrote, "there are a hundred failures. For every former trapper-farmer now adjusted to assembly-line work and city life, there are ninety-nine adrift in a new and hostile environment."[11]

In response to criticism of the policy, Congress passed the Indian Relocation Act, also known as Public Law 959, and established the Adult Vocational Training Program. The legislation authorized the federal government not only to pay the costs of transportation and to provide a daily per diem for up to four weeks but also to pay for the cost of shipping household goods and furniture. In addition, Congress provided health insurance for the families of those who secured employment. Finally, the legislation mandated the payment of tuition costs for vocational training in relocation cities and for Indigenous Americans employed in factories on or near reservations.

The relocation policy succeeded in moving large numbers of Indigenous Americans from reservations to cities. Between 1952 and 1972, approximately two hundred thousand moved to urban locations, about half of them on their own and apart from government assistance. Of this number, 30 to 40 percent returned to life on the reservation. Some returned to the reservation and then moved back to the cities at a later date. Approximately five thousand people, representing thirty-three tribes, relocated to Cleveland. In 1950, only

---

[10] Dorothy Van de Mark, "The Raid on the Reservations," *Harper's Magazine* (March 1956): 48-49.
[11] Ruth Mulvey Harmer, "Uprooting the Indians," *Atlantic Monthly* 197 (March 1956): 54-57, www.theatlantic.com/magazine/archive/1956/03/uprooting-the-indians/641221/.

6 percent of Indigenous Americans lived in urban contexts. Today, that number hovers around 78 percent.[12]

The policy did not succeed in assimilating Indigenous Americans fully into the American mainstream. While many chose to assimilate, others resisted by finding common cause with those of other tribes who were determined to preserve their cultures. The urban experience generated a pan-Indian consciousness that found expression in the establishment of urban Indian centers, which provided social services, preserved cultural identities, and advocated for Indigenous rights. Activists contributed to a shift in government policy from assimilation to self-determination, prompting President Lyndon Johnson to stop relocation in 1964 and, in 1968, to request that Congress end termination and relocation. The proposal stalled, but the Nixon administration and the new Congress ended the policies and pivoted to a policy of self-determination.

The assumptions, intentions, and implementation of the relocation program reflected attitudes and convictions that configured civilizing programs from the Washington administration onward. The impulse to civilize the Indian originated in the widely held belief, among the White population, that Indians were a primitive race whose way of life was incompatible with the expansion of civilization, the engine of progress that fueled it, and the transformation of wilderness lands into farms and real estate. Many White citizens believed that moral values and Christian mission obligated them to rescue Indians from extinction and help them along the road to civilization.

The civilization project took many forms. Early administrations believed that Indigenous people would recognize the copious benefits civilization offered when they were introduced to it and would readily embrace assimilation. When this did not occur, however, advocates believed the application of benign force would be necessary to bring Indians into the American mainstream. The common sentiment was that Indians were like children and needed a firm parental hand to help their societies mature. White reformers rarely respected Indigenous cultures and did not consider consulting with Indigenous communities. Add the settler government's

---

[12]Joe Whittle, "Most Native Americans Live in Cities, Not Reservations. Here Are Their Stories," *The Guardian*, September 4, 2017, www.theguardian.com/us-news/2017/sep/04/native-americans-stories-california.

insatiable desire for Indian land, and it was no coincidence that every major civilizing program resulted in a significant loss of the Indigenous land base.

CIVILIZING AND CHRISTIANIZING: PHASE ONE

Inculcating a sense of individual identity, the possession of land as private property, and conversion to Christianity constituted the three pillars of civilizing programs. White settler Christians believed that land, conceived as a possession and a commodity, constituted the material bedrock of American civilization. Private ownership of land opened land for development and thus provided the means by which assimilated Indians could generate capital and participate in the market economy of the settler society. Civilization programs therefore attempted to replace the communal character of Indigenous communities with a robust individualism, and the perceived nomadism of Indigenous peoples with European agricultural practices.

Christianity provided the value system that shaped American civilization. Christianity and civilization, in short, were fused in the settler mind. Civilizing was Christianizing, and vice versa. "We cannot too highly prize the influence of Christianity in promoting true civilization," proclaimed one missionary magazine in 1849. "We contend that a true Civilization cannot exist apart from Christianity."[13] Another society proclaimed:

> The truth is, that Christianity has little affinity with the indolent, migratory, nomadic habits of the Indians. The two cannot abide together. Unless the latter are changed to industry, a settled abode, and regular employment, the former can take no strong hold of heart or conscience. While faith and love are the great elements of the gospel, its great law is work, development, progress, in all that improves, adorns, and elevates social life.[14]

An Episcopal missionary summarized the rationale and plan of the civilization program succinctly in 1839:

> All the history of the past shows the difficulty of applying the means of improvement to *wandering* tribes. But, induce them to become fixed and

---

[13]"Influence of Missions on the Temporal Condition of the Heathen," *Baptist Missionary Magazine* 29 (1849): 101-5, quoted in Robert F. Berkhofer Jr., *Salvation and the Savage: An Analysis of Protestant Missions and American Indian Response, 1787–1862* (Atheneum, 1972), 8.

[14]*Report of the Select Committee of the Society for Propagating the Gospel Among the Indians and Others in North America* (Boston, 1856), 34.

permanent, and more than all, let them be *dependent on the produce of the ground for subsistence*; then they are within our reach, and from that moment they have a special interest in the country in which they live. *Industry* then becomes *necessary* to prolong life, and *private property* is invested with an interest, which the hunter know nothing of.[15]

As these comments demonstrate, and the rest of this chapter will confirm, Christian reformers, determined to do right by the Indian, effectively constituted the tip of the civilizing spear.

The United States embarked in earnest on civilizing the Indian during the administration of James Monroe. In his second annual message to Congress, Monroe called on Congress to "adopt some benevolent provisions" for civilizing the Indians within the boundaries of the United States. His rationale couched the policy as a necessary expedient to prevent their extinction.

> Experience has clearly demonstrated that independent savage communities can not long exist within the limits of a civilized population. The progress of the latter has almost invariably terminated in the extinction of the former. . . . To civilize them, and even to prevent their extinction, it seems to be indispensable that their independence as communities should cease, and that the control of the United States over them should be complete and undisputed.[16]

The success of the Brainerd School, a day school established by the American Board of Commissioners for Foreign Missions on Cherokee land, persuaded many members of Congress that education would be the Indians' salvation. Later in 1818, a House committee declared:

> One of two things seems to be necessary; either that these sons of the forest should be moralized or exterminated. . . . Put into the hands of their children the primer and the hoe, and they will naturally, in time, take hold of the plough; and, as their minds become enlightened and expand, the Bible will be their book, and they will grow up in the habits of morality and industry, leave the chase to those whose minds are less cultivated, and become useful members of society.[17]

---

[15]Quoted in Berkhofer, *Salvation and the Savage*, 70–71.
[16]James Monroe, "Second Annual Message," November 16, 1818, The American Presidency Project, www.presidency.ucsb.edu/node/205598.
[17]Quoted in John Reyhner and Jeanne Eder, *American Indian Education: A History* (University of Oklahoma Press, 2004), 43.

Congress followed up by passing the Civilization Fund Act in 1819. The legislation codified the collaboration between the church and government-sponsored assimilation. Echoing Monroe's proposal, the act declared that the legislation had been passed "for the purpose of providing against the further decline and final extinction of the Indian tribes, adjoining the frontier settlements of the United States, and for introducing among them the habits and arts of civilization." The act established a Civilization Fund of $10,000 annually, which would be allocated to benevolent societies and Christian missionaries. Congress looked to these groups to enlist "capable persons of good moral character, to instruct them in the mode of agriculture suited to their situation; and for teaching their children in reading, writing, and arithmetic."[18]

Education constituted the linchpin of the civilization program, and schools became its primary vehicle. Shortly after Monroe signed the act into law, Secretary of War John C. Calhoun sent circulars to Christian denominations and mission agencies, announcing federal assistance for the establishment of Indian schools. Christian organizations responded enthusiastically. In 1819, only four mission schools existed on or near Indigenous land. By 1824, there were thirty-two schools with 916 students. By 1830, the year that saw the passage of the Indian Removal Act, the number of schools supported by the Civilization Fund had risen to fifty-two, with a combined enrollment of 1,512 students.[19]

Religious instruction constituted an integral part of the curriculum. The school day typically began with Bible readings, prayer, and hymn singing. Instruction in the Bible constituted the core of the curriculum, as Christian civilization was founded on biblical principles. The connection was self-evident to the settler population, as "a really civilized people cannot be found in the world except where the Bible has been sent and the gospel taught; hence, we believe that the Indians must have, as an essential part of their education, Christian training."[20]

---

[18]Francis Paul Prucha, ed., *Documents of American Indian Policy*, 3rd ed. (University of Nebraska Press, 2000), 33.
[19]"Let All That Is Indian Within You Die!," *NARF Legal Review* 38, no. 2 (2013): 3, https://narf.org/nill/documents/nlr/nlr38-2.pdf.
[20]David Wallace Adams, *Education for Extinction: American Indians and the Boarding School Experience, 1875–1928* (University of Kansas Press, 2020), 23.

The study of biblical history drew students into the explanatory narrative of White Christian America and displaced Indigenous identities rooted in tribal myths and narratives. Taught as a compendium of propositions, principles, and moral precepts, the Bible instilled a work ethic, inculcated an appreciation for law and order, and molded Indigenous minds into the settler way of thinking.

All instruction was conducted in English, as assimilation into the new humanity of settler society required fluency in the language of White America. In the few boarding schools that existed, students were given haircuts and settler-style clothing. They typically sat on benches and learned to use a knife and fork.[21] "In the school and in the field, as well as in the kitchen," Methodist missionary John Pitezel exclaimed, "our aim was to teach the Indians to live like white people."[22]

Some Christian reformers regarded civilization as a gift that made amends for the atrocious treatment Indians had received from the United States. Prominent citizens such as Stephen Van Rensselaer and Jedidiah Morse were troubled by the "blots" on the "character of our ancestors and of our nation," and particularly

> the manner in which we have, in many, if not most instances, come into possession of their lands, and of their peltry: also, to the provocations we have given, in so many instances, to those cruel, desolating, and exterminating wars, which have been successively waged against them; and to the corrupting vices, and fatal diseases, which have been introduced among them, by wicked and unprincipled white people.

These "national sins," the writers believed, exposed the United States "to the judgments of that just Being, to whom it belongs to avenge the wrongs of the oppressed."[23] Divine justice, they believed, demanded that the United States redress the wrongs by extending "the blessings of civilization and Christianity, in all their variety, to the Indian tribes within the limits of the United States."[24]

---

[21] Berkhofer, *Salvation and the Savage*, 35-37.
[22] Quoted in Berkhofer, *Salvation and the Savage*, 10.
[23] Stephen Van Rensselaer, John Cotton Smith, Jonas Platt, and Jedidiah Morse, "Memorial of the American Board of Commissioners for Foreign Missions," in *The First Annual Report of the American Society for the Promotion of the Gospel* (New Haven, CT, 1824), 66.
[24] Van Rensselaer et al., "Memorial of the American Board," 66.

A speech by Morse demonstrates how Christian reformers wove together the various threads that justified civilization programs. Morse was an influential cleric, intellectual, and geographer. Shortly after the passage of the Civilization Fund Act, Secretary of War Calhoun enlisted Morse to visit and take an inventory of all Indian tribes and bands located within the boundaries of the United States and to issue a report on their condition. The report, published in 1820, includes a speech Morse delivered to a gathering of Odawas at Michilimackinac.

The address begins with a proclamation that "a glorious day is dawning. . . . Never before was the prospect for Indians so bright." Morse reports, "Your fathers, the christian white people" are "praying to God for their red brethren. They are devising plans for your happiness." He then informs the gathering that Congress has "put money into the hands of your Father, the President, to promote the welfare of the Indians."[25]

From here, Morse launches into a long account of the ways that God has prospered "the settlements of the white people . . . over a wide extent of the country of your father." The Indians, however, have declined to such an extent that they can no longer "associate with white people, as their equals." They face a dismal future, without a "posterity on the face of the earth."[26] Yet, Morse avers, Indians may yet become partakers in the blessings that all Whites enjoy. To help them, "your christian fathers, will send among you, at their own expense, good white men and women, to instruct you and your children, in every thing that pertains to the civilized and christian life." The choice they face, he tells the tribal leaders, is simple. "*Civilization* or *ruin*, are now the only alternatives of Indians."

Morse then delivers what he believes will be inspiring news.

> Among the means for your civilization, in addition to what have already been mentioned, we will bring you the best, the only *effectual,* means of making you truly happy—we will bring you the BIBLE, the best of all Books. We will teach you to read and understand it. This book is a revelation from God, and contains the words of eternal life. It reveals the true character of God, the Great Spirit, in whom you profess to believe, and of man, and the relation and duty of man to his

---

[25]Jedidiah Morse, "Appendix," in *A Report to the Secretary of War, on Indian Affairs* (New Haven, CT, 1822), 9.
[26]Morse, "Appendix," 11.

Maker, and to his fellow men. . . . We will bring you this blessed book. We will teach your children to read it, that they may be happy, and comfort you; that they may know how to live, and do good; and how to die, and to live forever.[27]

Morse did not report how the Odawas received his speech.

Civilizing and Christianizing: Phase Two

The development of the reservation system, in the aftermath of the Civil War, promised a more successful way of transforming Indian thinking and customs. White policymakers believed that, once concentrated on reservations, tribal peoples would eventually develop a farming economy. Reservations also ensured that children could be educated in reservation schools, free from the bad influence and wanton violence of frontier Whites.

By this time, anxiety about settler America's "national sins" was intensifying in reforming circles. The ferocity of Sherman and Sheridan's campaigns against the Plains nations brought the violence and mendacity of American western expansion into public view. Reformers were disgusted. The following comments, included in a report by treaty commissioners in 1876, express common misgivings about the practices by which the United States had dispossessed the land's Indigenous peoples.

> We are aware that many of our people think that the only solution of the Indian problem is in their extermination. . . . We are not simply dealing with a poor perishing race; we are dealing with God. We cannot afford to delay longer fulfilling our bounden duty to those from whom we have taken that country, the possession of which has placed us in the forefront of the nations of the earth. . . . A great crisis has arisen in Indian affairs. The wrongs of the Indians are admitted by all. Thousands of the best men in the land feel keenly the nation's shame. They look to Congress for redress. Unless immediate and appropriate legislation is made for the protection and government of the Indians, they must perish. Our country must forever bear the disgrace and suffer the retribution of its wrong-doing. Our children's children will tell the sad story in hushed tones, and wonder how their fathers dared to trample on justice and trifle with God.[28]

---

[27]Morse, "Appendix," 13-14.
[28]*Eighth Annual Report of the Board of Indian Commissioners for The Year 1876* (Washington, DC, 1877), 19, www.google.com/books/edition/Annual_Report_of_the_Board_of_Indian_Com/Lq7RAAAAMAAJ?hl=en&gbpv=0.

It had become apparent to Whites with humane sentiments that, barring intervention, the entire Indian race would soon die out from the effects of violence, disease, starvation, and loss of land. Something had to be done to solve the Indian problem.

Aggressive assimilation provided a means of assuaging White Christian guilt and setting things right. Assimilation into Anglo-American society ensured that Indian peoples would not be lost but absorbed. Civilizing them would enable them to become partakers of the blessings that God had bestowed on the settler nation. To accomplish this objective, the communal, lawless, and primitive societies of Indian peoples had to be rejected, and Indians had to adopt the thinking and practices of Anglo-American civilization. In particular, they had to be taught to value self-interest and self-reliance rather than community and generosity. Historian David Wallace Adams summarizes the reformers' convictions: "They must be inculcated with the values and beliefs of possessive individualism. They must come to respect the importance of private property, they must internalize the ideal of self-reliance, and they must come to realize that the accumulation of personal wealth is a moral obligation."[29]

The educational component of the civilization project had yielded mixed results by the 1860s. Several factors frustrated its objectives. First, the enrollment of children in both day and residential schools was voluntary; students enrolled at their parents' initiative and with their permission. The students themselves attended when they felt like it. Participation in traditional ceremonies, planting and harvesting, and the simple desire to enjoy a beautiful day generally took precedence over going to class. Parents, furthermore, often objected to the manual labor that formed an integral element of the curriculum, and they refused to authorize the corporal punishment that teachers believed was necessary to instill respect and discipline. Most vexing of all, the program of religious study, English-language instruction, and indoctrination into White values was constantly undone when students went home. There they spoke their tribal language, participated in their community's ceremonies, and reinforced their Indigenous identity. Generally speaking, Indigenous communities adopted what they

---

[29] Adams, *Education for Extinction*, 22.

found useful in the schools and set aside whatever they did not. One frustrated Indian agent remarked in 1878 "that to place these wild children under a teacher's care but four or five hours a day, and permit them to spend the other nineteen in the filth and degradation of the village, makes the attempt to educate and civilize them a mere farce."[30]

The failure of the civilization program required an explanation, one that put the failure on the shoulders of Indigenous people rather than on settler elites. The reformers rejected arguments from their opponents that Indians were an inferior race and intellectually incapable of advancing to a civilized state. The former belief received support from scientific racialism, which defined and categorized races in terms of their place on a continuum of biological evolution. On this continuum, skin color provided the index for classifying races as biologically superior or inferior.[31]

Reform-minded Whites also adopted an evolutionary perspective but rendered it in terms of social rather than biological development. They explained the Indians' "primitive" state in terms of arrested social development. The basis for this belief was a widely accepted notion that societies advanced incrementally in a straight line from savagery (associated with hunting and gathering) to barbarism (associated with pastoral societies) and finally to civilization (associated with settled land and property). Many reformers, in short, believed that Indigenous people were capable of civilization but were held back by the primitive practices and thinking of their cultures.

When asked whether Indians could be civilized, US Commissioner of Education William Torey Harris responded that Indians were presently at a tribal stage but possessed the capabilities required to advance toward a civilized state. "No yellow race," he remarked, "has passed through it. The black race has not passed through as it has come into the house of bondage. The nations of Europe and America have passed through it. It is a great thing to go through these stages."[32] Based on these views, reformers looked for ways to accelerate the process, confident that the Indian was the intellectual equal of the White man. "It follows," one reformer declared, "that the history and experience of the American Indian tribes represent, more

---

[30]Adams, *Education for Extinction*, 29.
[31]Reginald Horsman, *Race and Manifest Destiny* (Harvard University Press, 1981), 116-57.
[32]Quoted in Adams, *Education for Extinction*, 15.

or less nearly, the history and experience of our own remote ancestors when in corresponding conditions."[33]

The development of the reservation system and a renewed emphasis on education promised the means of accelerating the social evolution of Indian societies so they could partake in the blessings of civilization. As settler elites contemplated the challenge during the decades following the Civil War, a consensus emerged around three ideas. First, most Indigenous adults could not be civilized, as they were too habituated in their primitive practices and thinking. The education program must therefore focus on children, the younger the better. Children, second, must be taught to abandon their community's religious practices and to embrace Christianity, which expresses the most sublime truths and the most advanced ethical system. Finally, the education of children must be made compulsory, in order to mitigate parental influence and interference.

The policy developed in fits and starts. In article 2 of its treaty with the Navajos in 1868, the federal government required the nation to "pledge themselves to compel their children, male and female, between the ages of six and sixteen years, to attend school" as a condition for permission to leave Bosque Redondo and return to their homeland. The United States promised, in return, that it would provide "a teacher competent to teach the elementary branches of an English education."[34] Shortly thereafter, the Grant administration appointed mainline Christian denominations to oversee and manage reservations and replaced Indian agents with missionaries appointed by church boards. Congress supported the move by increasing funding for education.

The Grant administration transferred oversight of reservations to Christian bodies in part, because the Bureau of Indian Affairs was rife with graft and fraud. Christian missionaries, on the other hand, were regarded as the most exemplary and effective agents of the civilizing program. Therefore, the thinking went, missionaries could serve as more honest and trustworthy intermediaries between tribal nations and the government.

---

[33]Lewis H. Morgan, *Ancient Society* (1877), quoted in Elizabeth Prine Pauls, "Cultural Evolution," *Encyclopedia Britannica*, last updated August 19, 2008, www.britannica.com/topic/cultural-evolution.

[34]"Navajo Treaty of 1868," Native Knowledge 360°, https://americanindian.si.edu/nk360/navajo/treaty/treaty.cshtml.

The plan soon collapsed under its own weight and against strenuous opposition but nevertheless cemented denominational oversight of education at reservation schools.

Enter Captain Richard Henry Pratt. In 1875, Pratt, a young cavalry officer with eight years' experience in the West, was ordered to transport seventy-two Cheyenne, Kiowa, and Comanche prisoners of war from Fort Sill, in Indian Territory, to Fort Leavenworth, and from there to Fort Marion in St. Augustine, Florida. The experience moved Pratt, who fervently believed that assimilation was the only hope for Indian survival. Shortly after arriving at Fort Marion, Pratt hit on the idea of using the prisoners' confinement as an opportunity to set his charges on the path to civilization. Over the course of the next year, he ordered their leg irons removed, cut their hair, gave them discarded uniforms, organized younger prisoners into a military-style guard, and instituted a regimen of drills. Local teachers conducted prayer meetings, instruction in the Bible, and English-language instruction as a supplement to weekly lectures on civilization.

The transformation of the Indians astonished prominent visitors and journalists. When the War Department released the prisoners to return to their reservations, Pratt secured enrollment at Hampton Institute in Virginia for twenty-two of the group who did not want to go back, and he raised funds to support them. Hampton had been established to educate newly freed slaves, and Pratt briefly served as a recruiter of Indian students for the school. During that brief period, he petitioned government officials to allow him to open a school solely for Indians at an abandoned military compound near Carlisle, Pennsylvania. When his request was approved, Pratt set off for the West to persuade tribal leaders to send their children to the school. On November 1, 1879, Carlisle Indian Industrial School began its first year with an enrollment of 136 students, 84 of whom were Lakotas from the Pine Ridge reservation.

The curriculum at Carlisle replicated the strict military discipline Pratt had established to transform the traumatized and disoriented prisoners at Fort Marion. Upon arrival, a student's hair was cut. Each was given a new English name and a drab, military-style uniform. Students were forbidden to speak their native languages or to practice their tribal customs and ceremonies. Pratt's vision, in short, aimed to force students to make a clean, complete, and immediate break with their Indian ways and communities and to immerse them instead in a civilized environment. "In Indian civilization I am a Baptist," Pratt proclaimed to a conference of Baptist ministers, "because I believe in immersing the Indians in our civilization and when we get them under, holding them there until they are thoroughly soaked."[35]

The curriculum consisted of English-language instruction, reading, writing, and mathematics. Manual labor and vocational training took up about half the school day. Boys were organized into companies and drilled, while girls were taught domestic skills. Time was also set aside for religious instruction, music, and, later, sports. Students were effectively incarcerated and were not allowed to leave the premises without permission. During the summer months, the schools sent them to work as farmhands, day laborers, and domestic servants for White families, for which they were paid a token salary. Those who graduated attained the equivalent of a fourth-grade education.[36]

Pratt elaborated his program in a speech delivered at the national meeting of the National Conference of Charities and Correction in 1892. The speech aimed to confirm the reformer's argument that Indians could advance rapidly along the social continuum from the primitive to the civilized.

> A great general has said that the only good Indian is a dead one, and that high sanction of his destruction has been an enormous factor in promoting Indian massacres. In a sense, I agree with the sentiment, but only in this: that all the Indian there is in the race should be dead. Kill the Indian in him, and save the man.... It is a great mistake to think that the Indian is born an inevitable savage. He is born a blank, like all the rest of us. Left in the surroundings of savagery, he grows to possess a savage language, superstition, and life. We, left in the surroundings of civilization, grow to possess a civilized language, life, and purpose. Transfer the infant white to the savage surroundings, he will grow to possess a savage language, superstition, and habit. Transfer the savage-born infant to the surroundings of civilization, and he will grow to possess a civilized language and habit.[37]

---

[35] Quoted in Gene Demby, "The Ugly, Fascinating History of the Word 'Racism,'" *NPR*, January 6, 2014, www.wnyc.org/story/the-ugly-fascinating-history-of-the-word-racism/.
[36] Mary A. Stout, *Native American Boarding Schools* (Greenwood, 2012), 42.
[37] Captain R. H. Pratt, "The Advantages of Mingling Indians with Whites," in *Proceedings of the National Conference of Charities and Correction, at the Nineteenth Annual Session Held in Denver,*

Carlisle quickly became the prototype for a number of off-reservation boarding schools. The government opened four more within the next five years, and a total of twenty-five by 1902. Carlisle's curriculum was also adopted by the hundreds of missionary schools across the American landscape that received federal subsidies for educating Indians.[38] Many schools went beyond the stern discipline applied at Carlisle and devolved into horrific abuse. Punishment ranged from public humiliation, to isolation in a school guardhouse, to severe beatings and other sadistic punishments (such as being made to brush one's teeth with harsh lye soap or to stand with arms outstretched for long periods of time). Most schools suffered from chronic underfunding. As a result, students often were fed a bland diet with few vegetables or fruits. Widespread malnourishment was the result. Weakened immune systems, along with overcrowding and poor medical care, made boarding schools hotbeds of disease. Tuberculosis and a severe eye disease called trachoma were particularly virulent. Virtually every school had a graveyard.[39]

The psychological trauma was often severe. Teachers taught Indigenous children to loathe their cultures and thus themselves. They cast their kin and communities as savage, indolent, and heathenish. Cut off from their families, children commonly suffered homesickness, depression, and loneliness. Religious instruction reinforced their indoctrination into settler civilization by equating savagery with sinfulness and pressuring students to convert to Christianity.

Increasing reluctance by parents and intense competition for students precipitated the final measure necessary to complete the project. On March 3, 1891, Congress made Indian education compulsory. It authorized the commissioner of Indian affairs "to make and enforce by proper means such rules and regulations as will secure the attendance of Indian children of suitable age and health at schools established and maintained for their benefit."[40] Two years later, Congress dictated that the Secretary of the Interior "may in his discretion withhold rations, clothing and other annuities from Indian

---

Col., ed. Israel C. Barrows (Boston, 1892), 46-47, https://carlisleindian.dickinson.edu/sites/default/files/docs-resources/CIS-Resources_1892-PrattSpeech.pdf.

[38] The National Native American Boarding School Healing Coalition has published an interactive map of all presently known Indian boarding schools at https://boardingschoolhealing.org/interactive-digital-map/.

[39] Adams, *Education for Extinction*, 121-34.

[40] *The Statutes at Large of the United States of America* (Washington, DC, 1891), 26:1014, www.loc.gov/item/llsl-v26/.

parents or guardians who refuse or neglect to send and keep their children of proper school age in some school a reasonable portion of each year."[41] From this time forward, the United States "coerced, induced, or compelled Indian children to enter the Federal Indian boarding school system."[42]

The boarding school project received enthusiastic support from a group of wealthy Christian philanthropists who considered themselves "Friends of the Indian." From 1883 to 1916, the group met annually at a resort on Lake Mohonk, New York. The resort was partly owned by Albert Smiley, a wealthy Quaker and a member of the Board of Indian Commissioners. The annual meetings soon evolved into a reformer think tank devoted to promoting Indian rights, developing policies for rapid assimilation, and advocating for legislation that would lift up the Indians. Participants aspired to use their considerable political clout to sway public opinion and press policymakers in Washington to adopt legislation that (in their eyes) benefited the Indian. To that end, the Mohonk Conference published yearly reports of its recommendations "to inform the people of the United States as to the most direct practicable way in which the Indian question may be solved" and "to stimulate the thoughtful and right-minded citizens of the country to take immediate steps toward the solution of the problem."[43]

Three reform agendas emerged during the 1884 conference and defined the members' deliberations during many future gatherings. First, the conference declared that the reservation system was "one of the most serious hindrances to the civilization project," because it perpetuated a state of dependency on the government and reinforced a communal mindset and practices. The group thus asserted that the government must break up reservations into individual, private allotments. Second, the conference declared that "all adult male Indians should be admitted to the full privileges of citizenship by a process analogous to naturalization." The members therefore pushed for measures designed to "place the Indian in the same position before the law as that held

---

[41] *The Statutes at Large of the United States of America* (Washington, DC, 1893), 27:635. www.loc.gov/item/llsl-v27/.

[42] Bryan Newland, *Federal Indian Boarding School Initiative Investigative Report* (May 2002), 36, www.opb.org/pdf/EMBARGOED%20REPORT%20_%20Boarding%20School%20Initiative%20Volume%201%20Investigative%20Report%20May%202022_1652226619302.pdf.

[43] "Program of the Lake Mohonk Conference, September," 1884, in Prucha, *Documents of American Indian Policy*, 162.

by the rest of the population." In other words, the distinctions that separated Indians from settler citizens had to be dissolved so that Indian people could enjoy the benefits, protections, and obligations that all citizens enjoyed; Indians, in short, should be treated like all other citizens. Finally, the conference called for the mandatory enrollment of all Indian children in off-reservation boarding schools or in mission schools that had already "lifted up the tribe to civilization and fitted them to take lands in severalty."[44]

The Lake Mohonk conferences invited leading reformers such as Captain Pratt to present new proposals and practices. An early proposal to abrogate all treaties provides a window into the conferences' typical proceedings. In 1885, Lyman Abbott addressed the conference with a passionate plea to dissolve all treaties as a way of redressing wrongs and expressing repentance. Abbott, an influential clergyman, declared, "If we have made a bad contract it is better broken than kept." Noting that the United States no longer made treaties with Indigenous nations, he proclaimed, "We can no longer be bound by our forefathers; we must adapt our policy to the change of circumstances." "We evangelical ministers," he concluded, "believe in immediate repentance. I hold to immediate repentance as a national duty."[45]

Abbott did not succeed in persuading the conference members that Indians were ready for this drastic measure. Nevertheless, the conference invited representatives of the Indian Rights Association, an organization sharing Abbott's views, to address the conference the following year. Philip Garrett, an attorney on the organization's executive committee, pressed Abbott's proposal by questioning whether Indian treaties were actually binding:

> If an act of emancipation will buy them life, manhood, civilization, and Christianity, at the sacrifice of a few chieftain's feathers, a few worthless bits of parchment, the cohesion of the tribal relation, and the traditions of their race; then, in the name of all that is really worth having, let us shed the few tears necessary to embalm these relics of the past, and have done with them; and, with fraternal cordiality, let us welcome to the bosom of the nation this brother whom we have wronged long enough.[46]

---

[44]"Program of the Lake Mohonk Conference, September," 162-65.
[45]Francis Paul Prucha, *American Indian Treaties: The History of a Political Anomaly* (University of California Press, 1994), 347.
[46]Prucha, *American Indian Treaties*, 348.

Massachusetts senator Henry Dawes was a frequent and popular participant in the early conferences. Dawes was pushing for legislation that would divide reservation lands into individual allotments. His proposal resonated with the Lake Mohonk members, who considered the private ownership of property the foundation of the civilization project. Dawes summarized the allotment program succinctly and challenged the philanthropists to take the Indian "by the hand and set him upon his feet, and teach him to stand alone first, then to gather, and then to keep."[47] In 1887, with the strong backing of the Lake Mohonk conference, Congress passed the General Allotment Act, also called the Dawes Severalty Act.

As elaborated in chapter three, the Dawes Act had catastrophic effects on Indigenous communities. It also resulted in a significant loss of the remaining Indigenous land base. The surplus of land that remained after all the allotments were assigned was opened for settlement and sold. The sale of those lands to White settlers reduced the remaining Indigenous land base from 140 million acres to about 50 million. Surplus reservation land purchased by White settlers rendered many reservations a patchwork of tribal and settler plots. Equally devastating was the impact the legislation had on tribal families and communities, whose members sometimes ended up with allotments that were unfit for farming. Allotment, in short, generated a "severe social disorganization of the Indian family" and often put Indigenous property owners in a direr condition than they experienced before the act's passage. The damage done was exacerbated by the fact that a large portion of the funds gained from the sale of surplus land went to fund boarding schools. "The land policy," as one historian writes, was "directly related to the Government's Indian education policy because proceeds from the destruction of the Indian land base were used to pay costs of taking Indian children from their homes and placing them in Federal boarding schools—a system designed to dissolve the Indian social structure."[48] As David Treuer has remarked, "It is impossible not to feel a kind of sickness at the thought that the government stole Indian land in order to fund the theft of Indian children."[49]

---

[47]Prucha, *American Indian Treaties*, 23.
[48]Newland, *Federal Indian Boarding School Initiative*, 44.
[49]David Treuer, *The Heartbeat of Wounded Knee: Native America from 1890 to the Present* (Riverhead, 2019), 146.

Concurrent with allotment and the boarding school project, the federal government instituted a third measure of coercive assimilation. In 1883, Secretary of the Interior Henry Teller established a court system on reservations that was funded by Congress. The system aimed to abolish the "heathenish practices" that configured tribal culture and identity. If the government was to civilize the Indians, Teller declared, "they must be compelled to desist from the savage and barbarous practices that are calculated to continue them in savagery." Teller justified his decree by declaring that, despite the continued efforts of teachers and missionaries, "a few non-progressive, degraded Indians are allowed to exhibit before the young and susceptible children all the debauchery, diabolism, and savagery of the worst state of the Indian race." He went on to identify the heathenish practices that must be abolished: all ceremonies (particularly dances), polygamy, destroying or giving away property at the death of its owner, and the influence of medicine men, "who are always found with the anti-progressive party."[50]

Tribal police forces had already been established on many reservations. They were now tasked with enforcing a "Code of Indian Offenses" and remanding offenders to a "Court of Indian Offenses," which consisted of a tribunal of three judges approved by the Indian agent. Punishment for committing an "Indian offense" ranged from withholding rations and levying fines to hard labor and incarceration.[51] The Code of Indian Offenses, in short, criminalized tribal traditions, ceremonies, and customs and punished those who were caught participating in them.

During a fifty-year period, then, the settler government devoted the full weight of its resources and energy to an unrelenting and multipronged effort to erase Indian societies, via assimilation, from the face of the earth. And it did so despite clear evidence of failure from the very beginning of the project. By 1889, 3,800 students had enrolled at Carlisle Indian Industrial School. Only 209 had graduated.[52] There were, to be sure, success stories, which Pratt and other boarding school leaders touted as proof of success. Yet these same leaders said little about the degrading conditions to which students

---

[50]Prucha, *Documents of American Indian Policy*, 158-60.
[51]Hiram Price, "Rules Governing the Court of Indian Offenses, March 30, 1883," University of North Dakota, US Government Documents Related to Indigenous Nations, https://commons.und.edu/indigenous-gov-docs/131/.
[52]Adams, *Education for Extinction*, 63.

were subjected at Carlisle and other schools, and they hid instances of physical and sexual abuse. Instead of encouraging self-reliance, allotment drove thousands into poverty. As for criminalizing "heathenish practices," many found ways to continue practicing ceremonies and traditions, despite the potential consequences.

The calamitous effects of the civilization program did not become fully apparent until the 1920s. In 1924, Congress passed the Indian Citizenship Act, which granted citizenship to all Indigenous Americans living in the United States. The bestowal of citizenship arose in large part from the fact that twelve thousand Native Americans had enlisted in World War I, during which they fought on the front lines and took five times the casualties per capita as did US forces as a whole. Another ten thousand joined the Red Cross. Thousands more supported the war effort in other ways, even though 30 percent of the Indigenous population were not citizens. The grant of citizenship raised the question of how the new citizens were faring and pressed the government to address widespread reports of deficiencies, abuse, and neglect in the education and health-care institutions administered by the federal government. In 1926, the secretary of the interior enlisted the Brookings Institute to undertake an independent and comprehensive assessment of Indian life. Under the direction of Lewis Meriam, a team of eight investigators visited agencies, reservations, hospitals, and schools throughout Indian Country.

The panel published its findings in 1928 in a report titled *The Problem of Indian Administration*. Popularly known as the Meriam Report, the massive document revealed the destructive effects that the civilization program had brought to Indigenous peoples. The report opened with a summary statement that was both direct and understated: "An overwhelming majority of the Indians are poor, even extremely poor, and they are not adjusted to the economic and social system of the dominant white civilization." Death and infant mortality rates were high. Disease was "extremely prevalent." Fruit, vegetables, and milk were largely absent from Indigenous diets. Housing was ramshackle and overcrowded. Earned income was "extremely low," and many people were living "on lands from which a trained and experienced white man could scarcely wrest a reasonable living." Fatalism, resignation, and dependency gripped reservation populations. "The past policies of the government," the report declared, "have been of a type which, if long continued, would tend to pauperize any race."[53]

As for Indian education, "the survey staff finds itself obliged to say frankly and unequivocally that the provisions for the care of the Indian children in boarding schools are grossly inadequate." The writers went on to report that boarding schools spent an average of eleven cents a day to feed each child, on a diet that consisted mostly of starch and sugar. They characterized the manual labor that constituted a large part of the curriculum "as a matter of fact production work for the maintenance of the school," which likely violated child-labor laws. Health care was minimal, and good teachers could not be recruited because of the low salaries. "Routine institutionalism," the report noted, was "almost the invariable characteristic of the Indian boarding school." When graduated, "in many instances the child returns to his home poorly adjusted to conditions that confront him" and is poorly fitted for life.[54]

The shocking findings of the Meriam Report prompted policymakers to bring the civilization project to a full and immediate stop and to reorient federal policy toward tribal self-determination and empowerment. The administration of Franklin Delano Roosevelt launched a new policy agenda with the appointment of John Collier as commissioner of Indian affairs. Collier had campaigned for years to release Indigenous Americans from government control. He implemented a program that came to be known as the Indian New Deal. Its signature piece of legislation was the Indian Reorganization Act, which Congress passed in 1934.

The Indian Reorganization Act stopped allotment and provided for some of the land to be recovered, eventually increasing the land base from forty-seven to fifty-one million acres. More significantly, the legislation opened the way for Indigenous communities to draft constitutions and to reorganize tribal governments. The Indian Reorganization Act gave tribal communities the freedom to reject reorganization, and a number of them did so; suspicion about yet another government program to help the Indian was a key factor. Collier also pushed Congress to give $12 million in loans to stimulate economic development. He decriminalized tribal practices and opened up

---

[53] *Meriam Report: The Problem of Indian Administration (1928)*, National Indian Law Library, 1-14, https://narf.org/nill/resources/meriam.html.
[54] *Meriam Report*.

employment opportunities in the Bureau of Indian Affairs and the Indian Division of the Civilian Conservation Corps. The Indian New Deal, finally, began to close boarding schools, provided protections for Native American art, and facilitated the construction of one hundred day schools on tribal lands.

While reorganization affected many tribes negatively, the Indian New Deal signaled a new government policy directed toward the recognition of tribal sovereignty and support for economic, family, and community development. That is, until federal policy shifted yet again in the direction of assimilation, in the form of termination and relocation—and in a new program designed to remove and assimilate indigenous children.

In 1958, as termination and relocation were in full swing, the Bureau of Indian Affairs instituted the Indian Adoption Project. The project orchestrated the removal of Indigenous children from their families in sixteen western states for adoption by White families in the East and Midwest. Advocates spun the program as a humane project to rescue Indian children from dead-end lives on reservations and to give them instead the opportunity to enjoy a better life with caring adoptive parents.

Publicity and recruitment for Indian adoption employed a "plight narrative" that appealed to the liberal sentiments of families who wanted to redress historic wrongs and to create a colorblind America. Indian children, they were told, faced hopeless futures on reservations, which were caught in a perpetual cycle of poverty, unemployment, dependency, and a host of other socioeconomic ills. Children, the narrative went, were often forgotten victims of neglect, who were born to unwed mothers and deadbeat fathers who took no responsibility in childrearing. These children deserved better, and White families could give them a better life within the nurturing environment of a nuclear family.[55] The program thus drew on deep-seated stereotypes to justify the assimilation, by adoption, of Indian children into White settler society.

Popular journalists assisted the government in gaining public support and recruiting White families for the project. An excerpt from an article titled "My Forty-Five Indian Godchildren," published in *Good Housekeeping*, offers an example.

---

[55]Margaret D. Jacobs, *A Generation Removed* (University of Nebraska Press, 2014), 39-41.

Neither is there any balance scale that can weigh the difference between the life these children would have experienced had they been left to grow up, without parents, on an Indian reservation, and the life they will now know as adopted sons and daughters. But this much is certain: the bare earth will never be the floor of their house—unless they go camping for a lark. They will never live huddled together in tiny cabins with neither water nor heating. They will have more than eight years of schooling, and the chances of their dropping out will be 50 times less. They will not be ravaged by disease, and they can expect to live well beyond the 43 years that would have been their life expectancy on an Indian reservation. All the intangibles that are part of parental love and care will also be theirs.[56]

There was a financial motive behind the project. The 1950s saw a dramatic rise in the Indigenous American population of the United States at the same time that the federal government was looking for ways to cut expenses. Cuts in funding, along with the growing Indigenous population, left the Bureau of Indian Affairs with an increasing Indian population but with fewer financial resources. Sending children to boarding schools was costly. Adoption, however, provided a means of reducing the Indigenous population by transferring expenses to White families who adopted them. Indigenous children "posed a financial burden for the Bureau of Indian Affairs which was responsible for them until they reached majority." Adoptions, however, released the Bureau of Indian Affairs from its financial obligations for the children throughout the termination era, providing yet another cost-efficient way to address the Indian problem.[57] Contracts with the Child Welfare League of America, a consortium of fifty service agencies, assisted in the administration of the project. "As in the past," therefore, "many compassionate white Americans unwittingly supported and participated in a devastating government policy and practice."[58]

By the time the project ended in 1967, official reports put the number of adopted children at 395. That number, however, was challenged. A later

---

[56]Arlene Silberman, "My Forty-Five Indian Godchildren," *Good Housekeeping*, August 1966, 34, 36, 38, 40.

[57]Clair Palmiste, "From the Indian Adoption Project to the Indian Child Welfare Act," *Indigenous Policy Journal* 22, no. 1 (2011): 4; Jacobs, *Generation Removed*, 17-32, 37-64. See also "Indian Adoption Project," The Adoption History Project, https://pages.uoregon.edu/adoption/topics/IAP.html.

[58]Jacobs, *Generation Removed*, 40-41.

report by the Association of American Indian Affairs in 1997, for example, put the number of children adopted between 1964 and 1967 at 11,157.[59] Concerted pressure by Indigenous activists and their allies in the late 1960s and early 1970s precipitated congressional hearings on Indian adoption, leading to the passage of the Indian Child Welfare Act in 1978. The legislation put an end to the adoption project and established stringent criteria that render it difficult for Indigenous children to be adopted out of their families and communities.

The Indian Adoption Project reflected the unquestioned assumptions that configured civilizing programs: (1) American civilization is superior to Indigenous cultures, (2) White progressives know what is best for the Indian, and (3) Indians can survive and flourish only if they assimilate into the settler society and structure.

Good Intentions

It is a tragic irony that those in the settler state who most cared to advance the cause of Indigenous people developed policies that instead resulted in some of the greatest damage suffered by Indigenous communities. White missionaries and reformers held many of the assumptions that animated those who actively pursued the demise and extinction of the Indian. Along with the rest of settler society, reformers believed that the future belonged to the White man, who was opening up vast expanses of wilderness land for development and improvement. The destiny of the settler nation was manifest by its steady advance westward, its subjugation of resistant Indigenous nations, the advanced character of its technology, society, and art, and the loftiness of its laws, morality, and religion. Indians, by contrast, were captive to a static and primitive lifestyle, configured by lawlessness, indolence, and heathenish thinking, and were doomed to extinction.

Many in settler America were content to let history take its course. Others sought to accelerate the decline of the Indian by direct and violent measures. The reformers, however, were gripped by a sense of urgency and obligation. Moral imperatives, Christian convictions, and a sense of guilt called for measures that would ensure the survival and welfare of

---

[59]"Indian Adoption Project," 5.

Indigenous peoples and make amends for White settler sins by assimilating them into American society.

An arrogant paternalism shaped reforming approaches to the Indian problem. In the settler-reformer mind, Indians continued to cling to moribund practices and modes of thinking that were leading to their doom as a race. Reformers believed that, left to themselves, Indians could not, or *would not*, leave their childlike ways and mature as a race. It therefore fell to morally minded settlers to help them advance toward civilization, for their own good and by a firm parental hand if necessary. Their solutions—boarding schools, allotment, termination, relocation, and adoption—devastated and fractured Indigenous communities, bringing deep suffering and lasting trauma. Good Christian people intended to show compassion for the poor Indian but did not think it necessary to involve Indians in their deliberations. The result was enduring harm and hardship.

QUESTIONS FOR REFLECTION AND DISCUSSION

1. What do you think about Christian mission trips to Indigenous American reservations in light of what you have read in this chapter?
2. Have you seen expressions of paternalism in your church? In Christian missions? In yourself?
3. What role should settler Christians play in initiatives and conversations devoted to healing and reconciliation?
4. Can civilizing practices or programs be redeemed? If so, how could that happen?
5. What story from this chapter stays with you? Take a few moments to imagine yourself in the experiences of the affected people. What do you see? How do you feel?
6. What might have happened if Christian compassion had been expressed by recognizing the human dignity of Indigenous communities and individuals?

7

CONSTRUCTING THE INDIAN

Five Mythic Tropes

The Indian had to give up all that was his and all that was dear to him—to make himself over or die. He would not yield. He died. He would not receive his salvation by surrender; rather would he choose oblivion, unknown darkness—the melting fires of extermination.

Joseph K. Dixon, *The Vanishing Race*, 1914

On December 13, 2020, co-owner Paul Dolan announced that the Cleveland Major League Baseball team would no longer be called the Indians and would begin the process of determining a "new, non-Native American based name for the franchise." Dolan, who also served as the chairman and CEO of the franchise, reported that he had come to the decision after meeting with representatives of Native American communities and listening to their stories and experiences. The report came as welcome news to Indigenous American activists and organizations, some of whom commended the franchise for "the genuine commitment the team has made to listen to and learn from Indian Country."[1] Be that as it may, the thoughtful decision represented the culmination of decades-long pressure to compel the team to abolish the "Indians" moniker and the team's mascot, Chief Wahoo.

Beginning in the early 1970s, Indigenous activists staged yearly protests against the team name and mascot on Opening Day. They were joined in

---

[1] David Waldstein, "Cleveland Makes Name Removal Official, Saying It Is 'Moving Forward,'" *New York Times*, December, 14, 2020, updated September 21, 2021, www.nytimes.com/2020/12/14/sports/baseball/cleveland-name-change.html.

1991 by the Committee of 500 Years of Dignity and Resistance, a local group that arose to protest celebrations of the five hundredth anniversary of Columbus's first voyage to America.[2] Protests also occurred in Cleveland and Atlanta during the 1995 World Series between the Braves and the Indians, drawing additional, undesired attention to Indian logos and mimicry (such as the Tomahawk Chop and rally drums). The protests, for the most part, were met with silence from the franchises and fan bases.

Such was not the case, however, concerning college and university mascots. In 2005 the NCAA banned "mascots, nicknames or images deemed hostile or abusive in terms of race, ethnicity or national origin hostile or abusive" from postseason tournaments. The decision effectively barred offending teams from wearing team or band uniforms, displaying their logos, and allowing their mascots to perform during games. Teams with offensive mascots were also barred from hosting postseason games.[3] "What we are saying," explained executive chairman Walter Harrison, "is that we find these mascots to be unacceptable for NCAA championship competition."[4] The NCAA concluded its report by listing eighteen colleges and universities that continued to "use Native American imagery and references" and were subject to the new policy.

The Cleveland professional baseball franchise, for its part, resolutely defended the Indians team name, claiming that it was meant to honor Native Americans. To reinforce the claim, it promoted a false narrative about how the team name was changed from the Naps to the Indians in 1915. As the franchise told the story, the team decided on "Indians" to honor Louis Sockalexis, a member of the Penobscot nation who, in 1897, had a season that was the stuff of legends while playing for the Cleveland Spiders—only to see his promising career succumb to alcoholism. Never mind that his legendary season occurred eighteen years before the name change, or that Chief Wahoo's toothy grin and large nose did not communicate a sense of honor.

---

[2]Committee of 500 Years of Dignity and Resistance, www.committeeof500years.org.
[3]"NCAA Executive Committee Issues Guidelines for Use of Native American Mascots at Championship Event," NCAA, August 5, 2005, http://fs.ncaa.org/Docs/PressArchive/2005/Announcements/NCAA%2BExecutive%2BCommittee%2BIssues%2BGuidelines%2Bfor%2BUse%2Bof%2BNative%2BAmerican%2BMascots%2Bat%2BChampionship%2BEvents.html.
[4]"NCAA American Indian Mascot Ban Will Begin Feb. 1," *ESPN*, August 5, 2005, www.espn.com/college-sports/news/story?id=2125735.

By 2010, however, the writing was on the wall. In 2014, the franchise replaced Chief Wahoo with the "block C" on its visiting uniforms, although the Chief still appeared on the home uniforms. When the franchise reached the World Series again in 2016, hundreds of activists protested outside the ballpark during game one. Even so, the team declared that it had no plans to change. Then, in 2019, the franchise removed Chief Wahoo from team uniforms and the ballpark. In the aftermath of George Floyd's killing, and facing more protests, the team issued a statement that proclaimed its commitment to "keep improving as an organization on issues of social justice."[5] Five months later, Dolan announced the franchise's decision to rename the team.

The elimination of the name and mascot provoked outrage in a large part of the fan base, as it had for the fan bases of many collegiate teams that replaced Indian team names with inoffensive alternatives. Fans retorted that "Indian" was no less offensive a name than other ethnic team names, such as the Notre Dame Fighting Irish, the Minnesota Vikings, or the Boston Celtics. What was the big deal? Why, some asked, were Native American mascots offensive, but other ethnic mascots were not? One could, however, ask a different question: Namely, what was it about Chief Wahoo and the Indian team name that provoked immediate and intense consternation in the fan base when they were eliminated?

The answer, I suggest, lies embedded in the White settler psyche. Chief Wahoo is an expression of the "White man's Indian," a mythic construction of the Indian that plays an essential role in American national mythology and the construction of settler America's identity. Fans attending a Cleveland Indians baseball game assumed a dual identity within the ritual space of the ballpark. By identifying with the franchise and its mascot, fans identified *with* Indians and *as* Indians. During the game, they participated in ceremonies (such as the seventh-inning stretch) and watched a ritual contest performed in a dedicated and bounded space (delineated by a diamond and foul lines) and configured by a peculiar marking of time (defined by innings as opposed to the clock). The contest followed established protocols and ceremonies, from the rules of the game to mysterious signals directed from pitchers to catchers and from coaches to players. Fan participation took the

---

[5]Mandy Bell, "Indians Weigh 'Best Path Forward' for Team Name," MLB.com, July 3, 2020, www .mlb.com/news/statement-from-the-indians.

form of war hoops and rally drums, which generated shouting and displays of emotion that were inappropriate in normal space/time.

The fans who gathered for the ceremonial contest at the ballpark were part of a larger fan community whose members also identified with Indians and as Indians. This larger community participated remotely, through TV and radio. Like those attending the game, they often donned clothing adorned with team colors and the Chief's visage; some even cheered and jeered alongside their counterparts at the game. After the game was over, fans transitioned back into ordinary space and time and from their dual Indian/settler identities to the identities that defined their everyday lives.

Chief Wahoo was an Indian whom settler citizens constructed. The mascot and similar caricatures were probably the only Indians most fans ever encountered. Mimicking Indians, in a strange way, connected participants to the nation's colonial past, rehearsed the Indians' role in shaping White American identity, and granted access to the spirit of the land by imitating the land's original peoples. Taking on a dual settler/Indian identity in the liminal space/time of the ballpark, fans of the Cleveland Indians were, in Philip Deloria's elegant phrase, "playing Indian"; they were conjuring the Indian's mystical relationship to the land, "creating a sense of Americanness," and bringing to the surface deep-seated ambivalence about the settler identity.[6]

Chief Wahoo and other Indian mascots are more than names for a team. They embody archetypal symbols and tropes that thread through American national mythology. As such, these tropes shape White settler America's identity just as settler America has reshaped Indigenous land into a settler homeland. In a subterranean way, settler fans of the Indians assumed the identity of the land's original people, and through them renewed their identity as the inheritors of Indigenous land. By playing Indian, fans laid "claim to the characteristics Indians had come to represent in the white mind" and gained "access to organic Indian purity in order to make it one's own."[7]

This chapter shifts from recounting the methods of Indigenous erasure to exploring the ways that, through myth and symbol, settler America erased real Indigenous people from its memory and replaced them with mythic

---

[6]Philip J. Deloria, *Playing Indian* (Yale University Press, 1998), 35.
[7]Deloria, *Playing Indian*, 115.

figures that reinforced settler America's claim to the land. Identifying these mythic types and what they signify plays an important role in dismantling the American settler narrative and exposing its fictions. It is necessary, first of all, to understand the role that symbols and myth play in constructing and maintaining national identity.

CONSTRUCTING NATIONS

The United States became a nation during the heyday of European nationalism in the eighteenth century. Modern nationalism was (and is) a homogenizing and unifying movement, facilitated by social elites, in which diverse ethnic groups combine to form larger entities we know as nations. In France, for example, nationalizing elites sought to transform Gascons, Bretons, Burgundians, Corsicans, and other groups into *Frenchmen*. This required the identification of an essential *French* identity that united the various groups and reoriented loyalty and identity from the ethnic group to the nation. A similar challenge faced the American founders as they sought to transform thirteen bickering colonies into a United States of America, bound together by shared ideals of liberty, republican democracy, humane values, and providential destiny.

Nationalizing movements, then as now, develop a transcendent vision that has sufficient power to persuade people groups to see themselves as part of something bigger than themselves and to make sacrifices for the nation. Anthony D. Smith, one of the most prominent scholars in the field, argues that elites sift through and reappropriate deep cultural resources of myths, symbols, traditions, memories, and rituals for the purpose of crafting a convincing narrative of national identity. The resultant myth-symbol complex presents itself as a true vision of the nation: its sense of itself, its values, and its ideals.[8]

The notion of an ancestral homeland constitutes an essential component of the myth-symbol complex that characterizes modern nationalist movements. Smith elaborates:

---

[8] Anthony D. Smith, *Chosen Peoples: Sacred Sources of National Identity* (Oxford University Press, 2003), 256-59. See also Smith, *Ethno-Symbolism and Nationalism: A Cultural Approach* (Abingdon, 2009); Smith, "The Formation of National Identity," in *Identity*, ed. Henry Harris (Clarendon, 1995), 129-53.

Whatever else it may be, modern nationalism always involves an assertion of, or struggle for land. A landless nation is a contradiction in terms. . . . The creation of nations requires a special place for the nation to inhabit, a land "of their own." Not any land; an historic land, a homeland, an ancestral land. Only an ancestral homeland can provide the emotional as well as physical security required by the citizens of a nation.[9]

An ancestral homeland constitutes the setting for the constitutive events and experiences that have shaped the nation. It is the place where the nation's ancestors are buried, the place where memorable events occurred, and the landscape that has shaped the people. The sense of a homeland therefore "links memory to destiny," for "it is in the reborn land, the homeland which is renewed, that national regeneration takes place. The sacred land is also the promised land of our descendants and posterity."[10]

The identification of a people with its land thus reflects "an alleged and felt symbiosis between a certain piece of earth and 'its' community," a deep emotional and reciprocal bond, whereby the people reflect the attributes of the land and the land, in turn, is shaped by the activity of the people.[11] A homeland therefore constitutes "an historic and poetic landscape, one imbued with the culture and history of a group . . . whose character is felt by themselves and outsiders to derive from the particular landscape they inhabit."[12]

Yet, what about nations, such as the United States, that take the land from its original inhabitants? Such nations must address the question of why they, and not the Indigenous peoples of the land, possess an organic and reciprocal attachment to the homeland. Why does the land belong to the settler nation rather than the Indigenous nations? Conquest therefore creates a tension at the core of national identity and may explain in part why settler-colonial states seek to cleanse the land of its Indigenous inhabitants. As noted above, settler America resolved the tension positively by an appeal to transcendence (for example, divine election and national destiny) and negatively by rendering the Indigenous peoples as unworthy of the land. The

---

[9] Anthony D. Smith, *Myths and Memories of the Nation* (Oxford University Press, 1999), 149.
[10] Smith, *Chosen Peoples*, 270.
[11] Anthony D. Smith, *The Ethnic Origin of Nations* (Blackwell, 1986), 28.
[12] Smith, *Myths and Memories*, 140.

American settler narrative, in short, aims to reconcile an ambivalent national identity that, on the one hand, differentiates the settler state from the Indigenous peoples it displaced, and, on the other, affirms an organic and reciprocal bond to the land it has seized for itself.

Myth resolves the tension by ascribing certain characteristics to the settler nation and the opposite characteristics to the Indigenous Other. In American national mythology, five figures mediate the tensions raised by the theft of Indigenous land and by settler America's attachment to it. Four of the types occupy opposing poles of an axis. The Ignoble Savage and the Noble Savage constitute one of the opposing binaries. The Ignoble Savage, like the land in settler eyes, is wild, lawless, and dangerous. The Noble Savage, on the other hand, symbolizes the virtues the settler nation believes it has inherited from the peoples of the land, such as liberty, independence, and self-sacrifice.

The Indigenous Helper and the White Savage occupy a second binary, which addresses racial anxiety about mixing with the peoples of the land. The Indigenous Helper is a woman who welcomes and assists the settler vanguard and, in so doing, implicitly acquiesces to the civilization it brings. The White Savage, by contrast, is a settler who "goes Indian" and tacitly calls into question the perceived superiority of the settler way of life and the legitimacy of its land claims. The White Savage represents the dangerous allure of the Indigenous peoples, as well as the seductive, dangerous, and degraded character of the wilderness and of the people who occupy it.

Both binaries are situated within the overarching myth of the Vanishing American, which renders the Indigenous peoples as tragic victims of the inexorable advance of civilization. As a whole, the mythic types render the Indigenous peoples invisible by transforming them from real human beings in the present into figures that inhabit American mythology. Each in its way explains why the settler nation is the rightful possessor of the land rather than the Indigenous peoples.

The Vanishing American

The fantasy that the Indian would one day vanish from the American landscape constituted the one unquestioned myth shared by White Americans from the Constitution of the United States until well into the twentieth century. Whether by assimilation or by a slow death, few in the settler nation doubted that Indians would one day cease to exist as a race. The land that settler America envisioned as the homeland of its great and mighty empire was a land whose only Indians were ghosts.

The myth was rooted in experience. At the turn of the nineteenth century, most of the White population of the United States inhabited land that no longer contained viable Indigenous communities. Citizens living in the urban centers of the East rarely, if ever, encountered those who once occupied their land, except as nostalgic figures from the past, commemorated by place names, literature, and local folklore. Citizens along the advancing western frontier, on the other hand, observed that Indigenous communities found subsistence increasingly difficult as game became scarce and the government took their lands.

When Boston orator Charles Sprague spoke of Indians on Independence Day 1825, he saw a race that was not long for this world. "Not many generations ago," Sprague proclaimed, "where you now sit, circled with all that exalts and embellishes civilized life . . . lived and loved another race of beings." Now, however, "the hero of the pathetic tale, is gone! And his degraded offspring crawl upon the soil where he walked in majesty." Sprague continued:

> As a race they have withered from the land. Their arrows are broken, their springs are dried up, their cabins are in the dust. Their council-fire has long since gone out on the shore, and their war-cry is fast dying away to the untrodden west. Slowly and sadly they climb the distant mountains, and read their doom in the setting sun. They are shrinking before the mighty tide which is pressing them away; they must soon hear the roar of the last wave, which will settle over them forever.[13]

Jedidiah Morse expressed similar sentiments to the gathering of Odawas that he hoped would embrace Christianity and civilization.

> Your game is already diminishing, and e'er long will be gone, and you will waste away, and perish, as hundreds of tribes of your brethren in the country east of you, have successively perished before you. Once they were numerous

---

[13]Charles Sprague, *American Independence: An Oration Pronounced Before the Inhabitants of Boston, July 4, 1825* (Boston, 1876), 152, 154-55, https://archive.org/details/poeticalprosewri00spra /mode/2up.

and prosperous like you. Now there is not one of their posterity to visit, and weep over, the sepulchers of their fathers.[14]

With the subjugation of the Indigenous nations in the West and the closing of the frontier, the figure of the Vanishing American figured prominently in the settler mind. The perceived, imminent disappearance of the Indian generated a sense of urgency to document their societies for White posterity. Anthropologists traveled to Indigenous nations on "a desperate salvage operation," to preserve their cultures for the historical record before they vanished into the mists of time.[15] Indigenous people took a curtain call as entertainers for White audiences—most notably in Buffalo Bill Cody's Wild West Show—where they served as exotic objects of nostalgia, who passed along their dynamic spirit to White audiences in one final flourish before departing the stage of history.

The image of the Vanishing American was everywhere in the late nineteenth century. Sculptors memorialized him in statues and reliefs with names such as *The Dying Chief Contemplating the Progress of Civilization* (Thomas Crawford, 1853), *Destiny of the Red Man* (Adolph A. Weinmann, 1904), and *The Appeal to the Great Spirit* (Cyrus E. Dallin, 1908). Most popular by far was a sculpture titled *The End of the Trail* (1894) by James Earle Fraser. Replicas of the work were widely sold in plaster and bronze—and were still available for purchase at the time of this writing, through Walmart, Bed, Bath & Beyond, and other online merchants.[16]

Pictorial representations of Indigenous peoples and communities constituted another popular medium for preserving the Vanishing American for the historical record. Already in 1830, George Catlin journeyed west of the Mississippi to paint portraits of Indian peoples before they could be spoiled by White expansion. In five expeditions to the Great Plains (one of over two thousand miles), Catlin produced more than five hundred paintings and sketches, many of which he exhibited in the United States and abroad under the title of "Indian Gallery."

Several photographic studies around the turn of the twentieth century also announced the imminent extinction of Indigenous nations and aspired

---

[14]Morse, "Appendix," 10.
[15]Dippie, *Vanishing American*, 223.
[16]Fraser also designed the buffalo-Indian head nickel coin that circulated from 1913 to 1938.

to preserve a visual record of the last embers of Indigenous societies. The most elaborate of these was *The Vanishing Race*, by Joseph K. Dixon in 1913. The idea for the book originated in the mind of Rodman Wanamaker, a wealthy Philadelphia businessman. Wanamaker initiated and underwrote three expeditions to the West, in 1908, 1909, and 1913, for the purpose of compiling a photographic record of the Indigenous peoples and a written record of their stories and traditions. The expeditions produced eleven thousand photographs.

Dixon led the second and most ambitious expedition. Possessed by a flair for the dramatic, Dixon assembled a "Last Great Indian Council," which he presented as a gathering of remaining tribal chiefs for one last Indian council. The book that resulted from the council contained eighty photographs, with captions such as "The Final Trail," "The Sunset of a Dying Race," and "Vanishing into the Mists," along with commentary, travel notes, and biographical accounts of Indian chiefs.

Dixon dedicated the book "To the man of mystery, the earth his mother, the sun his father, a child of the mountains and the plains, a faithful worshipper in the great world cathedral, now a tragic soul haunting the shores of the western ocean, my brother the Indian."[17] A lengthy introduction articulates the range of stereotypes that characterized the White idea of the Indian, prompting one historian to characterize the Grand Indian Council as "the last rites for the First Americans" and the book as "in effect a souvenir album of the occasion."[18] The book's final chapter narrates a solemn ceremony in which the assembled chiefs somberly remember a noble past, while the "Indian cosmos sweeps a dead thing amid the growing lustre of the unfading stars of civilization and history."[19] When the council fire is extinguished, the chiefs mount up and depart into the sunset—but not without a poignant farewell by one chief on behalf of all—uttered opposite a photograph titled "The Empty Saddle":

> Brothers, the West! The West! We alone have the key to the West, and we must bravely unlock the portals; we can buy no lamp that will banish the night. We

---

[17]Joseph K. Dixon, *The Vanishing Race: The Last Great Indian Council* (Doubleday, Page, 1914), https://archive.org/details/vanishingracelas0000jose/page/n11/mode/2up.
[18]Dippie, *Vanishing American*, 212-13.
[19]Dixon, *Vanishing Race*, 212.

have always kept our time by the sun. When we pass through the gates of this dying day, we shall pass into a sunless land, and for us there shall be no more time, a forever-land of annihilating darkness.[20]

In this and countless other works, the myth of the Vanishing American rendered the Indian as a figure from the settler nation's past and not its present. As the image of the dying race became fixed in the settler mind, living Indians receded from the settler consciousness and were replaced by a nostalgic image constructed by White stereotypes. The Indigenous peoples thus disappeared from the White gaze, putting to rest the troubling questions that their persistent existence raised about the unsavory ways the settler nation had stolen their land. The myth assured the settler nation that it bore no responsibility for the demise of the Indian. Civilization had triumphed. The Indian had vanished beneath a roiling tide of progress that no human power could resist.

THE IGNOBLE SAVAGE

As noted previously, White settler attitudes, policies, and practices were implemented and justified by a worldview that rendered Indigenous societies as the antithesis of White civilization. In the settler mind, Indian communities were lawless, but White society was governed by laws. Indian communities were heathenish. White society was Christian. Indian societies were violent and impulsive. White colonists were peaceful and self-controlled. In short, the settler nation constructed an image of the Indian that was made up of negative ascriptions as opposed to the positive ascriptions that White colonists considered definitive of their race. By these opposing ascriptions, settlers defined themselves as the positive *this* against the negative *that* they believed defined Indian societies.[21]

Constructing Indians via negative ascriptions has roots in the colonial era, when Puritans defined themselves as an elect community in opposition to their Indigenous neighbors, whom they visualized as living a wild life in a wild land under the domain of Satan. The Puritans regarded Indian

---

[20]Dixon, *Vanishing Race*, 220.
[21]The idea of the savage is deeply rooted in the European psyche, with roots in ancient Greece and Rome. The continuity and changes in the image over time is elaborated by Robert A. Williams Jr., *Savage Anxieties: The Invention of Western Civilization* (Palgrave Macmillan, 2012).

societies as ungodly. Indians lacked proper moral restraint. They were "indulgent without measure with their children." They were lascivious, slothful, and "undutiful." They didn't wear pants. They were, in Cotton Mather's words, "doleful creatures who were the veriest ruins of mankind; who were to be found anywhere on the face of the earth" and Satan's "most devoted and resembling children."[22] Looking back at the Salem witch trials, Mather suggested that the causes probably lay with the Indians. "Their chief sagamores," he wrote, "are well known . . . to have been horrid sorcerers and hellish conjurers and such as conversed with demons." In Puritan eyes, Indians constituted "the irreducible, satanic other" against which the Puritan community defined itself as the elect of God.[23]

By the American Revolution, the Christian/satanic binary had been transformed into a civilized/savage one. A signal example occurs in the Declaration of Independence, which invokes Indigenous savagery in the final grievance leveled against the British Crown, namely that the king "has endeavoured to bring on the inhabitants of our frontiers, the merciless Indian Savages, whose known rule of warfare, is an undistinguished destruction of all ages, sexes and conditions." Never mind that settlers perpetrated most of the merciless savagery on the Ohio and Kentucky frontiers.

The Ignoble Savage was constructed by frontier sentiments. Settlers who lived in direct contact with Indigenous peoples often invoked the figure to present a "realist" perspective of the Indian. Many renderings of the Ignoble Savage explicitly sought to correct the Noble Savage of "Cooper's Indians" and to expose the latter figure as a naive fantasy concocted by eastern elites. One of the realists was Francis Parkman, the premier American historian of the mid-nineteenth century. Parkman traveled west in 1845 to get a firsthand experience with Indians and lived for a time with the Lakota and Pawnee. In the first chapter of his book *The Conspiracy of Pontiac* (published in 1851), Parkman took pains to debunk what was being "written foolishly, and credulously believed" about the Indian character. He expressed particular disdain for the "counterfeit image" that had been "'tricked out' by the rhapsodies of

---

[22]Quoted in Charles M. Segal and David C. Stineback, *Puritans, Indians and Manifest Destiny* (G. P. Putnam's Sons, 1977), 33; quoted in W. Scott Poole, *Satan in America: The Devil We Know* (Rowman & Littlefield, 2009), 16.

[23]James A. Morone, *Hellfire Nation* (Yale University Press, 2003), 76.

poets, the cant of sentimentalists, and the extravagance of some who should have known better." The Indian, he declared, was a study in contradictions, whose "habitual self-restraint" threw "an impenetrable veil over emotion," joining him "to the wild, impetuous passions of a beast or a madman." Parker sought to set the record straight.

> Ambition, revenge, envy, jealousy, are his ruling passions; and his cold temperament is little exposed to the effeminate vices which are the bane of milder races. With him revenge is an overpowering instinct; nay, more, it is a point of honor and a duty. His pride sets all language at defiance. He loathes the thought of coercion; and few of his race have ever stooped to discharge a menial office. A wild love of liberty, an utter intolerance of control, lie at the basis of his character, and fire his whole existence.

The Indian character, Parkman declared, "is hewn out of a rock. . . . He will not learn the arts of civilization, and he and his forest must perish together."[24]

Mark Twain, also a traveler to the West, took aim at the Noble Savage figure by declaring that the real Indian was really "nothing but a poor, filthy, naked scurvy vagabond, whom to exterminate were a charity to the Creator's worthier insects and reptiles which he oppresses."[25] In *Roughing It*, an account of his Western adventures, Twain minces no words in describing his encounter with the Goshoots of Utah.

> The Goshoots we saw . . . were small, lean, "scrawny" creatures; their complexions a dull black like the ordinary American negro; their faces and hands bearing dirt which they had been hoarding and accumulating for months, years, and even generations. . . . A silent, sneaking, treacherous looking race, taking note of everything covertly, like all the other "Noble Red Men" that we (do not) read about, and betraying no sign in their countenances; indolent . . . treacherous, filthy, and repulsive.

"Wherever one finds an Indian tribe," Twain continued, "he has only found Goshoots more or less modified by circumstances and surroundings—but Goshoots, after all."[26]

---

[24] Francis Parkman, *History of the Conspiracy of Pontiac, and the War of the North American Tribes Against the English Colonies After the Conquest of Canada* (Boston, 1851), 42, 43, 45, www.gutenberg.org/cache/epub/39253/pg39253-images.html.
[25] Quoted in Dippie, *Vanishing American*, 134.
[26] Mark Twain, *Roughing It* (Hartford, CT, 1872), 146, 149.

As discussed earlier, the evolutionary scheme that influenced White racial thinking in the nineteenth century situated Indians on a developmental continuum that categorized the Red race as primitive and childlike and the White race as advanced and mature. The thinking informed the Marshall Court's declaration, in *Cherokee Nation v. Georgia*, that Indigenous peoples were "domestic dependent nations" and that "the relationship of the tribes to the United States resembles that of a 'ward to its guardian.'" Justice William Johnson's supporting opinion in that case declared that the law of nations did not apply to Indigenous peoples, who were "nothing more than wandering hordes, held together only by ties of blood and habit, and having neither laws or government, beyond what is required in a savage state."[27]

Realist sentiments viewed the primitive character of Indians as fixed and immutable. Renowned newspaper man Horace Greely expressed the conviction succinctly:

> The Indians are children. Their arts, wars, treaties, alliances, habitation, crafts, properties, commerce, comforts, all belong to the very lowest and rudest stages of human existence. . . . They are utterly incompetent to cope in any way with the European or Caucasian race. Any band of schoolboys, from ten to fifteen years of age, are quite as capable of ruling their appetites, devising public policy, constituting and conducting a state or community, as an average tribe of Indians.[28]

The degrading view of the Indian that Greeley espoused could be set in milder terms more suitable to the Christian palate, especially when it was voiced along with an affirmation of Anglo-Saxon racial superiority. As the frontier was closing, many White Christians wondered about the nation's identity and mission. Influential clergyman Josiah Strong addressed their concerns in the widely read book *Our Country: Its Possible Future and Its Present Crisis*, published in 1885. With the successful spread of European colonialism, Strong proclaimed, "There are no more new worlds. The unoccupied arable lands of the earth are limited, and will soon be taken." The scarcity of new land would usher in *"the final competition of races, for which the Anglo-Saxon is being schooled."*

---

[27]Cherokee Nation v. Georgia, 30 U.S (5 Pet.) 1, 27 (1831).
[28]Horace Greeley, *An Overland Journey, from New York to San Francisco in the Summer of 1859* (New York, 1860), 151.

Strong believed that the Anglo-Saxon race stood on the threshold of a glorious future: "This race of unequaled energy, with all the majesty of numbers and the might of wealth behind it—the representative, let us hope, of the largest liberty, the purest Christianity, the highest civilization—having developed peculiarly aggressive traits calculated to impress its institutions upon mankind, will spread itself over the earth." "Whether the feebler and more abject races are going to be regenerated and raised up," he wrote, "is already very much of a question." That question provoked another, more profound question: "What if it should be God's plan to people the world with better and finer material?" Whatever the case, "Whether the extinction of inferior races before the advancing Anglo-Saxon seems to the reader sad or otherwise, it certainly appears probable."[29]

The figure of the Ignoble Savage constitutes arguably the most durable and deeply embedded image of the Indian in the settler psyche. Whether rendered as hopelessly dirty and disgusting or as socially primitive, the figure has played a key role in defining the settler nation by personifying the negative attributes that constitute the opposite of the settler nation's ascription of itself. The type explains why the Indigenous peoples were unworthy of the land the settlers took. The Ignoble Savage depicts Indians as a violent, degraded race, incapable of improvement and therefore unworthy occupants of the land.

THE NOBLE SAVAGE

The Noble Savage constitutes the antithesis of the Ignoble Savage. This type originally reflected romantic sentiments that valued emotion, intuition, authenticity, simplicity, honesty, and freedom—all qualities prized by the new and expanding nation. The Noble Savage was typically gracious in demeanor, imposing in physique, and steadfastly loyal to friends and family, even to the death. He was an admirable figure, who represented the values and freedom that distinguished the new republic in the New World from the despotism and decadence that settler America saw in the Old World. In this capacity, the Noble Savage "offered a thoroughgoing critique of European social

---

[29]Josiah Strong, *Our Country: Its Possible Future and Its Present Crisis* (New York, 1885), 174-75, 177.

institutions and cultural values."[30] The Noble Savage, in other words, personified the attributes settler America believed it had inherited from the Indigenous peoples—attributes that rendered settler America as a better version of European civilization and yet distinct from it.

Whereas the Ignoble Savage was constructed in the crucible of the frontier, the Noble Savage was fabricated by those parts of settler America where Indians were "safely dead and historically past," that is to say, by settler elites who lived a significant distance from the reciprocal violence that saturated the frontier.[31] Since few had any firsthand contact with Indigenous people, their views of the Indian were shaped more by nostalgia and idealism than by experience. Their temporal and geographical distance from Indigenous people made it possible for them to think of the Indian as the epitome of pristine American values and identity.

In the settler mind, the most noble of savages and the most worthy of admiration were those living in pristine societies that had not been contaminated by contact with White civilization. Admirers of the Noble Savage believed that civilization, for all its benefits, also brought vices that diminished the Indians' intuitive naivete. Settlers introduced civilization's vices (such as alcoholism and dishonesty), which eventually degraded Indigenous minds and actions. For this reason, George Catlin classified the Indians he painted into two categories, corrupted and uncorrupted, and developed a table that contrasted Indian attributes in their "primitive and disabused state" with those Indians acquired through contact with White people (for example, the binaries of virtuous/libidinous, temperate/dissipated, independent/dependent).[32]

Accounts by early travelers reinforced the idyllic virtue of precontact Indian life, as in one traveler's description of the Seminoles:

> They seem to be free from want or desires. No cruel enemy to dread; nothing to give them disquietude, but the gradual encroachment of the white people. Thus contented and undisturbed, they appear as blithe and free as the birds of the air, and like them as volatile and active, tuneful and vociferous. The

---

[30]Robert F. Berkhofer Jr., *The White Man's Indian: Images of the American Indians from Columbus to the Present* (Vintage, 1976), 90.
[31]Berkhofer, *White Man's Indian*, 76.
[32]Dippie, *Vanishing American*, 25-28.

visage, actions and deportment of a Seminole form the most striking picture of happiness in this life; joy contentment, love and friendship, without guile or affection, seem inherent in them.[33]

James Fenimore Cooper's *The Last of the Mohicans* features arguably the two most influential and well-known examples of the Noble Savage: Chingachgook and his adopted son Uncas. Chingachgook, the friend of protagonist Natty Bumppo, displays the "expanded chest, full formed limbs, and the grave countenance" of a warrior. He possesses a mystical understanding of nature, thinks with a moral clarity that outshines the colonial authorities, and is unfailingly true to his word and to his friends. Yet, he is haunted by the demise of his people. Early in the novel, he laments their fate: "Fallen, one by one. So all of my family departed, each in his turn, to the land of spirits. I am on a hilltop, and must go down into the valley; and when Uncas follows in my footsteps, there will no longer be any of the blood of the Sagamores, for my boy is the last of the Mohicans."[34]

Cooper describes Uncas as "upright, flexible and unrestrained in the attitudes and movements of nature. . . . There was no concealment to the dark, glancing, fearless eye, alike terrible and calm; the bold outline of his high, haughty features, pure in their native red. . . . An unblemished specimen of the noblest proportion of man." In the closing pages of the novel, after Uncas meets his death at the hands of Magua, a vengeful Huron, Chingachgook poignantly declares, "I am a blazed pine, in a clearing of the palefaces. . . . I am alone." The novel concludes with Tamenund, a Delaware elder, declaring: "Go, children of the Lenape. . . . The pale-faces are masters of the earth, and the time of the red-men has not come again. My day has been too long. In the morning I saw the sons of Unamis happy and strong; and yet before the night has come have I lived to see the last warrior of the wise race of the Mohicans."[35]

Less known to modern readers is *Hobomok, a Tale of Early Times*, by Lydia Maria Child. First published in 1824 and set between 1629 and 1632,

---

[33]William Bartram, *Travels Through North and South Carolina and Georgia, East and West Florida, the Cherokee country, the extensive territories of the Muscolgulges or Creek confederacy, and the country of the Chactaws* (London, 1792), 182, https://archive.org/details/travelsthroughno00bart/page/n5/mode/2up.
[34]James Fenimore Cooper, *The Last of the Mohicans* (Stringer & Townsend, 1856), 34, 39.
[35]Cooper, *Last of the Mohicans*, 65, 443.

the novel tells the story of Mary Conant, a free-spirited and strong-willed teenager, who lives in the Puritan town of Salem.[36] Mary falls in love with a young settler named Charles Brown, who is a Christian but not a Puritan. When her father learns of the relationship, he forbids Mary to wed the young man. Brown is subsequently banished from the colony and sent back to England. Unbeknown to all, however, a friendly Indian named Hobomok has fallen in love with Mary. When Mary receives news that Brown has died in a shipwreck, she impulsively marries Hobomok, whom she comes to love because of his tender devotion. She gives birth to a son, whom they call Little Hobomok. Her husband is so kind that she later confesses to a close friend, "I speak truly when I say that every day I live with that kind, noble-hearted creature, the better I love him."[37]

Brown, however, has not died. He returns three years later and meets Hobomok by chance on his way back to the colony. When Hobomok learns of his identity and of Brown's unabated love for Mary, an indescribable struggle grips him. He resolves, finally, to release Mary from their marriage so that she can marry Brown. "She was first his," he reasons. "Mary loves him better than she does me; for even now she prays for him in her sleep. The sacrifice must be made to her." After a brief but intense inner conflict, Hobomok tells Brown he "will go far off among some of the red men in the west. They will dig him a grave." Brown tries to dissuade him, but Hobomok's mind is set; Mary will be Brown's wife, and Little Hobomok will be Brown's son. He will leave and "be buried among strangers, and none shall black their faces for the unknown chief." With tears streaming down his cheeks, Hobomok asks only that Mary pray for him, "that when I die, I may go to the English-man's God, where I may hunt beaver with little Hobomok, and count my beavers for Mary." As the novel comes to an end, Hobomok assumes the form of the Vanishing American: "Without trusting another look, he hurried forward. He paused on a neighboring hill, looked toward his wigwam till his strained vision could hardly discern the object, with a bursting heart again murmured his farewell and blessing, and forever passed away from New England."[38]

---

[36]Lydia Maria Child, *Hobomok and Other Writings on Indians* (Rutgers University Press), 1986.
[37]Child, *Hobomok and Other Writings*, 121.
[38]Child, *Hobomok and Other Writings*, 123-24.

Drama proved to be a particularly popular vehicle for the Noble Savage in the nineteenth century. No less than fifty "Indian dramas" were written and staged during that span of time. The most popular was *Metamora; or, The Last of the Wampanoags*, which has been called "the major Indian play of the century" and whose protagonist has been hailed as the "most developed noble savage" of all. The script was written by John Augustus Stone, and it was first staged in 1829, with Edwin Forrest in the title role. The play became a sensation. Forrest reprised the title role to packed houses for the next forty years. It remains "the most performed Indian play in the history of the American theatre."[39]

Set during King Philip's War, the drama centers on Metamora, the son of Massasoit and a loyal friend of the colonists. Metamora possesses an imposing physique and is elegant in speech and manner. The chief displays an intuitive understanding of nature and an impassive demeanor. Over the course of the drama, however, Metamora falls victim to the violence, greed, and power of the colonists. He begins to realize that his people face doom at their hands. Eventually, he confides to his wife, Nameokee, that the colonists will not stop until they have made an end of the Wampanoags.

> When our fires are no longer red on the high places of our fathers; when the bones of our kindred make fruitful the fields of the stranger, which he has planted amidst the ashes of our wigwams; when we are hunted back like the wounded elk far toward the going own of the sun, our hatchets broken, our bows unstrung and war whoop hushed; then will the stranger spare, for we will be too small for his eye to see.[40]

Determined to preserve his people's future and dignity, Metamora becomes an implacable foe of the White man.

After the colonists defeat his warriors in battle, Metamora takes refuge in a mountain stronghold. When discovered, he slays his wife to spare her from enslavement and boldly faces the soldiers who have discovered him. They fire a volley, and he falls to the ground. His last words, unlike those of Hobomok, utter a curse rather than a blessing.

---

[39]B. Donal Grose, "Edwin Forrest, *Metamora*, and the Indian Removal Act of 1830," *Theatre Journal* 37 (May 1985): 185, https://doi.org/10.2307/3207064.

[40]John Augustus Stone, *Metamora; or The Last of the Wampanoags*, in *Dramas from the American Theatre 1762-1909*, ed. Richard Moody (Houghton Mifflin, 1966), 211.

My curses on you, white men! May the Great Spirit curse you when he speaks in his war voice from the clouds! Murderers! The last of the Wampanoags' curse be on you! May your graves and the graves of your children be in the path the red man shall trace! And may the wolf and panther howl o'er your fleshless bones, fit banquet for the destroyers! Spirits of the grave, I come! But the curse of Metamora stays with the white man![41]

The contrasting treatments of the Noble Savage elevate the virtue of self-sacrifice and represent the two roles that the figure plays in American national mythology. Positively rendered, as in the case of Hobomok, the Noble Savage personifies the virtues settler America acquires from the Indigenous peoples and invites emulation. As a mythic personification of pristine national ideals, the Noble Savage can therefore be invoked as a source of regeneration in times of crisis or uncertainty. The Noble Savage, in short, embodies the spirit of America in its pristine form and embodies virtues that express the settler nation's authentic self.

Rendered negatively, as in the case of Metamora, the Noble Savage represents the sins of the nation and in so doing levels a critique of settler civilization. In this form, the Noble Savage confronts the nation with the sins of its past, which serves as a vehicle for safeguarding the national mission and character in the present. He invites the settler reader or audience to express laudatory sympathy and a tinge of remorse for the wrongs committed against the Indigenous peoples, all from the safe distance of an irrecoverable past and with the knowledge that their demise was inevitable. In both cases, as the last scenes of the two literary works illustrate, "Noble Indians could exist before the coming of White society or they could help the White settlers and then die forecasting the wonders and virtues of the civilization that was to supersede the simplicity and naturalness of aboriginal life."[42]

THE INDIGENOUS HELPER

The Indigenous Helper appears at the beginning of the settler narrative and assists the first settlers who enter her people's land. Whereas the Ignoble Savage and the Noble Savage occupy, separately, opposite poles of an axis, the Indigenous Helper combines the settler/Indigenous binary in her person.

---

[41]Stone, *Metamora*, 226.
[42]Berkhofer, *White Man's Indian*, 91.

On one hand, she symbolizes the Indigenous people and the land they occupy. On the other hand, she assists and identifies with the settler society. The assistance she provides, along with her incorporation into the settler community, symbolically acknowledges the settler's right to the land and acquiesces to settler claims, their dreams, and their superiority. The helper thus confirms the colonizers' fiction that the Indigenous peoples willingly gave their land to the colonists.

The Indigenous Helper's role in national mythology explains why the story of Pocahontas is the settler nation's best-known Indian story. Pocahontas makes her appearance in the story of Jamestown, the first permanent English colony in the land. Literary works about Pocahontas were "recast and retold more often than any other American historical incident" prior to the Civil War, and her story continues to resonate up to the present day.[43] Pocahontas's role in the settler narrative is attested by the fact that two episodes from her story are depicted in the US Capitol. A painting of her baptism constitutes one of eight paintings circling the rotunda, and a sandstone relief over the west door depicts her intercession to save Captain John Smith from execution. The latter scene ironically faces and complements Thomas Crawford's bas-relief of the Vanishing American, which is located above the eastern door.

As with the Noble Savage, the story of an Indian woman who saved one colonist and married another has generated a large body of literary works. Pocahontas first appeared on the stage in James Nelson Barker's ballad-opera melodrama *The Indian Princess, or La Belle Sauvage*, which premiered in Philadelphia in 1808. As per the genre, the play incorporates stock characters. John Smith is a noble hero who impresses the Powhatans with his fighting prowess. When Powhatan warriors capture Smith and bring him to their village, a noble and a bloodthirsty savage argue before the chief about what to do with him.

Powhatan's son extols Smith, who "held lightning in his hand," and argues that he should be given the hand of friendship. The other warrior, however,

---

[43]Robert S. Tilton, *Pocahontas: The Evolution of an American Narrative* (Cambridge University Press, 1994), 1. Howard A. Snyder, *Jesus and Pocahontas: Gospel, Mission, and National Myth* (Cascade, 2015), 151-85, offers an excellent summation of the various faces Pocahontas has been given in American national mythology.

demands that Smith be killed to avenge the deaths of those he killed in battle, for their spirits "cry out for the stranger's blood." When the king orders Smith to be taken to the chopping block, Pocahontas shouts, "Oh, do not, warriors, do not! Father, incline your heart to mercy; he will wind your battles, he will vanquish your enemies." Then, when the warriors raise their tomahawks, she runs to the block and takes his head in her bosom, crying out, "White man, thou shalt not die; or I will die with thee!" Moved by her plea, the king spares Smith, who responds in gratitude: "O woman! Angel sex! Where'er thou art, Still art thou heavenly." The scene concludes with the son's declaration that he will "go among the white men; I will learn their arts; and my people shall be made wise and happy."[44]

The drama, produced with dazzling sets and lavish costumes, became enormously popular. It mattered little that the account on which it was based probably never happened. The story of Pocahontas sparing Smith first appears in the second edition of Smith's *General History*, published in 1624. At the time, Smith was living in disgrace in London, during the time of Pocahontas's visit to the city with her English husband, John Rolfe. The episode, however, does not appear in the original version of the volume, which Smith published in 1608. The episode is further suspect because Smith was an ardent self-promoter, who claimed to have experienced similar deliverances through the intercessions of prominent women in Turkey and Russia.[45] The historicity of the event thus remains questionable. The influence of the drama, however, is not. Approximately forty plays about Pocahontas were staged between 1825 and 1869 alone. Her rescue of Smith, her intercession before Powhatan, and her eventual conversion to Christianity combine to signal Indigenous acceptance of the colonial settlement and the eventual demise of her people.[46]

---

[44] James Nelson Barker and John Bray, *The Indian Princess or La Belle Sauvage* (Da Capo, 1972), 26-32.

[45] John Smith, *The Generall Historie of Virginia, New-England, and the Summer Isles* (New York, 1624), 47, 49.

[46] The Indigenous Helper appears in the person of Sacagawea at the second great point of beginning in the settler narrative, namely, the initiation of western expansion across the Mississippi River through the Corps of Discovery. And she appears as the Indian maid to commemorate the settlement of Tiffin, Ohio.

THE WHITE SAVAGE

Like the Indigenous Helper, the White Savage represents the settler/Indigenous binary. Yet, he does so as the negative to the Indigenous Helper's positive. The Indigenous Helper is a friendly Indian who recognizes the superiority of settler civilization, affirms its sense of law and order, and symbolically acquiesces to the transformation of Indigenous land into the colonizers' homeland. The White Savage, on the other hand, is a bloodthirsty settler who has fallen prey to the demonic influence of the wilderness and to the savagery of the people who live there. While the Indigenous Helper plays her role by extending hospitality and entering the settlers' space, the White Savage inhabits the chaotic space of the settler/Indigenous conflict zone. He embodies and resolves White anxiety about the allure of Indian cultures and personifies the pandemonium that ensues when the internal walls of the settler nation are compromised. Thus, in the settler mind, the most savage person of all is the White settler who rejects civilization and "goes Indian."

Like the Noble Savage, the White Savage appears in two forms. In one, he embodies the wanton violence that characterizes Indigenous societies in the settler mind. An experience of Indigenous savagery typically transforms him into a purveyor of excessive violence, propelled by an intense hatred for Indians. A striking example is the popular novel *Nick of the Woods or, The Jibbenainesay*, by Robert Montgomery Bird. First published in 1837, the novel was an immediate success. It was translated into four languages and went through twenty-nine editions. The novel tells the story of Nathan Slaughter, a Quaker living in Kentucky, who extends a hand of friendship to the Shawnees only to see a Shawnee war party kill his wife and five children and leave him for dead. Driven to avenge his family, Slaughter dresses up by night as a demonic spirit feared by the Shawnee in a quest to seek and kill every Shawnee who butchered his family. By day, he practices his Quaker faith and presents himself as a man of goodwill and good character, true to the Quaker "turn the other cheek" ethic. At night, however, he becomes "Nick" (as in, "Old Nick," a.k.a. Satan) and carries out a one-man genocide against the Shawnees.

Bird depicts the Shawnees with degrading and violent caricatures, including the use of the stupid Indian English that would be imitated by narrators for more than a century (for example, "Me Inju-Man!" "Me kill all white man!"). He peppers the tale with gratuitous descriptions of violence. In the novel's climactic scene, Slaughter confronts the elderly Shawnee chief Wenonga, who led the party that killed his family. Nick has been captured, bound, and imprisoned in a wigwam. Wenonga enters, "hideously bedaubed on one side with vermilion, on the other with black." A long conversation follows, during which Nick reveals himself and convinces Wenonga to cut his bonds. When he does so, Nick immediately grabs the chief's tomahawk and plunges it into his brain "with furious haste and skill." Then, "Another stroke, and another . . . and Wenonga trode the path to the spirit-land, bearing the same gory evidences of the unrelenting and successful vengeance of the white-man that his children and grandchildren had borne before him." Nathan, however, continues to vent his fury by burying the tomahawk in the chief's chest and fiercely cutting and jerking his scalp from his head. "The last proof of the slayer's ferocity was not given until he had twice, with his utmost strength, drawn the knife over the dead man's breast, dividing skin, cartilage, and even bone, before it, so sharp was the blade and so powerful the hand that urged it." Slaughter then flees, bearing the scalps of his family, which have been tethered to a pole in the wigwam, yet not before "he had, in the insane fury of the moment, given forth a wild, ear-piercing yell, that spoke the triumph, the exulting transport, and of long-baffled but never-dying revenge."[47]

Responding to criticism of the novel in the preface to the second edition in 1853, Bird claimed that he had depicted "real" Indians rather than fictional Noble Savages. "The Indian is doubtless a gentleman," he conceded, "but he is a gentleman who wears a very dirty shirt, and lives a very miserable life, having nothing to employ him or keep him alive except the pleasures of the chase and of the scalp-hunt." He portrayed Indians, he insisted, "as they existed . . . ignorant, violent, debased, brutal."[48]

The novel sets before readers a vision of the demonic power of the wilderness, of the violence that saturates it, and of the chaos that threatened the settler identity if the Indian was not subdued. Nick is a devout Christian

---

[47] Robert Montgomery Bird, *Nick of the Woods or, The Jibbenainosay: A Tale of Kentucky* (New York, 1837), 201-7, https://archive.org/details/nickofwoodsstory00birdrich/page/4/mode/2up.
[48] Bird, *Nick of the Woods*, iii-v.

White man by day but by night transforms into a hideous creature driven by the retaliatory violence that defines Indigenous justice in settler eyes. Nick's Jekyll-and-Hyde character demonstrates that the Indian can never be reconciled with a peaceful, civilized nation and must be rejected. The novel, furthermore, imbues settler violence with moral legitimacy. "What Slaughter had suffered personally, in extreme form, the whole country had suffered collectively. . . . In return, the United States might expropriate and kill and even scalp them."[49]

Perhaps more threatening to settler identity, however, was the White settler who identified with Indigenous people rather than with their fellow Whites. The vexing fact that many Whites on the frontier preferred to live in Indian societies, and sometimes even to fight with them against settlers, challenged settler fictions about the unequaled beauty, nobility, and morality of Christian civilization. The magnitude of this threat to White racial identity is attested by the measures that the Plymouth colonists took to eliminate a rival colony established nearby by Thomas Morton in 1624. Morton arrived in New England on a trading mission sponsored by the English Crown. Upon arrival, he and a partner founded a colony he named Merrymount. The colony respected Indigenous customs and protocols and thus scandalized the Pilgrims of Plymouth. Merrymount adopted a communal polity with no hierarchy of leadership. The colony welcomed everyone, whether colonist or Indian, and traded equitably with the Algonquian tribes. The Merrymount colonists also rejected Christian sexual mores and participated in Indigenous ceremonies. Morton himself criticized the Plymouth colonists for building forts and dealing unfairly with the surrounding tribes.

The Pilgrims of the Plymouth colony were outraged. Their anger reached a fever pitch when Morton revived a pagan English festival, erected a maypole, and began to trade guns to the Indians. Plymouth governor William Bradford sent Myles Standish to Merrymount to apprehend Morton. Standish and his forces burned Merrymount to the ground and took Morton to Plymouth, where Pilgrim authorities charged him with violating a ban on the sale of guns and rum to the Indians. They quickly convicted him and sent him back to England. Once in England, Morton took his case to the

---

[49]Drinnon, *Facing West: The Metaphysics of Indian-Hating and Empire-Building* (University of Oklahoma Press, 1997), 158.

public by publishing a three-volume set titled *The New English Canaan* in 1632. In it, he condemns and satirizes Puritan militarism and expansionism, unfair trading practices, injustice in the courts, and economic inequities. Worse in Puritan eyes, he writes admiringly about Indigenous societies, presenting them as more noble and peaceful in many respects than Christian colonies.[50] William Bradford, however, played up the licentiousness and lawlessness of Merrymount, epitomized by the Maypole festivities, which he characterized as "drinking and dancing for many days together, inviting Indian consorts, dancing and frisking together like so many fairies, or furies rather; and worse practices."[51] All of this made Morton an inchoate form of the White Savage.

The fullest expression of the type during the revolutionary period was fleshed out in the person of Simon Girty. Simon, along with his brothers Joe and Jim, was a son of an Irish immigrant who was captured and adopted into the Seneca nation during the French and Indian War. Girty initially served the colonists as a frontier scout and translator during the early years of the Revolutionary War. As the war went on, however, he grew disgusted by the colonists' perfidy and joined the British and their Indigenous allies. He subsequently fought along with the Shawnees and other tribes for the duration of the Revolution and throughout the ensuing Indian Wars.

Girty's defection to the British, along with the fact that he dressed and lived like an Indian, cemented his reputation as a renegade. But it was his presence among the Delawares during the torture and death of Colonel William Crawford that catapulted him into a mythic icon. Crawford, a close associate of George Washington, led a force into Ohio in 1782, under orders to destroy Indigenous towns. A coalition of Indigenous forces routed his troops, and Crawford himself was taken captive by Shawnees. The Shawnees handed Crawford over to the Delawares (Lenapes), who subjected him to death-by-torture in revenge for the Gnadenhutten massacres.

---

[50]Thomas Morton, *New English Canaan or New Canaan* (Washington, DC, 1838). Probably from an original printed in London by Charles Green in 1632. The original publication date is disputed; see https://archive.org/details/newenglishcanaan00mor.

[51]Quoted in Richard Slotkin, *Regeneration Through Violence: The Mythology of the American Frontier 1600–1860* (University of Oklahoma Press, 1973), 64. Slotkin offers a trenchant account of how Merrymount expressed the sum of all Pilgrim fears.

A sensational account of Crawford's death, based on the recollections of an eyewitness who escaped from the Delawares, was published the following year.[52] The author, Hugh Henry Brackenridge, used the story to portray Indian savagery and cruelty. His account narrated Crawford's death in gruesome detail and portrayed Girty, who was present, as an inhuman monster. In Brackenridge's account, Girty revels in Crawford's suffering and callously rebuffs Crawford's pleas to put him to death and end his suffering. The book, along with Moravian missionary John Heckewelder's characterization of Girty as "the wicked white savage," transformed Girty into the quintessence of treachery and brutality. Scores of literary treatments followed, which depicted Girty as far surpassing the Indians in cruelty and bloodlust. Within a few decades, popular opinion held him responsible for stirring up peaceful Ohio Indians against the settlers. Mothers used his name to chastise unruly children. Girty the renegade became "the Fiend of the Frontier" and "Dirty Girty."[53]

Zane Grey completed the transformation of Girty into the archetypal White Savage in his Frontier trilogy.[54] Grey's enormously popular historical novels rendered a romanticized and fanciful portrait of the frontier that contributed as much as any literary works to the mythology of the West. Set along the Ohio River Valley during the American Revolution, the three novels depict the original Wild West, employing plot lines and stock characters that became staples of later Western literature and films: silent protectors, spunky lasses, Indian friends and foes, and a heartless, evil villain (Girty). In *Betty Zane*, Grey gives Girty an extensive introduction. Noting that Gitty "spoke most of the Indian languages," Zane reports that he gained a reputation "for his assisting the Indians in marauds, for his midnight forays, for his scalpings, and his efforts to capture white women, and for his devilish cunning and cruelty." Then Grey comments on "the Deathshead of the frontier." "It is difficult to conceive of a white man's being such a fiend in human guise. The only explanation that can be given is that renegades rage

---

[52]Henry Brackenridge, *Narratives of a Late Expedition Against the Indians, with an Account of the Barbarous Execution of Col. Crawford . . .* (Philadelphia, 1783).
[53]Daniel P. Barr, "A Monster So Brutal: Simon Girty and the Degenerative Myth of the American Frontier, 1783–1900," *Essays in History* 40, no. 1 (1998): 1-14, https://doi.org/10.25894/eih.515.
[54]*Betty Zane* (1903); *The Spirit of the Border* (1906); and *The Last Trail* (1909), in Zane Grey, *The Zane Grey Frontier Trilogy* (Tom Doherty Associates, 2007).

against the cause of their own blood with the fury of insanity rather than with the malignity of a naturally ferocious temper."[55]

Fiendish descriptors follow in the next two novels. After Girty captures a missionary and two girls, Grey describes Girty's menacing approach to one of the girls, whom Girty calls "the purtiest lass, 'cpetin mebbe Bet Zane, I ever seed on the border." Zane writes that Girty's "little, yellow eyes glinted; he stroked his chin with a bony hand, and his dark, repulsive face was wreathed in a terrible, meaning smile." Later we see Girty in a wigwam with another captive woman, who is tied to a log. Her hair is tangled and matted. "On her face and arms were many discolored bruises," and she shook her head meaninglessly, with "a vacant expression" that was "proof her mind had gone." In the end, Girty is felled by heroic Indian fighter Lewis Wetzel and watches helplessly as a buzzard gradually circles down and suddenly "fastened sharp talons in the doomed man's breast."[56] Thus Girty suffers a tortuous death that befits his cruelty.

SAVAGES, ALL

The Indian who inhabits settler mythology is not a real, present, flesh-and-blood human being but rather a caricature constructed from the fabric of centuries-long settler expansion. By constructing mythological Indian types, White settler America erased real people, real cultures, and real communities from its vision with as much vigor as it sought to erase them from the land. Stock caricatures and mythic figures replaced living people and assigned them to the nation's past, rendering them invisible in the present. The types contribute to the narrative that facilitates settler denial and supports the myth of innocence. The mythic Indian allays pangs of settler guilt by assuring the settler nation that the Indigenous people gave up their land willingly and then died out, victims of their determination to cling to lifeways that were incompatible with the advancing Christian civilization.

It is difficult to underestimate the energy that settler America exerts to continue the myths and maintain Indigenous invisibility. This explains in

---

[55]Grey, *Frontier Trilogy*, 168-69.
[56]Grey, *Frontier Trilogy*, 375, 422, 509. For a study of how the Indigenous Helper and White Savage persist in contemporary American cinema, see L. Daniel Hawk, "Indigenous Helpers and Renegade Invaders: Ambivalent Characters in Biblical and Cinematic Conquest Narratives," *Journal of Religion & Film* 20, no. 3 (2016), https://digitalcommons.unomaha.edu/jrf/vol20/iss3/24.

part, I suggest, the explosive outrage that erupts whenever the caricatures are challenged. To challenge the myth is to challenge settler denial. Challenges bring repressed narratives to the surface, rendering living Indigenous Americans visible.

The narrative of repression and denial is founded on the myth of the Vanishing American. The myth explains why "we order our lives in *this* way, since there is clearly an alternative."[57] Opposing constructions of the Indian thus thread the memories that form the core of settler national mythology. The Ignoble Savage and the Noble Savage address tensions that haunt settler identity with the land. They depict, negatively, a disordered and wasteful land that had to be subdued and ordered, and, positively, the dynamic, pristine spirit that White settler America inherits from the Indigenous nations. The Indigenous Helper and the White Savage occupy the poles of a second axis, which addresses settler America's ambivalent identity as rightful occupants but outsiders.

The types medicate the conflicted settler soul by presenting hybrid, opposing figures who, positively, affirm Indigenous acknowledgment of the superiority of settler civilization and, negatively, personify the dangerous, seductive, and corrupting power of the wilderness. Richard Slotkin's description of the identity anxiety that gripped the Puritans of New England can be extended over the entire course of the settler project: "The strangeness of the Indian was a threat to the outer man and Puritan society; the Indian's familiarity, his resemblance to the primitive inner man, was a threat to the Puritan's soul, his sense of himself as English, white, and Christian."[58]

And so it goes. White America's impulse to "play Indian" manifests the behavior of a nation fixated on a macabre attempt to master the unruly people who haunt its plagued psyche. The mythic Indian plays an integral role in shaping national mythology. The prominence and persistence of the figures attest to their deep articulation of settler identity, as does the furor they invoke when challenged.

---

[57]Slotkin, *Regeneration Through Violence*, 55.
[58]Slotkin, *Regeneration Through Violence*, 558.

Questions for Reflection and Discussion

1. Can you think of instances where one or more of these types appear in modern film or literature (for example, the Indigenous Helper in the persons of Stands with a First in *Dances with Wolves*, Neytiri in *Avatar*, and Mollie Kyle in *Killers of the Flower Moon*)?

2. What images of Indians do you recall seeing in literature, film, or advertising? Do they appropriate any of the mythic types? In what ways?

3. Did you ever "play Indian" as a child or an adult? If so, why do you think you did?

4. Are Indigenous team names and mascots offensive, or are they innocent? What do you think about the argument that they honor Indigenous Americans?

5. How do you think literary and artistic representations of the Indian shaped American society and culture? Do you know of additional expressions beyond those discussed in this chapter?

6. What can be done to resist or abolish offensive Indigenous caricatures?

8

MIRRORING CONQUEST

Reading Joshua and the American Settler Narrative

All the goods in these towns, along with the livestock, the Israelites plundered for themselves. But they massacred every human being with the edge of the sword until they had eradicated them. They did not leave one breathing thing alive. As Yahweh commanded Moses his servant, so Moses commanded Joshua, and so Joshua did. He did not deviate from a single word that Yahweh commanded Moses.

Joshua 11:14-15

For many years, I taught a Sunday school class in Ashland that was composed of free thinkers. On those occasions when the divinely directed massacres in the book of Joshua came up, one of the members would consistently proclaim, "I cannot worship a God who would command people to do something like that!" Approving nods would usually follow.

Joshua gives good reason for this exclamation. The book recounts a campaign of invasion, expulsion, and genocidal violence against the indigenous peoples of Canaan, propelled by obedience to divine commands and with no expression of remorse save that Israel did not finish the job. It tells a story that is all too familiar to a world haunted by the specter of genocidal violence. Then there are the ways the biblical script parallels the American mythology of Manifest Destiny and echoes settler America's determination to erase Indigenous peoples from the land it believes God has given it. The associations between the two narratives appear obvious. God delivered America's Christian forebears from tyranny by a passage through the waters and into a wilderness inhabited by heathen, whom they slaughtered and expelled in order to establish a new nation in their land. Just like biblical Israel.

A large volume of literature has arisen to address the ethical problem the Israelite conquest poses to Christian faith and mission. How on earth can a program of divinely ordained genocide be reconciled with Jesus' teachings about loving one's neighbor? Shouldn't Christians, like those who were in my Sunday school class, be outraged by the book of Joshua? And should we not be outraged as well with the corresponding American script?

In this chapter I will employ a patristic metaphor to read the book of Joshua. "Holy Scripture," wrote Gregory the Great, "presents a kind of mirror to the eyes of the mind, so that our inner face may be seen in it. There we learn our own ugliness, there our own beauty."[1] Following Gregory, I will read Joshua as a mirror that reflects the American settler narrative and its conceits. I propose that Joshua constitutes a critical biblical resource for generating Christian conversation about Christians' complicity with the American colonial enterprise. Joshua, as I see it, reflects a version of Christian America's narrative and its justifying mechanisms.

Ignorance and Denial

George Bush was one of the most eminent biblical commentators of his time. Converted to Christianity while a student at Dartmouth College, Bush attended Princeton Seminary and was ordained a Presbyterian minister. In 1831, he accepted an appointment as professor of Hebrew and Oriental literature at New York University, a newly chartered private research university in New York City. From that position, he embarked on a wide-ranging and often controversial career as an educator and lecturer. In 1832, Bush published his first book, *The Life of Mahomet*. His subsequent publications included a Hebrew grammar, expositions on the millennium, a proposal to return the Jews to their ancestral land, and an argument against the bodily resurrection of Christ. He also published a series of widely read biblical

---

[1] Translated from Latin and quoted in Kathryn A. Duys, "Song in Monastic Culture: The Lectio Divina in Gautier de Coinci's Miracles de Nostre Dame," in *Cultural Performances in Medieval France: Essays in Honor of Nancy Freeman Regalado*, ed. Eglal Doss-Quinby, Roberta L. Krueger, and E. Jane Burns (D. S. Brewer, 2007), 129.

commentaries that includes *Notes, Critical and Practical, on the Book of Joshua* in 1844.[2]

Bush's Joshua commentary follows the conventions of the time. Each unit begins with a review of commentators. It then moves to a detailed reading of the Hebrew text, discusses connections with other biblical texts, provides geographical and historical information, and explains its theological and moralistic lessons. Concerning the story of Rahab, for example, Bush comments that no one is so vile (as a Canaanite harlot) that they may not become a saint, that faith always produces good works, and whatever is done for God's people will be rewarded.[3] When the spirits of darkness assail the children of God, he writes, "to whom shall they betake themselves but to Christ, their true Joshua?" Joshua's victories, moreover, are anticipations of a time "when the last enemy shall be destroyed" and "all the envy, the opposition, the hatred, the malice that was cherished against the Saviour and the saints, will have become extinguished forever." And the massacres that the Lord commands? They are divine judgment against "a nation of incorrigible idolaters, whose morals, from the most remote periods, were polluted to the utmost degree."[4]

Bush wrote and published his commentary on Joshua during a pivotal era in settler America's history. By 1840, the US government had largely completed the process of removing Indigenous nations in the East to lands west of the Mississippi. Fervor for colonial expansion across the Mississippi was intensifying, as was a belief in America's Manifest Destiny. The abolitionist movement was gaining momentum and political power. Christian opponents of Indian relocation in the previous decade continued to press for justice for Indigenous peoples.

Few individuals leveled a more biting critique of White settler America than William Apess, a Pequot Methodist preacher in New England during the 1830s. In an essay titled "An Indian's Looking-Glass for the White Man," Apess calls out the hypocrisy of settler Christianity.

> Can you charge the Indians with robbing a nation almost of their whole Continent, and murdering their women and children, and then depriving the

---

[2] George Bush, *Notes, Critical and Practical, on the Book of Joshua*, 2nd ed. (New York, 1852), https://archive.org/details/notescriticalpr1852bush/page/n5/mode/2up.
[3] Bush, *Notes Critical and Practical*, 72-73.
[4] Bush, *Notes Critical and Practical*, 113, 124, 71.

remainder of their lawful rights, that nature and God require them to have? And to cap the climax, rob another nation to till their grounds, and welter out their days under the lash with hunger and fatigue under the scorching rays of a burning sun? I should look at all the skins, and I know that when I cast my eye upon that white skin, and if I saw those crimes written upon it, I should enter my protest against it immediately, and cleave to that which is more honorable.[5]

Prominent New England clerics in the East also denounced US expansionism and the violence that accompanied it. When, in 1837, the prospect of Texas annexation became an object of discussion, Boston Unitarian leader Ellery Channing wrote an open letter to Henry Clay, in which he declared:

> There is no Fate to justify rapacious nations, any more than to justify gamblers and robbers, in plunder. . . . We are *destined* (that is the word) to overspread North America; and, intoxicated with the idea it matters little to show we accomplish our fate. To spread, to supplant others, to cover a boundless space, this seems our ambition, no matter what influence we spread with us. Why cannot we rise to noble conceptions of our destiny?[6]

Bush, in other words, did not write his commentary in a vacuum. He did not make a connection between Joshua and the associated narrative that was playing out in settler American discourse and practice. While debates raged about western expansion and national destiny, and as many in settler America viewed Indians as a primitive people and incorrigible idolaters, Bush confined his comments on Joshua to the moral lessons and theological truths that could be extracted by a close grammatical reading of the text. By restricting the interpretation of Joshua to spiritual and moral matters, Bush satisfied the expectations of his White settler readers while insulating them from troubling associations between the Bible they revered and the parallel script that was playing out in their time.

Bush was not alone in sidestepping associations between the biblical conquest and US westward expansion. While it is commonly claimed that settler

---

[5] William Apes, "An Indian's Looking-Glass for the White Man," in *The Experiences of Five Christian Indians of the Pequod Tribe* (Boston, 1833), 56, https://archive.org/details/experiencesoffiv00apes/page/n3/mode/2up.

[6] Quoted in Anders Stephanson, *Manifest Destiny: American Expansion and the Empire of Right* (Hill and Wang, 1995), 50-51.

America justified its conquest and dispossession of Indigenous nation with recourse to the book of Joshua, the truth is that there are virtually no cases where anyone did so in public literature, aside from a smattering of reports from the frontier and a sermon preached to militia leaders in 1678.[7] Likewise, references to Indians as Canaanites are conspicuously absent in the public discourse of the nation that considered itself "God's New Israel."

What are we to make of this stunning silence, especially since biblical typology contributed significantly to the development of the settler narrative? Hadn't Providence delivered the chosen people from tyrannical oppression and brought them through the water to settle a promised land? Did it not follow that the Indigenous people were Canaanites who should be driven from the land? Evidently not. Exodus imagery appeared prominently in American mythology from the Revolutionary period onward.[8] Exodus metaphors rolled off the settler tongue, but conquest metaphors appear to have stuck in its throat. While Christian settlers embraced the idea of the New World as a New Canaan, they steadfastly avoided casting the Indigenous people as Canaanites. Even Cotton Mather, Puritan New England's greatest typological interpreter, avoided the association. "Amalekites" and "Ammonites," sometimes. "Canaanites," never.

Put simply, there is virtually no reference to the biblical conquest narrative in settler America's vast web of justifications for colonial expansion. A single work from the postrevolutionary period, Timothy Dwight's *The Conquest of Canaan*, employs Joshua and the Canaanites as types in an allegorical poem that celebrates Connecticut's liberation from British control.[9] That appears to be the sum of it. Rather than justifying the settler nation's narrative with recourse to the biblical conquest, settler America resolutely

---

[7]Samuel Nowell, *Abraham in Arms: Or, the First Religious General with His Army, Engaging in a War for Which He Had Wisely Prepared, and by Which, Not Only an Eminent Victory Was Obtained, but a Blessing Gained Also; Delivered in an Artillery-Election-Sermon, June 3, 1678* (Boston, 1678), https://quod.lib.umich.edu/e/eebo2/A52557.0001.001?rgn=main;view=fulltext, referenced in Richard Slotkin, *Regeneration Through Violence: The Mythology of the American Frontier 1600–1860* (University of Oklahoma Press, 1973), 87-88.

[8]When asked to design the national seal for the new nation, Franklin proposed the image of Moses parting the Red Sea. Thomas Jefferson, on the other hand, proposed that the great seal should depict the Israelites entering the Promised Land.

[9]Timothy Dwight, *The Conquest of Canaan: A Poem in Eleven Books* (Hartford, CT, 1785), https://archive.org/details/cocana00dwig/page/n5/mode/2up.

avoided connecting the dots; there was no appeal to biblical precedent to justify its program of violence and dispossession.

Postcolonial scholar Bill Templer describes this avoidance as "a powerful repression or bracketing out of the Canaan complex . . . so that it is rarely cited by name, in *explicit* reference to Joshua and his exploits."[10] Yet, why repress the Joshua paradigm, when it promises a direct biblical precedent? Templer elaborates:

> Judeo-Christian tradition seems to have built a fortress of discursive repression and encryptment around its primary biblical narrative of colonial slaughter. There seems to be an explicit understanding of the Joshua paradigm here. It informs the colonial present and its agendas without specific concrete reference, perhaps a kind of discursive tactic to avoid explicitly invoking the most violent genocidal chapter in the Biblical narrative.[11]

Templer's proposal suggests the intriguing possibility that settler silence about Joshua constitutes an intentional and pervasive act of denial. Why did the New Israel repress the biblical conquest account when that account provided a biblical warrant for its colonial program? Perhaps because the biblical account of unprovoked invasion, wanton slaughter, and forceful dispossession—all for the sake of gaining land—clashed with the ethical sensibilities of Christian America. The massacres of men, women, and children depicted in Joshua reflected the primitive, savage violence that settler America associated with Indians but not with itself. Connecting colonial violence with what Christian settlers read in Joshua threatened to unmask justifying fictions. Reading Joshua as a script for imperial expansion perhaps raised too many troubling questions. Better to repress and deny.

We cannot rule out the possibility, furthermore, that the repression and silence, to some extent, might have been unconscious and unintentional. That is, the Joshua script may have operated at a subterranean level to shape settler thinking, even though settler Christians rejected any conscious association with it. In either case, making the association today promises to bring repressed practices, thinking, and denial mechanisms to the surface.

---

[10]Bill Templer, "The Political Sacralization of Imperial Genocide: Contextualizing Timothy Dwight's *The Conquest of Canaan*," *Postcolonial Studies* 9, no. 4 (2006): 382.
[11]Temple, "Political Sacralization," 383.

The shared script follows a common plot: (1) would-be settlers invade a land with a divine mandate to take it (the land promise in Joshua; the doctrine of discovery and creation mandate in the United States); (2) the invaders subdue the Indigenous peoples with massive violence; (3) the invaders remake the land through the demarcation of boundaries and the erection of memorials (tribal allotments and standing stones in Joshua, and the delineation of state, country, and township borders in the US, and the erection of public monuments); (4) residual Indigenous populations are removed in order to protect the nation from their influence (for example, Joshua's address [Josh 23:1-16] and, in the US, Indian relocation and the reservation system).[12]

Joshua is a sophisticated narrative that tells the story of invasion, expulsion, and settlement by weaving together three distinct voices. Each voice presents a specific account of what happened and reflects on what the story means. The intratextual conversation within the book invites the modern reader to acknowledge that there is no single right way to narrate a nation's past. Rather, as the vast corpus of literature on US history attests, there are many ways to narrate a nation's memories and many understandings of what the past means. Recognizing the unique conversation of voices that Joshua generates honors the way the narrative renders Israel's past and provides trajectories for talking together about how narratives of US history advance particular understandings of the past.[13]

MANDATE AND BLESSING

The book of Joshua constitutes three main sections, with a brief introduction. The first chapter introduces the themes that will shape the account of Israel's invasion (Josh 1:1-18). The first unit of the book then depicts Israel as an irresistible force that wipes out the indigenous peoples, with God fighting for Israel (Josh 2:1–12:24). After subduing the entire land, the narrative delineates the boundaries and settlement of tribal lands (Josh 13:1–21:42). The book then concludes with a series of endings,

---

[12]For more on the parallel scripts, see L. Daniel Hawk, "The Myth of the Emptied Land: Biblical Conquest and American Nationalism," *Word & World* 35, no. 1 (2017): 252-62.

[13]The three narrative voices reflect Joshua's complex compositional history. For a detailed review, see Thomas B. Dozeman, *Joshua 1–12*, Anchor Yale Bible 16B (Yale University Press, 2015), 5-80.

each of which presents a specific point of view on the meaning of the invasion and its implications for Israelite identity and occupation of the land (Josh 21:43-24:33).

The Prologue (Josh 1:1-18)

Four speeches introduce the book: Yahweh to Joshua (Josh 1:2-9); Joshua to the Israelite leaders (Josh 1:10-11); Joshua to the tribes of Reuben, Gad, and half-Manasseh (Josh 1:12-15); and those tribes to Joshua (Josh 1:16-18). The speeches appropriate the language of Deuteronomy, the book that immediately precedes Joshua in the canon, including several direct quotations from it (compare Josh 1:3-4 with Deut 11:24-25 and Josh 1:6 with Deut 1:8). As a whole, the speeches articulate Deuteronomy's distinct theological vision. Specifically: Yahweh will give the land of Canaan to the Israelites in fulfillment of Yahweh's promise to their ancestors; Israel and its leader must devote meticulous and constant attention to following "this scroll of the law" (a phrase Deuteronomy uses with reference to itself; Deut 28:58; 29:1; 31:24); the fulfillment of the land promise, finally, is contingent on Israel's strict obedience to the commands of Moses and Joshua. As a whole, the speeches echo Deuteronomy's tendency to think in terms of wholes and units. Israel will take *every* place their foot touches. Joshua must act in accord with the *entire* law and *all* that is written in it. The tribes promise Joshua that they will do "*all* you have commanded" and declare that they will obey Joshua in *all* matters just as they obeyed Moses.[14]

Directly relevant is the Deuteronomic command that specifies what Israel must do with the peoples of the land (Deut 7:1-2; compare Deut 20:16-17).

> When Yahweh your God brings you into the land that you are to enter and occupy, and Yahweh forces out many nations ahead of you—the Hittite, the Girgashite, the Amorite, the Canaanite, the Perizzite, the Hivite and the Jebusite—seven nations stronger and more numerous than you, and Yahweh your God gives them to you, then you must attack them and wipe them out.

The Hebrew term I have translated "wipe out" (*herem*) casts the extermination of the Canaanites as an act of religious devotion; Moses

---
[14] The italicized words translate the same Hebrew term.

commands Israel to obliterate the indigenous nations as demonstrations of obedience to the conquering god. As a whole, then, the opening speeches present the account of Israel's invasion through the theological lens of Deuteronomy.

THE CONQUEST NARRATIVE (JOSH 2:1-12:24)

The first unit renders Israel's victories over the first three Canaanite towns as object lessons on unity and obedience. Yahweh wins spectacular victories over Canaanite kings in the central highland region of the land through displays of divine power at Jericho and at Gibeon (Josh 6:1-27; 10:1-15) and by a stratagem at Ai (Josh 8:1-35). Israel participates in the victories by following Yahweh's commands through Joshua. The three accounts establish a template for the subsequent battle accounts that report victories in the southern region: (1) Yahweh gives the town to Joshua, (2) Joshua takes the town, and (3) Joshua implements the Deuteronomic commandment and exterminates the entire population (Josh 10:28-42). The unit concludes with an account of Joshua's defeat of a large coalition of kings in the north of Canaan. The narrator describes the forces of this coalition as a "great mass of people, like the sand on the seashore, with a huge number of horses and chariots" (Josh 11:4). Here again we are told that Yahweh delivers Canaanite forces to Joshua, who defeats the kings, wipes out the people in their towns, and burns down Hazor (Josh 11:1-15).

Taken together, the accounts of victories and massacres accentuate Yahweh's initiative, Joshua's strict obedience to Yahweh's commands, and Israel's wholehearted compliance with divine directives. Joshua and Israel act as one, meticulously follow Yahweh's directions, and as a consequence win victory after victory until the land is swept clean of indigenous peoples. The narrator punctuates the totality of conquest in summaries that conclude the campaigns in the south and the north of Canaan.

> Joshua conquered the entire land: the highlands, the Negev, the Shephelah, and the slopes, along with all of their kings. He left no survivors. He wiped out every breathing thing, exactly as Yahweh the God of Israel commanded. He defeated them from Kadesh-barnea to Gaza and the whole territory of Goshen. All these kings and their land Joshua conquered at one time, because Yahweh the God of Israel fought for Israel. (Josh 10:40-41)

Joshua put every human being to the edge of the sword until he had exterminated them. He did not allow a single breathing them to survive. As Yahweh commanded Moses his servant, so Moses commanded Joshua, and so Joshua did. He did not neglect a single thing that Yahweh commanded Moses. (Josh 11:14-15)

The narrator then extends the scope of victories to the entire land, with the comment that "Joshua conquered the entire land, in compliance with everything Yahweh said to Moses, and Joshua gave it as a permanent possession to Israel, as it was apportioned to the tribes" (Josh 11:23). The conquest narrative concludes with an expansive description of all the land east of the Jordan that Israel had previously taken under the leadership of Moses (Josh 12:1-6). Then, in a final flourish, the narrator lists thirty defeated kings and towns (Josh 12:7-24).

THE SETTLEMENT NARRATIVE (JOSH 13:1–24:33)

In the light of repeated and emphatic assertions of totality, it comes as a surprise when Yahweh makes a stunning declaration near the end of Joshua's life: "You are old. Your days are numbered, and there is a vast amount of the land yet to be possessed" (Josh 13:1). There follows a description of large areas of land that remain outside Israel's occupation. Yahweh follows the description with another puzzling declaration: "I will drive them out before the Israelites" (Josh 13:6). Yahweh then directs Joshua to apportion the land to the tribes who will settle west of Canaan. The second section of the book, therefore, begins with a striking contradiction. If Joshua conquered the entire land and defeated all its kings, what are we to make of the report that much of the land remains to be taken? And why does Yahweh now speak about expelling the Canaanites rather than exterminating them?

The narrator heightens the sense of discontinuity in subtle ways as the narrative relates the allotment of tribal lands and boundaries. The description of tribal lands east of the Jordan includes a note that "the Israelites could not expel the Geshurites and Maacathites," who live in Israel "to the present day." Likewise, a footnote to the description of Judah's territory reports that "the Judahites could not expel the Jebusite inhabitants of Jerusalem. So, the Jebusites live with the Judahites to this very day" (Josh 15:63). The comment clashes with a prior report that Joshua killed the king of Jerusalem and routed his forces (Josh 10:1-14, 23-26).[15] Another footnote reports that the Ephraimites could not expel the people of Gezer, who also remain into the narrator's present (Josh 16:10). And still another report lists Manassite towns whose indigenous occupants could not be expelled because "the Canaanites were determined to live in the land" (Josh 17:12). The last tribe listed, that of Dan, contains a list of the towns allotted to it, but then reports that the tribe was forced out of its territory and conquered another, unallotted town far in the north (Josh 19:40-48).

The section also includes vignettes that portray a less energetic and united Israel than we encounter in the conquest account. The Joseph tribes want more territory than they have been allotted. Yet, they refuse to expand into the Jezreel Valley because, they complain, the Canaanites who occupy the region have iron chariots (Josh 17:14-18; cf. Josh 11:1-9). Soon thereafter, the narrator reports an assembly of the entire nation at Shiloh, where Joshua rebukes the seven remaining tribes for their reluctance to occupy the land Yahweh has given them (Josh 18:1-7). The allotments defining two of the tribes (Simeon and Issachar) describe no territory at all but only a list of towns.

So, what happened? Did Israel enter the land as an irresistible force, in unified obedience to Yahweh, who won spectacular victories? Or did the Israelites have a tougher go of it? Did the Israelite nation sweep across the land as a single, unified force, or did individual tribes subdue and occupy Canaanite regions with varying degrees of energy and success? Did Israel take all the land and annihilate all its peoples? Or did large sections of the land remain outside Israel's control, and did numerous peoples successfully resist? What did Israel's God direct the Israelites to do to the indigenous peoples of the land, wipe them out or expel them?

The last question is a good place to start. In every declaration of the land promise, outside Deuteronomy and Joshua, Yahweh commands the Israelites to expel the peoples of the land. At Sinai, Yahweh promises to "expel" (*gerash*) the indigenous nations of Canaan and commands the Israelites to

---

[15]Deepening the ambiguity is the later note that Jerusalem is allotted to Benjamin, not Judah (Josh 19:28).

demolish their sacred sites and smash their standing stones. Yahweh promises to send the hornet to expel the peoples but declares that the process will not take place within a single year. Rather, Yahweh declares that the peoples will be driven out gradually, until the Israelite population has grown large enough to take possession (Ex 23:28-31).[16]

Yahweh elaborates in more detail as Israel prepares to invade the land (Num 33:50-56). "You must expel all of the inhabitants of the land who face you.... You must take possession of the land and occupy it in their place, because I have given the land to you so that you can take possession of it" (Num 33:52-53). Additional references to expulsion also occur briefly in Deuteronomy (Deut 11:22-25) and toward the end of Joshua (Josh 23:5, 9, 13). Finally, expulsion describes what the tribes of Israel attempt to do in still another version of the story that begins the book of Judges (Judg 1:1-36).

The language of wiping out, then, constitutes a divergence from the program of expulsion that describes how Israel is to take the land. The change in style and program signals that the conquest narrative represents an overtly stylized account. This becomes clear when the narrative is compared with the military literature of the ancient Near East. The comparison reveals that Deuteronomy's account of a unified and total conquest employs literary conventions attested among the nations of Israel's world. These conventions include the use of hyperbole, declarations that the nation's deities were fighting for the people, and reports of massacres as acts of devotion to deities. Typical as well are claims that military leaders launched campaigns in response to divine commands, that the deity promises that the enemy will not prevail, and reports that the deity employed weather phenomena (such as hail) against the enemies.[17]

The Merneptah Stele offers a particularly relevant example of the totalizing rhetoric employed in ancient battle accounts. The stele details Merneptah's victories over the Libyans and over peoples in Canaan. The stele dates to the latter years of the thirteenth century BCE, a time that coincides with

---

[16]The verb here (*gerash*) is an approximate synonym of that which occurs in Joshua (*yarash*).
[17]Lawson K. Younger, *Ancient Conquest Accounts* (Sheffield Academic Press, 1990), 240-63; John Van Seters, "Joshua's Campaign of Canaan and Near Eastern Historiography," *Scandinavian Journal of the Old Testament* 4 (1990): 1-12; Lori Rowlett, *Joshua and the Rhetoric of Violence*, Journal for the Study of the Old Testament Supplement Series 226 (Sheffield Academic Press, 1996), 49-70.

what was likely the early era of Israel's judges. Near the end of the account, the stele reports, "Israel is laid waste (and) his seed no longer exists." Merneptah thus claims that he obliterated Israel, leaving no one to carry the nation into the future.[18] History, of course, does not bear that out.

Two narrative voices, then, present different accounts of what Moses commanded Israel to do, what happened, and what the story means. The dominant narrative voice, which I will refer to as the Theologian, uses conventional rhetoric and motifs to depict a dramatic and comprehensive conquest of the land. Its goal is to glorify Joshua and Yahweh through the narrative. Using hyperbole and other rhetorical devices, the Theologian crafts the story of conquest into a narrative confirmation of Deuteronomy's distinct theological program and perspective. The second narrative voice, which I will refer to as the Historian, employs a straightforward, unembellished style. The voice counters the Theologian's stylized narrative, as if to say, "It didn't happen quite that way."

The two narrative voices share common themes and affirmations. Both claim that Yahweh fought for Israel and gave the land to Israel to fulfill promises to the nation's ancestors. Both narratives also manifest a deep anxiety about the seductive allure of the Canaanites, which is expressed principally by admonitions that Israel maintain a strict distance from the indigenous peoples. The language of the Deuteronomic commandment demonstrates this concern by warning Israel against making agreements with the peoples of the land immediately after the command to wipe out those very peoples (Josh 7:1-5). "You must not make a covenant or show them any favor. You must not give your daughters to their sons nor take their daughters for your sons. That will draw your sons away from following me and serving other gods. That will kindle Yahweh's anger, and Yahweh will quickly make an end of you" (Josh 7:2-4).

How can one intermarry or make agreements with people one has wiped out? The arresting addition of commands to remain separate, in a nutshell, reveals those commands to be the real concern. "Wiping out," in other words, reinforces the imperative that Israel must have no contact with the peoples of the land. Why? Because Israel is "a people holy to Yahweh your

---

[18]Frank Yurco, "3,200-Year-Old Picture of Israelites Found in Egypt," *Biblical Archaeology Review* 16, no. 5 (1990): 27.

God," whom Yahweh has chosen "out of all the peoples in the world to be his people, his treasure" (Josh 7:5-6). The Theologian's use of *herem* language to report Israel's victories in the land therefore renders the conquest narrative as a dramatic demonstration of Israel's singular devotion to God; reports that Joshua wiped out the inhabitants of Canaan underscore, symbolically, the urgency of separation from the Canaanites.

The Historian articulates the concern for separation in a farewell address that Joshua delivers late in the narrative (Josh 23:1-16). In the speech, Joshua speaks of expelling the Indigenous peoples and warns Israel to keep its distance from them, "so that you will not enter these nations who survive among you, or speak the names of their deities, or swear by or serve them, or worship them" (Josh 23:7). Joshua reiterates the Mosaic admonition against intermarriage in a different form. He assures Israel that Yahweh will continue to expel the indigenous peoples if Israel obeys Yahweh. If Israel does not remain separate, Joshua warns, the indigenous peoples will entrap and torment the Israelites until they "vanish from this good land that Yahweh God" has given them (Josh 23:12-13). The rhetoric of Deuteronomy and of Joshua thus reinforces a single command: Every vestige of Canaanite presence must be erased.

The Humanist

A third narrative voice subverts the ethnic anxiety expressed by the Conquest and Settlement voices. It appears in Joshua 2–12 and in counterpoint to the triumphalist reports of massacred Canaanites. This narrative voice, which I will refer to as the Humanist, levels a subtle critique of the ideology of exclusion and violence promoted by the other two voices. The Humanist does this through stories that dissolve the ethnic boundaries that mark Israelites as chosen and worthy of life and Canaanites as dangerous and subject to extermination. The Humanist, in short, is more concerned with challenging constructions and stereotypes than with validating Israel's possession of the land.

The Humanist adopts a sophisticated, two-pronged strategy that sets the humanity of Canaanites and Israelites front and center. First, it presents three vignettes that introduce the first three battle accounts (at Jericho, Ai, and Gibeon). The first and third vignettes depict Canaanites who display attributes prized by Israel. The middle vignette flips the script and depicts an Israelite who perpetrates a gross sacrilege against Yahweh. Second, the narrator gradually presents Canaanite kings, rather than Canaanite difference, as the threatening power Israel faces in the land.

Each of the three vignettes occurs immediately before the account of Israel's victory at the site. The story of Rahab the Canaanite prostitute occurs before Yahweh's spectacular victory over Jericho (Josh 2:1-24). The story of a pedigreed Israelite named Achan is intertwined with the account of Israel's ambush and victory over the king of Ai (Josh 7:1-26). And the story of Gibeonite elders precedes the spectacular defeat of five Canaanite kings in the environs of the town (Josh 9:1-27). Each of the vignettes relates an encounter with Canaan that reverses the bad Canaanite/good Israelite construction.

Rahab's story (Josh 2:1-24) appears immediately after the speeches that begin the book. The episode begins when Joshua sends two hand-picked (although anonymous) spies to reconnoiter Jericho. The spies enter Jericho and spend the night in the house of Rahab, a Canaanite prostitute. When men sent by the king appear at Rahab's door seeking the spies, she tells them that the men have already left and sends them away. She then goes up to the roof, where she has hidden the spies under stalks of flax.

The episode centers on two conversations between Rahab and the spies. In the first (Josh 2:8-14), Rahab acclaims Yahweh's victories over the Amorite kings east of the Jordan, confesses Yahweh's supremacy, and asks the spies honor her kindness by sparing her family when the Israelites take the city. The spies immediately agree but later modify the agreement by stipulating that she must tie a crimson cord in a window. If her family stays in the house while the Israelites are killing the townsfolk, they declare, everyone within the house will be spared. She agrees and lets the spies down through the window of her house.

In the course of the story, Rahab displays the attributes of energy, opportunism, and cleverness prized by the Israelites and as exemplified by Jacob the patriarch. She recounts God's mighty works and acclaims the supremacy of Israel's God. In so doing, she articulates the essence of Israel's confession. The spies, however, do not even mention Yahweh. The narrator portrays them in passive and self-serving ways (lying down, preparing to sleep, dangling from a cord). The spies readily break the Mosaic commandment in order to save their lives and later protest that they made the forbidden agreement under duress (Josh 2:14). As the story develops, a striking shift in perspective takes place. A Canaanite prostitute takes the form of an exemplary Israelite, while Israelite spies demonstrate the diffidence and disobedience that will later prompt a rebuke from Joshua (Josh 18:2-3; 24:19-22). Rahab's experience of deliverance, marked by a red thread in the window of her house, caps the sense that she is as worthy of life and dignity as those who will invade her land.

The story of Achan (Josh 7:1-26) incorporates the same plot elements that configure Rahab's story but reverses them. The account opens with a comment that Achan committed a sacrilege by taking plunder from Jericho that had been devoted to Yahweh. The narrator introduces Achan with a long genealogy that accentuates his Israelite identity. There follows a brief report in which overconfident Israelites try to conquer Ai and are routed. When Joshua questions Yahweh about the defeat, Yahweh responds angrily that the Israelites have taken devoted plunder and have become, like the people of Jericho, *herem*. Yahweh then directs Joshua to expose the offender by casting lots. When the lot falls to Achan, Joshua demands that he confess. Achan does so and reveals that the plunder is hidden in the ground beneath his tent. When messengers excavate and present the plunder, "all Israel" stones Achan and his family to death. They then heap a pile of rubble over their bodies, thus identifying them with the king of Ai, over whom a pile of rubble will also be heaped (Josh 7:2; 8:29). Rahab and her family thus experience deliverance and live among the Israelites "to the present day." Achan and his family, however, are put to death and interred under a pile of rubble, which, like Rahab and her descendants, remains "to the present day" (Josh 6:25).

The third vignette concerns elders from the Hivite town of Gibeon. The elders don tattered clothing and carry worn-out wineskins and moldy bread. They present themselves to Joshua and the Israelite elders as travelers from a distant city. They request a peace treaty. Like Rahab, they acclaim the mighty acts of Yahweh and succeed in wangling an agreement that spares their lives—in this case with Joshua and the Israelite elders. Days later, the Israelites discover that the delegation came from a nearby Canaanite town. The situation prompts a dilemma. Should the Israelites honor the treaty and break the commandment or break the treaty and keep the commandment?

The elders decide to honor their oath and do not attack Gibeon and its villages. Joshua, however, stipulates that the Gibeonites must serve as woodcutters and water bearers for the nation and its sanctuary, which they do "to this very day."[19] Like Rahab, the Gibeonites display resourcefulness, trickery, and initiative to gain a place in the land. Joshua and the elders, however, appear to be easy dupes.

Each vignette concludes with an image that alludes to a significant event in Israel's story. The crimson cord Rahab puts in her window recalls the blood on the lintel that spared Israelite households while the Destroyer killed the Egyptian firstborn (Ex 12:21-24). The heap of rubble over Achan and his family resembles the pile of rubble Israel makes of Ai and other Canaanite towns. The Gibeonites' worn-out clothing and sandals link them to the covenant Moses renews on the plains of Moab (Deut 29:1-29). There Moses proclaimed that the Israelites' clothing did not wear out during its wilderness experience, echoing the ruse of the Gibeonite delegation (Deut 29:5; cf. Josh 9:5). Joshua's declaration that the Gibeonites are to be woodcutters and water drawers explicitly evokes a group included in the Israelite community at the covenant renewal (Deut 29:11; cf. Josh 9:21, 27).

Each of the vignettes reverses the bad Canaanite/good Israelite polarity. Rahab and the Gibeonites are good Canaanites. Achan is a bad Israelite. Taken together, the three stories portray indigenous peoples who act like Israelites and continue to live in the land and a sacrilegious Israelite who shares the fate of the Canaanites. The sophisticated rendering of the three accounts effectively dissolves the ethnic boundaries that bless Israelites and condemn Canaanites. In these vignettes, Israel sees its face reflected in that of the Indigenous Other. We do not see wicked peoples who need to be driven away and killed but rather human beings who bear an uncanny resemblance to the chosen people and who continue to live with them in the land.

It is worth noting that Yahweh says nothing when the Israelites egregiously disobey the Deuteronomic commandment to wipe out the peoples of the land, even though Yahweh has called Israel to meticulous obedience to "this book of the law." There is not the slightest hint of condemnation in

---

[19]For a more thorough description of the plot parallels that bind the three vignettes together, see L. Daniel Hawk, *Joshua*, Berit Olam (Liturgical Press, 2000), 19-33.

any of the cases. The placement of the stories, immediately before each of the first three battle accounts, therefore puts human faces on the men, women, and children who are slaughtered in the battle that follows. In Rahab and the Gibeonites, in other words, we encounter fellow human beings and not caricatures.

A second thread in the Humanist's strategy defuses the ethnic antagonism that shapes the Theologian's and Historian's accounts by gradually guiding the reader to see Israel's enemies in political rather than ethnic terms. The first king, at Jericho, signals malicious intent by sending men to apprehend the Israelite spies (Josh 2:2-3). At Ai, the king leads his forces into an Israelite ambush, resulting in the deaths of his troops (Josh 8:1-23). A report that a coalition of kings prepares to attack Gibeon then explicitly portrays kings as aggressors (Josh 9:1-2). Their defeat and deaths lead in turn to formulaic reports that mark Joshua's defeat of kings and towns in southern Canaan (Josh 10:22-36). From there, the narrator shifts to the north, with a report that the king of Hazor unites the kings of the whole region into a massive army, "as numerous as the sand on the seashore" (Josh 11:1-5). These kings Joshua also defeats, so that "all the towns of those kings, as well as the kings themselves, Joshua conquered and put to the edge of the sword, wiping them out as Moses, Yahweh's servant, had commanded" (Josh 11:12). The conquest account then concludes with a list of thirty-one kings Joshua defeated (Josh 12:7-24). The narrator's strategy thus presents the kings of the land, and not the land's peoples, as the threat that confronts Israel in the land.[20]

The ethical critique of the conquest thus begins within Joshua himself. The Humanist prompts readers to see those who are massacred as human beings rather than as faceless victims of conquest and expulsion. By juxtaposing personal vignettes and battle accounts, the Humanist unsettles the othering of Canaanites that justifies their extermination. Seeing others as fellow human beings makes killing them a more difficult enterprise. And by shifting the reader's gaze to kings, the Humanist tacitly diminishes the idea that indigenous others are enemies.

---

[20]For a detailed elaboration of this narrative strategy, see L. Daniel Hawk, "Conquest Reconfigured: Recasting Warfare in the Redaction of Joshua," in *Writing and Reading War*, ed. Brad E. Kelle and Frank Ritchel Ames, Symposium Series 42 (Society of Biblical Literature, 2008), 145-60; Lawson G. Stone, "Ethical and Apologetic Tendencies in the Redaction of the Book of Joshua," *Catholic Biblical Quarterly* 53 (1991): 25-36.

THE JOSHUA SCRIPT

The book of Joshua and the American settler narrative share a common plot. First, settlers invade the land as an irresistible force, driven by destiny, and take indigenous land from resistant people who are unworthy of it. Second, the settlers remake and reorder the land by delineating boundaries and erecting monuments. Third, the settlers cleanse the land of residual Indigenous presence, thus rendering the land as the sole and exclusive arena for the new humanity the settlers represent.

The American settler narrative includes two mythic figures who reprise the role of Rahab: Pocahontas and Sacagawea. Both mirror the Indigenous Helper, who appears at the beginning of Joshua in the person of Rahab. Likewise, the renegade Simon Girty echoes the treacherous Achan. Rahab welcomes and helps Israelite spies, just as Pocahontas and Sacagawea do for European settlers, thus expressing the Indigenous peoples' implicit acquiescence to the invaders. Achan's story, on the other hand, issues a stern warning about the seductive power of Indigenous ways, corresponding to the figure of Girty, the White Savage.

Because Joshua and the American settler narrative constitute variations on a common script, reading the two together opens space for decolonizing discussions of the settler narrative. Rather than a lamp that lights the way, Joshua should be read as a mirror that reflects the settler narrative and exposes what it hides. It constitutes a revelatory text that cannot and must not be dismissed. Rather, Israel's conquest narrative provides a vehicle by which troubling truths may be raised, particularly within communities that regard Joshua as a sacred text. The three narrative voices within Joshua remember Israel's past differently and for different reasons. The same can be said of the American settler narrative, which appears in the form of history, mythology, and critique. Recognizing the intratextual conversation the three voices of Joshua generate therefore promises a way to engage in difficult conversations about the settler past and present and about Christian complicity with the colonial project. How might viewing the settler narrative as mythology, history, and critique reveal about the role of each the ways US history is told?

The interpretive approach advocated by influential literary critic Edward Said offers a model for conducting such conversations. Said envisions interpretive communities that constitute ensembles of readers from diverse locations, perspectives, and experiences. These interpretative ensembles create a nonhierarchical discursive space that dissolves the subject/object binary and decenters the mechanisms that privilege "right" or dominant interpretations of the text. They generate an interpretive program that facilitates a fluid and lively interchange of interpreters, each of whom speaks from the particularities of their experiences.

As a metaphor for the approach, Said turns to baroque music and to the contrapuntal compositions that are an expression of it. Contrapuntal composition intertwines multiple independent melodic lines, in counterpoint to each other, to create a complex fabric of sound. "Various themes," he writes, "play off one another, with only a positional privilege given to any particular one; yet in the resulting polyphony there is a concert and order, an organized interplay that derives from the themes, not from a rigorous or formal principle outside the work." As a hermeneutical practice, contrapuntal reading creates an alternate discursive space, which contrasts with the uneven, partial, and polarized character of postimperial discourse. It rejects the rhetoric of blame and the politics of confrontation that infuse it. Contrapuntal reading decenters the dominant discourse by seeking out and including those voices that have been silenced, empowering them to represent themselves and speak their truths and experiences.[21]

By creating a discursive space that allows differences to emerge and all voices to be heard, a contrapuntal reading of Joshua can facilitate the integration of distinct, intertwined voices without harmonizing, contesting, or creating new centers. "The point of contrapuntal reading," as Alyssa Jones-Nelson helpfully summarizes, "is not to distil a single, agreed-upon meaning from a given text but to allow different streams of meaning to coexist, to recognize that difference does not necessarily entail conflict, and that 'truth can be opposed to truth.'"[22]

---

[21] Edward Said, *Culture and Imperialism* (Vintage, 1993), 18, 51, 67.

[22] Alyssa Jones-Nelson, *Power and Responsibility: Reading the Book of Job with Edward Said* (Routledge, 2012), 85. Writing of the model's potential for biblical interpretation, R. S. Sugirtharajah remarks: "To read contrapuntally means to be aware simultaneously of mainstream scholarship and of other scholarship which the dominant discourse tries to domesticate and speak and act against. . . . Such readings are undertaken, not with a view to refuting or contesting, but as a way of showing a substantial relationship between the center and the periphery." *The Bible and the Third World* (Cambridge University Press, 2001), 280.

We may think of Joshua itself as a narrative that invites a contrapuntal conversation. Each of the three voices offers a distinct account of Israel's origin in the land and what that past means for the present. The interplay of themes and perspectives renders a polyphony that resists a single, determinative, dominant meaning.

The Theologian presents a stylized account of the past that uses literary conventions, Deuteronomic motifs, exaggeration, mythic tropes, and metaphors to construct biblical Israel's narrative. The narrative glorifies Israel's God and depicts the nation as obedient to the divine law that orders it. A united Israel wipes out all the Indigenous inhabitants, in obedience to God's initiative and directives, through Joshua. The Theologian proclaims that Israel is chosen by God to take the land and to establish there a new community birthed from deliverance and promise. Yahweh and Israel enter the land together. Yahweh fights for Israel, wins victories over mighty indigenous nations, and gives the land to Israel to fulfill promises to the nation's ancestors. Israel sweeps the land clean of Indigenous peoples, artifacts, and deities, creating a space solely devoted to God and occupied by a new human community.

The Historian counters the Theologian's mythologized account with a relatively unembellished narrative that identifies vast areas of the Promised Land outside Israel's possession. It presents Israel as less unified, less obedient, and less successful in driving out indigenous populations. While the Theologian presents Israel's possession of the land as a fait accompli, the Historian relates a work in progress. Indigenous populations successfully resist and remain on the land into the narrator's present. The Historian presents readers with an Israel that does not display the energy, unity, or commitment the Theologian attributes to it. Even so, the Theologian and Historian share certain common convictions: (1) Yahweh fights for Israel, (2) Yahweh has given the land to Israel, (3) Indigenous presence constitutes an existential threat to the settler nation, and (4) Indigenous presence must be erased.

Employing Joshua as a mirror extends the textual conversation into decolonizing conversations among and between settler and Indigenous Christians. How do participants read the stylized settler narrative in the light of American national mythology? What histories lie behind its mythic renderings? What do are readers to make of the dehumanization of Indigenous people, and how should they respond to it? Reading Joshua together, attuned to the book's intratextual conversation about the past, can play a critical role in exposing and demystifying the script that justifies settler America and the system it validates.

Richard Slotkin, who has written extensively about the literature and mythology of the United States, trenchantly observes, "A people unaware of its myths is likely to continue living by them, though the world around that people may change and demand changes in their psychology, their world view, their ethics, and their institutions."[23] I find Slotkin's words particularly apt. Exposure and acknowledgment constitute a necessary step in unmasking the settler narrative, as exposure confronts the myth of innocence that justifies the settler structure. Exposure reveals repressed truths that fuse settler identity with Christian identity, White settler ideologies with Christian mandates, and White racial superiority with myths of election.

QUESTIONS FOR REFLECTION AND DISCUSSION

1. Are there any redeeming aspects of White settler colonialism and its justifying fictions?

2. What would be the impact, if any, if White settler Christians challenged Manifest Destiny and declared that the United States acquired its land by illegitimate means?

3. Has complicity with colonial violence shaped the thinking and practice of the American church? If so, in what ways?

4. How has what you've read in this book changed the way you think about American history?

5. Do you see the three narrative voices in Joshua in contemporary US histories and memories: (1) a mythologized voice that glorifies the nation and expresses its identity and virtues, (2) a historical voice that aspires to recount what happened, and (3) a humanizing voice that critiques the violence and ethnic separatism of the other two voices?

---

[23]Slotkin, *Regeneration Through Violence*, 4.

9

BEYOND INNOCENCE

Dismantling the Settler Narrative

There is no separation between past and present, meaning that an alternative future is also determined by our understanding of our past.

Nick Estes, *Our History Is the Future*

On June 20, 2023, the city of Columbus, Ohio, launched a $3.5 million initiative titled the Reimagining Columbus Project. Its purpose was to reenvision the city's public space and commemorative landscape, to promote diversity through investing in new public art, and to tell the truth about colonialism and racism. "By reckoning with symbols of our city's namesake, Christopher Columbus," the project declares, "and creating a more inclusive public art landscape, our city has an opportunity to create and more fully recognize, understand, and celebrate our multiplicity."[1] The project was supported by a $2 million grant from the Mellon Foundation's Monument Project for the purpose of "recontextualizing" a twenty-foot statue of Christopher Columbus that stood outside City Hall until its removal in 2020. The city of Columbus designated the remaining $1.5 million to support new public art that promotes diversity in the city's public spaces.

In a press release announcing the project, Mayor Andrew J. Ginther declared, "Today, we take the next step in rewriting our narrative. We take responsibility to tell the truth about colonialism and racism, and to tell the stories of the people who have been overlooked and erased from the telling of our history." Elizabeth Alexander, the president of the Mellon Foundation,

---

[1] Reimagining Columbus, www.reimaginingcolumbus.com.

affirmed the value of the project by noting, "Through the monuments and memorials that mark them, our civic spaces are where many of us first learn about the American story."[2] With the partnership, Columbus joined other cities that aspire to "uplift the stories of people who haven't been represented in our symbolic landscape."[3]

The Mellon Foundation launched the Monument Project in 2020, as statues of Confederate generals, Christopher Columbus, and other figures were being vandalized, toppled, and removed. The project recognizes the inextricable connection between the historical narrative of the United States and its commemorative spaces. The foundation has pledged $500 million to reconfigure those spaces and to reimagine them in ways that more accurately reflect the nation's values and diversity. The project abstract comments:

> Monuments and memorials—the statues, plaques, markers, and place names that commemorate people and events—are how a country tells and teaches its story. What story does the commemorative landscape of the United States tell? Who are we instructed to honor and uplift, and who do we not see in these potent symbols? Does the civic landscape show an accurate picture of our nation, or propagate a woefully incomplete story?[4]

The project answers these questions by explaining that monuments and memorials "shape powerful narratives that say some of us ought to be visible and celebrated, and some of us ought to be invisible and ignored."[5] The $500 million pledged to the project underscores the urgency of the contemporary conversation about race, power, and the American narrative.

The Reimagining Columbus initiative manifests a dramatic and contentious transformation that has taken place in a relatively short time. Until recently, citizens of the city celebrated their association with Christopher Columbus. The statue in front of City Hall was a gift from the citizens of Genoa, Italy, in 1955. It was unveiled in front of Columbus City Hall to a crowd of one hundred thousand and amid a four-day celebration of

---

[2] News Release, City of Columbus, June 20, 2023.
[3] Reimagining Columbus.
[4] "The Monuments Project Initiative," The Monuments Project, www.mellon.org/article/the-monuments-project-initiative.
[5] "The Monuments Project FAQs," The Monuments Project, www.mellon.org/article/the-monuments-project-initiative-faqs.

Columbus Day.[6] Citizens celebrated again in 1992 to mark the quincentennial of Columbus's first voyage in 1492. The main attraction, on that occasion, consisted of three life-size replicas of the *Niña*, the *Pinta*, and the *Santa Maria*, which lay at anchor near the mouth of the Scioto River. The ships were located near the site of Salt-Lick Village, an Ohio Seneca town.

In 1774, Virginia militia attacked the town, slaughtered six residents, and took another fourteen captive. Then they plundered the town and burned it to the ground. The militia, under the command of Colonel William Crawford, attacked the town in retaliation for Tachnedorus's (Chief Logan) raids on white settlements. The militia attacked when most of the warriors were away.[7] The massacre has long since faded from settler memory, although ironically two statues and a monument honor the memory of Chief Logan elsewhere: a statue at Chief Logan State Park in West Virginia; a twenty-foot tribute carved from a fallen oak tree in Bath, Ohio; and a monument at Logan Elm State Memorial near Circleville, Ohio, where the Cayuga orator is said to have delivered his famous speech. No historical marker, however, commemorates what happened at Salt-Lick.

Renunciations of Columbus's brutal enslavement, torture, and massacre of Caribbean peoples, along with the celebration of Columbus as an icon of colonialism and White supremacy, generated mounting pressure to remove the statue. In 2017, a group of protestors rallied in front of City Hall and demanded that the statue be removed. At the time, Mayor Ginther refused, remarking, "There are many perspectives on the Christopher Columbus statue, but let's not be distracted from the need to address the real problem: the racial divide in our community and across this country."[8] By 2020, however, Ginther's defense of the statue was no longer convincing. In July of that year, Columbus State College announced that it would remove a statue of Columbus located on its grounds. Two days later, Ginther

---

[6] Tyler Buchanan, "Columbus Statues in Columbus: Their Legacy and Future," *Ohio Capital Journal*, June 23, 2020, https://ohiocapitaljournal.com/2020/06/23/columbus-statues-in-columbus-their-legacy-and-future/.

[7] Andrew Lew Feight, "William Crawford & the Destruction of Salt-Lick Town," Scioto Historical, https://sciotohistorical.org/items/show/2.

[8] Michelle Rotuno-Johnson, "Protestors Call for Removal of Christopher Columbus Statue," *NBC4i*, August 19, 2017, www.nbc4i.com/news/protesters-call-for-removal-of-christopher-columbus-statue/.

announced that the statue at City Hall would be removed "as soon as possible."⁹ Coinciding with the removal of the City Hall statue in 2020, the council passed a resolution to observe Indigenous Peoples' Day (as opposed to Columbus Day) on October 12.

THE EMPIRE STRIKES BACK

While the city of Columbus was contemplating what to do with the Columbus statue, the Ohio State Legislature was pondering legislation designed to defend the White settler narrative. In 2023, State Senator Jerry Cirino (Republican) introduced a bill titled the Higher Education Enhancement Act (SB 83), which among other things required state institutions of higher learning to "prohibit any mandatory programs or training courses regarding DEI [diversity, equity, and inclusion]" and to guarantee "intellectual diversity." Among a wide-ranging list of dictates were stipulations that no institution may "influence or require" students and personnel to "endorse or express" a particular "ideology, social stance, or view of a social policy." The bill also mandated sanctions against personnel who interfere "with the intellectual diversity rights of another." Finally, the bill required state institutions to develop and require a three-credit-hour course on American government or history, which includes a list of prescribed documents. Steve Demetriou (Republican) and Josh Williams (Republican), who introduced a companion bill in the House, declared that the legislation was necessary because "across Ohio and the nation, universities and colleges have become the epicenter of indoctrination of young Americans."[10]

When the bill stalled in the House, Cirino reintroduced a modified version in January 2025 as the Enact Advance Ohio Higher Education Act. The legislature passed the bill in a relatively short time, and Governor Mike DeWine signed it into law on March 28. Besides the dictates mentioned above, the law requires that state institutions of higher learning "ensure full intellectual

---

⁹Bill Bush, "Christopher Columbus Still in Hiding as City Council Pauses Return to Public View," *Columbus Dispatch*, July 26, 2022, www.dispatch.com/story/news/politics/2022/07/26/christopher-columbus-statue-ohio-city-no-return-public-view-soon/10131853002/.

[10]"Williams, Demetriou Legislation Will Provide Educational Freedom for College Students," Ohio House of Representatives, 135th General Assembly, April 12, 2023, https://ohiohouse.gov/members/steve-demetriou/news/williams-demetriou-legislation-will-provide-educational-freedom-for-college-students-114212.

diversity" and requires instructors to maintain neutrality on "controversial beliefs or policies." (What constitutes intellectual diversity is nowhere defined.)[11] Upon passage by the legislature, Cirino proclaimed that the bill enhanced academic freedom, returned "our public universities and colleges to their rightful mission of education rather than indoctrination," and raised Ohio to "the top of the heap of higher education reform nationally."[12]

The legislative initiatives in the Ohio Senate and House corresponded to others introduced in state legislatures around the United States, all of which aimed "to silence discussions of race, gender, inequality, and any version of America history that's different from the White founders, rational, and 'divinely-inspired' America mythology."[13] Less than two years into the presidency of Joe Biden, 537 bills had been introduced in federal, state, and local governments, 241 of which were enacted into law. Supporters submitted so-called anti–critical race theory or diversity, equity, and inclusion legislation in every state except Delaware. Forty-one percent of these (including the bills introduced in the Ohio State Legislature) referred to "divisive concepts" and banned teaching that held individuals responsible for past acts committed by members of their race or sex.[14] By April 2023, twenty-eight states had adopted so-called anti–critical race theory legislation related to classroom instruction.[15]

A coalition of conservative think tanks, led by the Heritage Foundation, developed a template for the restrictive legislation and assisted Republican

---

[11] "Senate Bill 1," Ohio Senate, 136th General Assembly, https://ohiosenate.gov/legislation/136/sb1; see also Richard Vedder, "Ohio Senate Bill 1 Takes the Lead Against Woke Schools," *Wall Street Journal*, March 27, 2025, www.wsj.com/opinion/ohio-senate-bill-1-takes-the-lead-against-woke-schools-4e75c166?mod=latest_headlines&msockid=2fd323bca2c460e7255b3607a3a561b4.

[12] "Senate Passes Cirino's Landmark Higher Education Legislation," Ohio Senate, 136th General Assembly, February 12, 2025, https://ohiosenate.gov/members/jerry-c-cirino/news/senate-passes-cirinos-landmark-higher-education-legislation; see also Jessie Balmert, "Ohio Gov. Mike DeWine Signs Higher Ed Bill That Eliminates DEI, Bans Faculty Strikes," *Columbus Dispatch*, March 28, 2025, www.dispatch.com/story/news/politics/2025/03/28/dewine-signs-higher-ed-bill-that-eliminates-dei-bans-faculty-strikes/82688476007/.

[13] Hialy Gutierrez, "Alarming New Report Shows Attacks on Public Education Are Coordinated by Right-Wing Think Tanks," *Religion Dispatches*, May 28, 2024, https://religiondispatches.org/alarming-new-report-shows-attacks-on-public-education-are-coordinated-by-right-wing-think-tanks/.

[14] Olivia B. Waxman, "Exclusive: New Data Shows the Anti-Critical Race Theory Movement Is 'Far From Over,'" *Time*, April 6, 2023, https://time.com/6266865/critical-race-theory-data-exclusive/.

[15] Katharina Buchholz, "Anti-CRT Measures Adopted by 28 U.S. States," *Statista*, April 19, 2023. www.statista.com/chart/29757/anti-critical-race-theory-measures/.

lawmakers in crafting bills designed to succeed in their state legislatures. At the same time, local organizations popped up to push the legislation and take control of local school districts.[16] Efforts coalesced around a conspiracy narrative that described a shadow movement bent on indoctrinating America's youth and turning them against the nation.[17]

The strategy for the legislative defense of the settler narrative, against its purported critical race theory detractors, drew inspiration from two measures taken by President Donald Trump toward the end of his first term in office. On September 1, 2020, as polls indicated a close race with Joe Biden, conservative activist Chris Rufo appeared on Fox News's *Tucker Carlson Tonight* and called on President Donald Trump to issue an executive order that would "stamp out" the critical race theory "cult of indoctrination," which he called "an existential threat to the United States." The next morning, Rufo received a call from the White House. He flew to Washington and assisted in drafting Executive Order 13950, which shut down diversity, equity, and inclusion training in the federal government and contractors working for it.[18]

At the same time, Trump floated the idea of inculcating students with a "patriotic education." On September 17, he announced the creation of an eighteen-member "1776 Commission," which would develop a curriculum to counter "the twisted web of lies" being taught in American classrooms.[19] Trump announced the establishment of the commission, which included no credentialed historian, a day before the election. On that occasion, he defined its purpose: namely, to counter a history of the United States that taught students

---

[16] July Carrie Wong, "The Fight to Whitewash US History: 'A Drop of Poison Is All You Need,'" *The Guardian*, May 25, 2021, www.theguardian.com/world/2021/may/25/critical-race-theory-us-history-1619-project; Paige Williams, "The Right-Wing Mothers Fueling the School-Board Wars," *New Yorker*, October 31, 2022, www.newyorker.com/magazine/2022/11/07/the-right-wing-mothers-fuelling-the-school-board-wars.

[17] Olivia B. Waxman, "'Critical Race Theory Is Simply the Latest Bogeyman.' Inside the Fight over What Kids Learn About America's History," *Time*, July 16, 2021, https://time.com/6075193/critical-race-theory-debate/.

[18] Benjamin Wallace-Wells, "How a Conservative Activist Invented the Conflict over Critical Race Theory," *New Yorker*, January 18, 2021, www.newyorker.com/news/annals-of-inquiry/how-a-conservative-activist-invented-the-conflict-over-critical-race-theory; Sam Dorman, "Chris Rufo Calls on Trump to End Critical Race Theory 'Cult of Indoctrination' in Federal Government," *Fox News Flash*, September 2, 2020, www.foxnews.com/politics/chris-rufo-race-theory-cult-federal-government.

[19] Alana Wise, "Trump Announces 'Patriotic Education' Commission, a Largely Political Move," *NPR*, September 17, 2020, www.npr.org/2020/09/17/914127266/trump-announces-patriotic-education-commission-a-largely-political-move.

"to hate their own country" and to view its heroes as villains. Trump's inflammatory rhetoric accentuated the sense of existential threat. The commission's mandate aimed to silence any entities that interrogated the settler narrative:

> This radicalized view of American history lacks perspective, obscures virtues, twists motives, ignores or distorts facts, and magnifies flaws. Resulting in the truth being concealed and history disfigured. Failing to identify, challenge, and correct this distorted perspective could fray and ultimately erase the bonds that knit our country and culture together.[20]

The commission met once before being disbanded hours into the administration of President Joe Biden, only to be reinstated by the second Trump administration.

To This Very Day

The inflammatory rhetoric. The loaded language. The evocation of conspiracy. The dark warning of a threatening movement "to recast American history." All reveal a deep anxiety about contemporary interrogations of the American settler narrative, as well as a determination to defend it. The magnitude of existential angst raised by questioning the settler narrative underscores the crucial role the narrative plays in legitimizing the White colonial structure of the United States. Questioning the narrative threatens to expose suppressed truths. Exposed truths in turn illuminate the narrative's mechanisms of denial and justification. Efforts to demystify the narrative must therefore be shut down, by legislative intervention if necessary.

Shielding the settler narrative from interrogation also shields the White settler America and its operations in the present day. The contemporary program of settler domination takes many forms. Federal efforts to acquire and control Indigenous land, for example, are evident today in projects to build new dams, authorize pipeline construction, and open reservation land for mining and drilling. Indigenous communities, and particularly Indigenous women, suffer violence in numbers that far exceed those of the general population. And much of the logic that informed *Johnson v. M'Intosh* continues to receive implicit support from the doctrine of discovery through

---

[20]"Executive Order on Establishing the President's Advisory 1776 Commission," November 2, 2020, https://trumpwhitehouse.archives.gov/presidential-actions/executive-order-establishing-presidents-advisory-1776-commission/.

rulings that dismiss attempts to acknowledge or to restore Indigenous sovereignty over tribal lands.

The construction of the Dakota Access Pipeline, across the Missouri River and upstream of the Standing Rock Sioux reservation, provides perhaps the best-known recent instance of the settler regime's determination to control Indigenous land and communities. In 2014, Energy Transfer Partners, a Texas-based developer, announced the construction of a pipeline that would transport crude oil from shale oil fields in northern North Dakota to a terminal in southern Illinois. The original route submitted by the Army Corps of Engineers routed the pipeline across the Missouri River north of Bismarck, North Dakota. A second plan, however, rerouted the pipeline so that it would instead cross the river a half mile upstream from the Standing Rock reservation.

The latter plan generated significant opposition from an array of tribal councils and Indigenous grassroots organizations. In 2015, the Standing Rock Sioux Tribe passed a resolution declaring that the planned route of the Dakota Access Pipeline would "pose a serious risk to the very survival of our Tribes and … would destroy valuable cultural resources," including sacred places, burial sites, and petroglyphs. The resolution cited promises made in the 1868 Treaty of Fort Laramie that guaranteed the "undisturbed use and occupation" of the Great Sioux reservation, most of which had never been ceded to the United States.[21]

On July 15, 2016, Oceti Sakowin Youth and Allies organized a two-thousand-mile relay run from Standing Rock to Washington, DC, where they delivered 140,000 signatures supporting the shutdown of the project.[22] Encampments situated by the Missouri River swelled to over four hundred people, Indigenous and non-Indigenous, many of whom traveled from distant locations. A corresponding legal campaign sought to halt the construction of the pipeline through the court system, beginning with a complaint against the Army Corps of Engineers, which was filed on July 27.[23]

---

[21] Wakíŋyaŋ Waánataŋ (Matt Remle), "Feb 26, 2016—Standing Rock Sioux Tribe Passes Resolution Opposing the Dakota Access Pipeline," *Last Real Indians*, February 26, 2016, https://lastrealindians.com/news/2016/2/26/feb-26-2016-standing-rock-sioux-tribe-passes-resolution-opposing-the-dakota-access-pipeline.

[22] The Oceti Sakowin constitute the seven nations of the Great Sioux Nation (Dakota, Lakota, and Nakota). The struggle to protect the water marked the first gathering of all seven nations since the Battle of Greasy Grass (Little Big Horn).

[23] This summary draws from the detailed firsthand account of Nick Estes, *Our History Is the Future: Standing Rock Versus the Dakota Access Pipeline, and the Long Tradition of Indigenous Resistance*

Events escalated quickly in August. Hundreds of water protectors, so named to reflect their purpose in resisting the pipeline, conducted marches to the construction site and lifted up prayers. Hundreds more joined the camps, swelling their number to over ten thousand.[24] On September 2, a tribal heritage official notified the court that he had identified eighty-two stone features and archaeological sites in the area, along with twenty-seven burial sites. Some were endangered by the ongoing construction.[25] The next day, a group of water protectors came to the destruction site and saw bulldozers demolishing a burial ground. They pushed through a fence and were met with tear gas and attack dogs from agents of TigerSwan, a private security firm hired by Energy Transfer Partners to assist law-enforcement personnel.

On September 6, US District Judge James Boasberg ordered a temporary halt to construction across the Missouri, pending a decision on the tribe's lawsuit against the Corps of Engineers. Two days later, however, North Dakota Governor Jack Dalyrimple declared a state of emergency, called in five hundred National Guardsmen, and issued a call for assistance from other law-enforcement jurisdictions. Seventy-six responded. By mid-October, 140 arrests had been made at demonstrations and blockades. No significant violence took place until November 21, when four hundred water protectors set a dozen fires near a bridge and attempted to cross it in subfreezing weather. The police fired rubber bullets and tear gas into the groups and sprayed them with water cannons.[26] All told, more than 830 criminal cases resulted from resistance at the site.[27]

In December, the Corps halted construction of the pipeline and announced that it would undertake an environmental impact study "with full public input and analysis" before allowing construction to resume. On January 24, 2017, however, President Donald Trump issued an

---

(Verso, 2019). See also Rebecca Hersher, "Key Moments in the Dakota Access Pipeline Fight," *NPR*, February 22, 2017, www.npr.org/sections/thetwo-way/2017/02/22/514988040/key-moments-in-the-dakota-access-pipeline-fight.

[24]Estes, *Our History Is the Future*, 3.

[25]Ben Davis, "How a Pipeline Is Threatening Native American Culture in North America," ArtNet, https://news.artnet.com/art-world/standing-rock-cultural-desecration-640799.

[26]Madison Park and Mayra Cuevas, "Dakota Access Pipeline Clashes Turn Violent," *CNN*, November 26, 2016, www.cnn.com/2016/11/21/us/dakota-access-pipeline-protests/index.html.

[27]"Future of Controversial Dakota Access Pipeline's River Crossing Remains Unclear," Associated Press, September 8, 2023, https://apnews.com/article/north-dakota-access-pipeline-standing-rock-76e6fbf35e5f70c5e58b97a5ccee3920.

executive order directing the Corps to expedite the process. The study was completed on February 17, and the pipeline became operational in June of that year.

On July 6, 2020, the district court for the District of Columbia vacated the Army Corps' decision to grant an easement for the pipeline and ordered that it be shut down within thirty days. The following September, the Corps announced that it would prepare another environmental impact statement.[28] A draft of the environmental impact statement was released three years later, in September 2023. The legal status of the project nonetheless remains in limbo. Meanwhile, the pipeline has remained operational, transporting 600,000 to 650,000 barrels of oil per day.[29]

Pipeline projects like the Dakota Access Pipeline typically bring another danger beyond the threat to water and the destruction of ecosystems and living spaces. Pipeline construction is usually accompanied by man camps. The camps typically consist of temporary modular housing in or near tribal lands. They can number up to a thousand workers. The booming numbers of pipeline workers who occupy the camps, an overwhelming majority of whom are male, correlate with a significant increase in sex trafficking and sexual violence in the surrounding Indigenous population. A study of man camps on the Fort Berthold reservation in North Dakota reported that sexual assaults of Indigenous women increased by 75 percent, with no corresponding increase in assaults outside the pipeline zone.[30] In short, man camps are "well documented to be hotbeds of sexual violence."[31]

Many factors contribute to the violence. The need for workers often leads to lax hiring standards; one study found that a large percentage of camp men were convicted sex offenders.[32] The rapid increase in population also strains local and tribal law enforcement. Tribal police, furthermore, may not arrest

---

[28] For a detailed summary of the litigation, see "The Dakota Access Pipeline (DAPL)," Environmental & Energy Law Program, 2024, https://eelp.law.harvard.edu/2017/10/dakota-access-pipeline/.
[29] "Future of Controversial Dakota Access Pipeline's River Crossing."
[30] "New Report Finds Increase of Violence Coincides with Oil Boom," First Peoples Worldwide, University of Colorado Boulder, March 14, 2019, www.colorado.edu/program/fpw/2019/03/14/new-report-finds-increase-violence-coincides-oil-boom.
[31] Ana Condes, "Man Camps and Bad Men," *Northwestern University Law Review* 116, no. 2 (2021): 517.
[32] "New Report Finds Increase."

non-Indigenous people for a number of serious crimes, including rape and murder. Colonial stereotypes that view Indigenous women as embodying a "savage sexuality" persist, leading offenders to view raping an Indigenous woman as less serious than raping a White woman. Finally, researchers have noted a widespread belief that those perpetrating crimes against Indigenous women face no serious consequences. The belief appears to be well founded, as the response to assaults, from law enforcement at all levels, is typically slow and ineffective.[33]

Overall, Indigenous women and children are victimized by violent crimes at an alarmingly high rate. According to a study published by the National Institute of Justice, more than four out of five American Indian and Alaskan Native women reported that they had experienced violence at some point in their lives; 38 percent of women reported experiencing violence in the year prior to the study. More than half of all Indigenous women have been victims of sexual assault. One-third have been raped. More than two-thirds of the perpetrators are non-Indigenous.[34] One activist writes, "Rape is seen as inevitable for many American Indian women; they 'talk to their daughters about what to do when'—not if—'they are sexually assaulted,' and young American Indian women often 'live their lives in anticipation of being raped.'"[35]

Indigenous women are murdered at a rate ten times that of the general population.[36] Thousands of Indigenous women also go missing. A report published in 2017 counted 5,646 American Indian and Alaska Native women as currently missing.[37] Approximately 1,500 missing American Indian and Alaska Native women have been included in the National Crime Information Center, and approximately 2,700 cases of homicide have been reported to the federal government's Uniform Crime Reporting Program. The Bureau of Indian Affairs estimates that approximately 4,200 reported cases

---

[33] Condes, "Man Camps," 523, 530, 519.
[34] André B. Rosay, "Violence Against Indian and Alaska Native Women and Men," National Institute of Justice, June 1, 2016, https://nij.ojp.gov/topics/articles/violence-against-american-indian-and-alaska-native-women-and-men.
[35] Condes, "Man Camps," 521.
[36] "Violence from Extractive Industry 'Man Camps' Endangers Indigenous Women and Children," First Peoples Worldwide, University of Colorado Boulder, January 29, 2020, www.colorado.edu/program/fpw/2020/01/29/violence-extractive-industry-man-camps-endangers-indigenous-women-and-children.
[37] Rosay, "Violence Against Indian and Alaska Native Women and Men."

of missing and murdered Indigenous women and girls remain unsolved.[38] The actual number in both cases is likely much higher, as the crimes are probably underreported to a significant degree.

The stunning number of missing and murdered Indigenous women and girls echoes, in a new key, the settler violence that accompanied frontier expansion, particularly so in the contact zones around man camps and White settlements. As in US military campaigns and frontier assaults, White men target Indigenous women and children. As on the frontier, White perpetrators often inflict violence with the belief that they will suffer no consequences. In addition, the response of local, state, and federal authorities today echoes the inattentiveness, confusion, ineptitude, and unresponsiveness that have historically characterized settler law enforcement in response to Indigenous people.

The mother of Hanna Harris, who was killed on the Northern Cheyenne reservation, puts the situation succinctly: "Bad people commit these horrible crimes against Native women, but it is the system that allows it to happen generation after generation."[39] In short, "the legal systems in place in Indian Country do little to offer either protection or justice to American Indian women."[40] The template of settler violence persists: Indigenous invisibility, settler outrage when egregious cases of violence pierce the public consciousness, but often little if any substantive action.

The US government took a significant step to address the violence with the adoption of the Not Invisible Act in October 2020. Introduced as a bill by the four Indigenous members of the Senate, the act called for the establishment of a cross-jurisdictional advisory commission representing a spectrum of law-enforcement personnel, tribal leaders, service providers, families, and survivors. The commission was charged with making recommendations for improving intergovernmental coordination, strengthening resources for victimized families, and reducing the number of missing

---

[38]"Missing and Murdered Indigenous People Crisis," U.S. Department of the Interior: Indian Affairs, www.bia.gov/service/mmu/missing-and-murdered-indigenous-people-crisis.
[39]Jacqueline Agtuca, Elizabeth Carr, Brenda Hill, Paula Julian, and Rose Quilt, "MMIW: Understanding the Missing and Murdered Indigenous Women Crisis Beyond Individual Acts of Violence," National Indigenous Women's Resource Center, www.niwrc.org/restoration-magazine/june-2020/mmiw-understanding-missing-and-murdered-indigenous-women-crisis.
[40]Condes, "Bad Men," 532.

persons and murders and the amount of trafficking of American Indian and Alaska Native peoples.

The commission began work in 2022, under the supervision of Secretary of the Interior Debra Haaland and in coordination with the Department of Justice. Six subcommittees addressed key topic areas. On November 1, the commission issued its recommendations under the title *Not One More*.[41] The document set the violence suffered by Indigenous people within the broader context of the White settler government's colonial actions:

> The United States government's failure to fulfill its trust responsibilities to Tribal nations, coupled with historic policies that sought to disconnect AI/AN people from their land, language, and culture, have given rise to a public health, public safety, and justice crisis in Tribal communities. The crisis is most notably reflected in the federal government's failure to effectively prevent and respond to the violence against AI/AN people, particularly in the context of missing, murdered, and trafficked AI/AN people. Despite the best efforts of many individuals across law enforcement (LE), the judiciary, and social services, long-standing institutional failures must be acknowledged and addressed.[42]

In response to the study, Secretary Haaland and Attorney General Merrick Garland called for a "Decade of Action and Healing" and "a commitment to carry forward the stories and memories of the victims, families, and survivors highlighted in the report."[43]

Dismantling Settler Narratives

At this point, you may be asking, What do I do with this? By reading this far, you've taken the first step. You've had the courage to read through material that you've likely found painful. You've cared enough to learn about difficult truths. You may have experienced heartbreak at the inhumanity on display in this book. You've stayed with the narrative to this point. You have therefore already done important work.

---

[41] *Not One More: Findings & Recommendations of the Not Invisible Act Commission*, November 1, 2023, www.niwrc.org/sites/default/files/files/34%20NIAC%20Final%20Report_version%2011.1.23_FINAL_0.pdf.
[42] *Not One More*, 8.
[43] *Section 4(c)(2)(C) Response of the Departments of Justice and the Interior to Not One More: Findings and Recommendations of the Not Invisible Act Commission*, March 2024, www.justice.gov/tribal/media/1341181/dl?inline.

In what follows, I would like to make a few suggestions about continuing the journey toward justice and peacemaking that you've begun with this book. I will begin by addressing the inner work that must be done, as elaborated in the work of Miroslav Volf. I will then move to the work of Elaine Enns and Ched Myers, who have developed a model for exploring how one's family and personal history is entwined with the larger history of settler colonialism and its attendant trauma. I will then offer a few examples of work being done by Christian bodies before concluding with specific suggestions.

Double Vision

In *Exclusion and Embrace*, Miroslav Volf presents a promising theological framework for shaping thinking and practice toward the work of healing and justice.[44] Volf argues that violence is ultimately rooted in the exclusion of others and a determination to cleanse them from our communities. By way of Christian response, he asserts that both perpetrator and victim can be reconciled through solidarity with the Crucified One and by following his example. What kind of selves, he asks, do we need to be to live in harmony with others? And how can theologians foster "the kind of social agents capable of envisioning and creating just, truthful, and peaceful societies, and on shaping a cultural climate in which such agents will thrive"?[45]

Volf asserts that following Christ brings about "an all-encompassing change of loyalty, from a given culture with its gods to the God of all cultures." This identity roots individuals in a particular culture but creates a distance that makes room to receive others and to judge the evil in one's own culture. The warped will to create a pure world generates the willful exclusion, demonization, and bestialization of those deemed outside the boundaries. Evil thereby binds victim and violator in acts of violation that render no one innocent. In Western civilization's impulse to pursue inclusion by excluding what it regards as barbaric, Volf sees a wrongly centered self that must be decentered by nailing it to the cross. The Christian self thus becomes a recentered self, rooted in the self-giving love and example of the suffering Messiah. "The question is," Volf writes, "how to live

---

[44]Miroslav Volf, *Exclusion and Embrace: A Theological Exploration of Identity, Otherness, and Reconciliation*, rev. and updated ed. (Abingdon, 2019).
[45]Volf, *Exclusion and Embrace*, 10.

with integrity and bring healing to a world of inescapable noninnocence that often parades as its opposite."⁴⁶

Divine self-giving exemplifies an embrace that overcomes a world of sinful exclusion. It receives estranged enemies into eternal communion, freeing both oppressors and victims from an unending cycle of violence and enmity. The cross unites different bodies into one body, forming a new self that is oriented toward the practice of embrace rather than exclusion. Volf describes embrace as *"the will to give ourselves to others and 'welcome' them, to readjust our identities to make space for them, is prior to any judgment about others, except that of identifying them in their humanity."* Embrace creates the indispensable condition for justice, for *"the embrace itself—*full reconciliation—cannot take place until the truth has been said and justice has been done."⁴⁷

Germane to our study are Volf's reflections on the connection between embrace, justice, and truth. Embrace creates a space in one's heart to receive others. Embrace exposes exclusion as evil, subverts the hierarchies that maintain nonsymmetrical relationships, and defuses the power of evil that "lies in the perverse truth it tells about the warped well-being it creates."⁴⁸ The will to embrace makes it possible for parties at enmity to tell and hear the truth from all sides and to agree on justice.

Opening one's heart to receive others opens one's eyes to see things from the perspective of the other and to be transformed by what one sees. Volf calls this practice "double vision." Seeing with double vision enables parties to speak and receive the truth. The pursuit of truth along this path requires a resolve to find it and requires us to unmask our deceptions. Practically speaking, this entails a process that begins by stepping outside ourselves in order to observe ourselves, and then crossing social boundaries temporarily into the world of the other. Inhabiting the world of the other, in turn, also requires that we receive the other into our world—so that their perspective stands next to ours. The practice is constantly repeated, as no judgment is ever final.⁴⁹

---

⁴⁶Volf, *Exclusion and Embrace*, 80.
⁴⁷Volf, *Exclusion and Embrace*, 19. Italics original.
⁴⁸Volf, *Exclusion and Embrace*, 85.
⁴⁹Volf, *Exclusion and Embrace*, 240-44.

Volf's model challenges White settler Christians to situate the exposure, dismantling, and decentering of colonial narratives within the framework of Christian witness and mission. Volf establishes a way to reject colonial programs of exclusion and to recenter Christian witness in the self-giving love of the Crucified One. To make room for others in our selves is also to make room for the *stories* of others. Making room thus calls Christians to reorient our own narratives, to recenter ourselves, and to create communities in which oppressors and victims together pursue healing, justice, and well-being.

Following Volf, the path to embrace calls us first to interrogate our personal narratives and to unmask the deceptions that configure them. For White settler Christians, as I have argued, this unmasking requires the exposure of deeply embedded mechanisms of denial and claims of innocence. Interrogation constitutes a first practice needed to reveal the ways that White settler Christians have been and still are shaped by the settler narrative.

Haunted Histories

In *Healing Haunted Histories*, Elaine Enns and Ched Myers present a model for interrogating our narratives and thus situating decentering and recentering within the larger work of decolonization. Their work focuses on the interconnection between the individual, the communal, and the political, primarily at the local level. Enns and Myers refer to Indigenous dispossession as the "primal sin" of settler colonialism, which settler Christians "cannot *not* face and hope to be a healthy and just people." They orient their project "*to* and *from* our settler faith communities in the hope that we will struggle harder to rescue the gospel from Christendom, colonization, and white supremacy, even as we are being rescued *by* that gospel. A discipleship of decolonization means facing the ways that we and our ancestors have been complicit in colonial violence."[50] Two convictions ground their project, namely:

> 1. We will not seek healing until and unless we recognize *we* are sick, especially those of us who are privileged within a sick system.
>
> 2. The cure is found in the shared struggle to turn our pathological personal and political history around, because it's killing us.[51]

---

[50] Elaine Enns and Ched Myers, *Healing Haunted Histories* (Cascade, 2021), xxvi–xxvii.
[51] Enns and Myers, *Healing Haunted Histories*, 41.

Enns and Myers call White settler Christians to excavate their personal and family histories to discover what truths those histories reveal about their complicity with settler colonialism and what resources for healing their stories bequeath to them. Delving into one's family story of settlement facilitates a restorative solidarity with Indigenous peoples and opens a path to reconciliation that cannot be separated from the restoration of justice and the practices that enact it.

Enns and Myers orient the process along three local story lines. *Landlines* relate how and why one's settler ancestors came to the land and whom they displaced. *Bloodlines* look into the family histories and communal stories of settlement that have been contrived or distorted. *Songlines* explore the traditions and practices that foster resilience and inspire the pursuit of justice and liberation. Following these lines challenges settlers to consider the extent to which they enjoy a good life in the land at the expense of the people whom they have dispossessed. It also provides the basis for dealing with the moral injury that settlers carry as a consequence of their complicity with colonial violence. The process thereby offers a release from paralyzing toxic shame, animating healthy guilt and facilitating a revision of each story line in restorative modalities.

The value of this tripartite module has been illustrated, I trust, in the threads of my own story that I shared in the first chapter. Of particular import for our study is Enns and Myers's discussion of the "strategies of defensiveness" that settlers employ to maintain their innocence and avoid "response-ability" for pursuing restorative solidarity. These include rejoinders such as (in my words):

- I don't know. I don't want to know. And I don't care.
- Colonial violence is not my fault. I'm not privileged. Get over it.
- What's done is done. Let's move on.
- Dispossession and violence were the inevitable consequences of human migration. It's been happening since the dawn of human history.
- The establishment of European civilization in the land benefited settler and Indigenous peoples alike.

- Colonial settlers were mainly good people who interacted benevolently with Indigenous people. Colonial violence and governmental mendacity were regrettable aberrations.
- White settlers are the present-day victims of unfairness and persecution.
- I have a Native American ancestor.
- I value Indigenous cultures (which I demonstrate by purchasing Native-themed merchandise, reading about Native peoples, mimicking ceremonies and practices, etc.).[52]

To these defensive measures, I add two more, each of which reflects subterranean patterns of thought that reflect long-standing settler denial.

Indians are a problem: The "Indian problem" casts Indigenous peoples primarily as problems to be solved rather than human beings to be respected. Finding a way to fix the problem is paramount, so that settler Americans can bring closure, put to rest the nagging reminders of colonial violence and dispossession, and move on. The settler script, in sum, views Indians as a problem that White settler America must fix so that it can be released from the burden of national sin and guilt.

We know how to fix the problem: The history of settler America's relations with Indigenous people has been littered with plans to fix the Indian problem: from removal, to boarding schools, to privatizing Indigenous lands, to termination. The one consistent element in these and other reforming programs has been a refusal to listen and interact with Indigenous people themselves. This has been driven by the paternalistic attitude that assumes that White settlers know what is good for Indigenous people. The consequences? Devastating policies generated by well-intentioned Whites who believed they had the answer.

Challenging Colonial Narratives

A growing number of Christian bodies are taking steps to tell the truth about the past, to acknowledge Christian complicity with the colonial project, and to dismantle the settler structure that perpetuates unequal relations with Indigenous nations. To date, more than two dozen Christian denominations and groups have repudiated the doctrine of discovery, confessed their

---

[52] Enns and Myers, *Healing Haunted Histories*, 214-23.

Beyond Innocence 231

complicity with the colonial project, and voiced commitments to pursuing healing relationships with Indigenous nations of the United States and around the world. In 2018, the World Council of Churches, representing seventy-three Christian bodies that encompass the range of Christian traditions, denounced the doctrine of discovery "as fundamentally opposed to the gospel of Jesus Christ and as a violation of the inherent human rights that all individuals and peoples have received from God" and called each member denomination to reflect its national and church history.[53]

The church bodies that have specifically repudiated the doctrine of discovery, consisting primarily of mainline denominations, have taken various measures to initiate repentance and to repair damaged relationships. The work of my denomination, the United Methodist Church, is but one example. I point to three initiatives in particular. First, the denomination held an "Act of Repentance Toward Healing Relationships with Indigenous Peoples" in conjunction with its General Conference in 2012. During the service, Professor Tink Tinker addressed the conference and issued a challenge: "There is a lot of history that has been concealed," he declared. "You have to go and dig it up."[54]

The denomination's subsequent work to "dig it up" included two significant initiatives, aimed at identifying, acknowledging, and making amends for Methodist collusion with colonial erasure. At the same conference, delegates passed a resolution calling for full disclosure about the Sand Creek massacre, which had been led by a Methodist clergyman. Four years later, the General Conference welcomed descendants of Sand Creek survivors and committed to learning and teaching the history of the atrocity, and "entering into a journey of healing" with the descendants. That initiative stalled but resumed again in 2024, when a task force met with tribal leaders to take concrete steps toward healing.[55]

---

[53] World Council of Churches, "World Council of Churches Repudiates the Doctrine of Discovery," Doctrine of Discovery Project, July 27, 2018, https://doctrineofdiscovery.org/world-council-of-churches/.

[54] Kathy L. Gilbert and Linda Bloom, "GC2012: Starting Along the Path to Repentance," UM News, April 27, 2012, www.umnews.org/en/news/gc2012-starting-along-the-path-of-repentance.

[55] Joey Butler and Jim Patterson, "United Methodist Church Restarts Response to Sand Creek Massacre," October 30, 2024, www.unitedmethodistbishops.org/newsdetail/church-restarts-response-to-sand-creek-massacre-18719533.

The second initiative has involved an investigation into residential boarding schools with Methodist connections. The work has involved identifying schools, tracking down documents, and conducting interviews for the purpose of discovering what happened at the schools and how they executed the program of assimilation. A report was presented at a meeting of the United Methodist Historical Convocation in September 2024. It aimed to provide a foundation for further research that might "push forward the dual project of remembrance and reconciliation" and "begin to unravel the many mistaken assumptions that led to and continues to proliferate colonial violence and Indigenous silence."[56]

As I have noted, however, initiatives like these continue, for the most part, to operate at the edges of denominational systems, church networks, and other Christian bodies. Although gaining momentum, the work of justice and reconciliation is often pushed to the edge. Those moved to expose, interrogate, and demystify colonial practices and narratives, and to seek healing pathways, remain few but resolute.

This is why your voice and participation matter. My hope is that this overview of the settler-colonial project and its justifying narrative will encourage you to join in the work of interrogation and exposure. Here are a few suggestions for taking the next steps.

1. Explore your family history and the history of the Indigenous people who once lived on your land. Discover how their land was taken, how the logic of elimination played out in their erasure, and how local histories denied or justified their erasure. Think about how your local histories have shaped your outlook. You can usually find local histories in historical societies or libraries. You may also be able to find digital copies on the Internet Archive at https//archive.org.

2. Participate with Christian organizations that are pursuing the work of justice and reconciliation with Indigenous people. If your faith community is not doing this work, consider ways to encourage them to do so.

---

[56] Ashley Boggan D., *The United Methodist Church and Indigenous Boarding Schools: A Progress Report* (General Commission on Archives and History, 2024), 10. For a fuller account, see Crystal Caviness, "Spotlighting UMC's Role in Indigenous Boarding Schools," UM News, September 28, 2024, www.umnews.org/en/news/spotlighting-umcs-role-in-indigenous-boarding-schools.

3. Discover the vibrancy and vitality of Indigenous cultures today. Read Indigenous historians such as Roxanne Dunbar-Ortiz, Ned Blackhawk, Joseph M. Marshall III, and David Treuer, and award-winning poets such as Natalie Diaz, Joy Harjo, and Layli Long Soldier. Watch films by Sherman Alexie and others who tell the stories of Indigenous America today. Become informed about issues and topics that concern Indigenous America and get Indigenous perspectives on current events through *Indian Country Today*, *Native News Online*, and other media. Read Christian theologians such as Randy Woodley, George Tinker, and Chris Hoklotubbe, whose work is profoundly shaping biblical interpretation and Christian theology. Read through the First Nations Version of the New Testament.[57]

4. Support and participate in efforts to raise awareness about US colonial history. Oppose legislative and social efforts to restrict whose stories can be told and how they should be told.

5. Seek out and participate with groups working to dismantle the colonial structure that continues to privilege the descendants of White settlers.

6. If you live in proximity to Indigenous communities or urban centers, attend events open to the public and participate in any groups that are hosting Indigenous/settler conversations.

7. Invite others to join a Bible study based on the book of Joshua and the American settler history, or a discussion group on the present book.

Dreams and Visions

On Saturday, September 19, 2019, I joined a crowd of about six hundred people who gathered in Upper Sandusky, Ohio. The occasion was the return of the deed to a Wyandotte mission building and burial grounds, which the Wyandottes entrusted to the Methodist Episcopal Church (a forerunner of the United Methodist Church) when they departed their Grand Reserve in 1843. The group included ninety to one hundred citizens of the Wyandotte Nation of Oklahoma and an undetermined number of individuals from

---

[57]*First Nations Version: An Indigenous Bible Translation of the New Testament* (InterVarsity Press, 2021).

Wyandotte bands in Kansas and Michigan. Besides a number of United Methodist dignitaries, the group included descendants of John Stewart, the African American lay preacher whose ministry among the Wyandottes led to the formation of the Methodist Mission Society in 1820.

The mission building and burial grounds had come to the attention of Thomas Kemper, the general secretary of the Board of Global Missions, as the agency was planning to mark its two hundredth anniversary in 2020. Kemper discovered that the United Methodist Church still held the deed to the mission building and grounds, which the Wyandottes had transferred for fear that the settler population would desecrate the area. It seemed fitting to return the land as an expression of repentance and commitment to the denomination's long-standing relationship with the Wyandottes.

Wyandotte Chief Billy Friend was taken aback when contacted about returning the mission and burial grounds to the nation. He later remarked, "Very seldom do people want to give things back to us." Friend had been bringing Wyandotte elders and youth to the mission since 2007 to teach them their history and connect them to the land. The return of the mission building and land therefore carried deep meaning. "It was where our ancestors had gathered," Friend said, "especially for the last time, before they left Ohio."[58]

The day was sunny, and the atmosphere was festive. I arrived early and participated in an impromptu meeting with a small group of colleagues. The celebration began with a service of remembrance at John Stewart United Methodist Church. The Wyandotte nation princess prayed the Lord's Prayer in sign language. There were songs on a hand drum and expressions of goodwill. The sanctuary was packed.

After the service, the congregation left the church and walked about a mile to the mission and burial ground, led by Wyandotte veterans. The route passed the site where the council house once stood and where some of the tribal members who had not embraced Christianity were buried. As the procession passed, Wyandotte people sprinkled tobacco on the headstones and site.

The procession ended at a large tent near the mission. There were speeches by Chief Friend and the leaders of the Anderon Nation of Michigan and the Wyandot Nation of Kansas, and by United Methodist and local leaders. After

---

[58] Annemarie Cuccia, "The Wyandotte Nation's Long Road to Land Back," NonDoc, September 28, 2022, 4, https://nondoc.com/2022/09/28/the-wyandotte-nation-long-road-to-land-back/.

Beyond Innocence

the transfer of the deed back to the Wyandotte nation, the Wyandottes gifted the church and local leaders with blankets. Young men danced in regalia. Chief Friend blessed the land with a pipe ceremony. There were many other expressions of goodwill. The day felt like a healing moment, marking a historic injustice but also affirming a lasting friendship.

Although I grew up in Tiffin, I was born in Upper Sandusky. The city is a little more than an hour's drive from Ashland. Prior to the September gathering, I had visited the mission building and burial grounds several times, mainly to attend services that were held there on Sunday mornings in the summer. On one occasion, I lingered for some time after the service, enjoying the stillness of a summer morning as I sat near a fenced plot where many Wyandotte leaders had been laid to rest.

The mission building is the oldest active church building in Ohio. It was constructed in 1824 under the supervision of Rev. James Finley, who was appointed to succeed John Stewart as a pastor to Wyandotte Methodists. Finley became an advocate for the nation and a fierce critic of the government's removal policy. In 1826, he took two Wyandotte Christian leaders with him on a speaking tour throughout the East to raise support for the nation. He invited both leaders to preach along the way. In *Life Among the Indians*, Finley expressed his unabashed admiration for the Wyandottes and the other Ohio nations he had visited:

> I do not believe that there are a people on the earth, that are more capable of appreciating a friend, or a kind act done toward them or theirs, than Indians. Better neighbors, and a more honest people, I never lived among. They are peculiarly so to the stranger, or to the sick or distressed. They will divide the last mouthful, and give almost the last comfort they have, to relieve the suffering. This I have often witnessed.[59]

Just north of Upper Sandusky stands another historic site. That one marks the scene of the battle where an Indigenous coalition routed the military expedition led by Colonel William Crawford in June 1782. George Washington had sent Crawford to destroy Indigenous town along the Sandusky River and to devastate their fields of corn and vegetables. As with the

---

[59] James B. Finley, *Life Among the Indians or, Personal Reminiscences and Historical Incidents Illustrative of Indian Life and Character* (Cincinnati, 1860), 407.

Sullivan campaign, Washington aimed to drive Britain's Indigenous allies out of the Revolutionary War. Crawford's force of about five hundred militia was met and surrounded by a large Indigenous force. When they tried to retreat during the night, it quickly turned into a disorganized flight. Crawford himself became separated from his men and, as reported previously, was captured by Shawnee fighters.

Both sites were in my mind as I drove back from Upper Sandusky. I thought about the good life I have enjoyed in the land and the good life that had been taken from the Wyandotte people who once called the land their home. I wondered how things might have turned out differently had more authentically Christian sentiments guided relations between Indigenous and settler peoples. The past cannot be changed, but the celebration in Upper Sandusky gave a glimpse of what can be when relationships are honored, people are respected, and reciprocity is valued. It offered a brief anticipation of that day when the Creator will wipe away all tears, death will be vanquished, and sorrow and suffering will be no more.

Questions for Reflection and Discussion

1. What does healing and reconciliation between peoples look like, practically speaking?
2. From what do White settler Christians need to be healed?
3. What might Volf's model of double vision look like in practice?
4. What efforts to defend the settler narrative are taking place in your location or state? Who is pushing them? How would you answer those who accuse their opponents of revising history?
5. What organizations in your area are engaged in decolonial work?
6. What now? How will you put what you have read into action?

ACKNOWLEDGMENTS

THE JOURNEY THAT CULMINATED in the writing of this book has been a long one. Robert Lyon, late professor of New Testament at Asbury Seminary, oriented my thinking toward the central role that justice plays in the biblical vision and Christian mission through his teaching and example. When scholarly colleagues challenged me to consider the ethical implications of my early work on the book of Joshua, I appropriated the justice orientation to read Joshua in conversation with the American master narrative of Manifest Destiny. As I pursued that project, I was invited by Joe Duggan to join the inaugural meeting of what became the Postcolonial Roundtable. Norman Gottwald, likewise, invited me to participate in the work of the Center and Library for the Bible and Social Justice. Both individuals gave me welcome encouragement, and the organizations played a vital role in shaping my thinking.

When, in the early 2000s, I began speaking at Ohio churches and conferences about pursuing justice with the Indigenous nations of this continent, I met Ken Brandes. Ken was a connector who had a deep passion for peace and reconciliation and facilitated a number of conferences toward that end. The conferences introduced me to individuals who became friends and teachers, especially Terry and Darlene Wildman, Kimberlee Medicine Horn Jackson, Mike Peters, and Jack Lyons. My attendance at a number of annual symposiums convened by the Native American Institute for Indigenous Theological Studies (NAIITS) introduced me to another set of valued relationships. I particularly thank Terry LeBlanc for frank conversations and communications, and Adrian Jacobs, who has been a valuable interlocutor as I've grappled with the faith implications of my work on the book.

I'm indebted to those who served with me on the East Ohio Committee on Native American Ministries (United Methodist Church). In the more than ten years that I chaired the committee, we did some very good work together. I also learned from my friendships with colleagues on the North Central Jurisdiction CONAM (UMC), particularly Fred Shaw, Carol Lakota Eastin, and Michelle Oberwise Lacock.

Gene and Sandy Heacock have been kindred spirits through much of my journey, as well as cherished friends and guides along the way. Joe and Janice Daltorio also shared common spiritual cause with me, which was expressed in prayer walks at a number of key sites in Ohio.

I'm deeply grateful to the administration and trustees of Ashland Theological Seminary, who granted me a study leave during which I drafted the majority of the manuscript. It is a privilege to teach and write in this uniquely supportive and collegial seminary community.

I am grateful as well to InterVarsity Press for taking on this unusual project with enthusiasm. The editorial acumen of Jon Boyd and the careful work of the editorial team at IVP have made this a much stronger volume.

Finally, I'm grateful for the support and encouragement I've received from my wife Linda throughout the journey. Her love, patience, and understanding have provided constant support. I could not have traveled this path if she had not been walking with me.

FOR FURTHER READING AND RESEARCH

COLLECTIONS OF PRIMARY SOURCES

Online
Avalon Project: Documents in Law, History, and Diplomacy. https://avalon.law.yale.edu/.
Doctrine of Discovery. https://doctrineofdiscovery.org/.
Founders Online. National Archives. https://founders.archives.gov/.
Gilder Lehrman Institute of American History. www.gilderlehrman.org/.
Internet Archive. https://archive.org/.
Legal Information Institute. Cornell Law School. www.law.cornell.edu/supremecourt/text.
National Indian Law Library. https://narf.org/nill/index.html.
National Museum of American History. Behring Center. https://americanhistory.si.edu/explore/stories/TRR.
Papers of the Winthrop Family. www.masshist.org/publications/winthrop/index.php/view/PWF04d089.
Tribal Treaties Database. Oklahoma State University. https://treaties.okstate.edu/treaties/.

Print
Calloway, Colin G. *First Peoples: A Documentary Survey of American Indian History*. 2nd ed. Bedford/St. Martin's, 2004.
Cherry, Conrad, ed. *God's New Israel: Religious Interpretations of American Destiny*. Rev. and updated. University of North Carolina Press, 1998.
Prucha, Francis Paul, ed. *Documents of American Indian Policy*. 3rd ed. University of Nebraska Press, 2000.
Segal, Charles M., and David C. Stineback, eds. *Puritans, Indians, and Manifest Destiny*. Putnam's Sons, 1977.

General Histories

Blackhawk, Ned. *The Rediscovery of America: Native Peoples and the Unmaking of U.S. History*. Yale University Press, 2023.

Brown, Dee. *Bury My Heart at Wounded Knee: An Indian History of the American West*. Holt, Rinehart & Winston, 1970.

Cozzens, Peter. *The Earth Is Weeping: The Epic Story of the Indian Wars for the American West*. Vintage, 2017.

Dippie, Brian W. *The Vanishing American: White Attitudes and U.S. Indian Policy*. University of Kansas Press, 1991.

Dunbar-Ortiz, Roxanne. *An Indigenous Peoples' History of the United States*. Beacon, 2014.

DuVal, Kathleen. *Native Nations: A Millennium in North America*. Random House, 2024.

Hämäläinen, Pekka. *Indigenous Continent: The Epic Contest for North America*. Liveright, 2023.

King, Thomas. *The Inconvenient Indian: A Curious Account of Native People in North America*. University of Minnesota Press, 2013.

Richter, Daniel. *Facing East from Indian Country: A Native History of Early America*. Harvard University Press, 2001.

Stannard, David E. *American Holocaust: The Conquest of the New World*. Oxford University Press, 1992.

Treuer, David. *The Heartbeat of Wounded Knee: Native America from 1890 to the Present*. Riverhead, 2019.

Wilson, James. *The Earth Shall Weep: A History of Native America*. Grove, 1998.

Representative Online Encyclopedias

Anchor: A North Carolina History Online Resource. www.ncpedia.org/anchor/anchor.

Encyclopaedia Britannica. www.britannica.com/topic/Encyclopaedia-Britannica-English-language-reference-work.

Encyclopedia of Alabama. https://encyclopediaofalabama.org/.

Encyclopedia Virginia. https://encyclopediavirginia.org/.

New Georgia Encyclopedia. www.georgiaencyclopedia.org/.

New World Encyclopedia. www.newworldencyclopedia.org/entry/Info:Main_Page.

Utah History Encyclopedia. www.uen.org/utah_history_encyclopedia/.

Resources (News, Lessons, Lesson Plans)

American Indian Magazine. www.americanindianmagazine.org/about-magazine.

Bureau of Indian Affairs. www.bia.gov/.

Doctrine of Discovery Project. https://doctrineofdiscovery.org/.

Indian Country News. https://ictnews.org/news.

Indianz. https://indianz.com/.

The National Native American Boarding School Healing Coalition. https://boarding schoolhealing.org/.
Native America Today. https://nativeamericatoday.com/.
Native Knowledge 360°. https://americanindian.si.edu/nk360/.
Native News Online. https://nativenewsonline.net/.
Research Guides. Library of Congress. https://guides.loc.gov/.

SPECIAL TOPICS

Adams, David Wallace. *Education for Extinction: American Indians and the Boarding School Experience, 1875–1928.* University of Kansas Press, 2020.

Augustine, Sarah. *The Land Is Not Empty: Following Jesus in Dismantling the Doctrine of Discovery.* APG, 2021.

Berkhofer, Robert, Jr. *Salvation and the Savage: An Analysis of Protestant Missions and American Indian Response, 1787–1862.* University of Kentucky Press, 1965.

Berkhofer, Robert, Jr. *The White Man's Indian: Images of the American Indian from Columbus to the Present.* Vintage, 1976.

Bowden, Henry Warner. *American Indians and Christian Mission: Studies in Cultural Conflict.* Chicago History of American Religion. University of Chicago Press, 1981.

Calloway, Colin G. *The Indian World of George Washington.* Oxford University Press, 2018.

Charles, Mark, and Soong-Chan Rah. *Unsettling Truths: The Ongoing, Dehumanizing Legacy of the Doctrine of Discovery.* InterVarsity Press, 2019.

Dunbar-Ortiz, Roxanne, and Dina Gilio-Whitaker. *"All the Real Indians Died Off": And Twenty Other Myths About Native Americans.* Beacon, 2016.

Enns, Elaine, and Ched Myers. *Healing Haunted Histories: A Settler Discipleship of Decolonization.* Cascade, 2021.

Hager, Shirley N., and Mawopiyane. *The Gathering: Reimagining Indigenous-Settler Relations.* University of Toronto Press, 2021.

Hansen, David Phillips. *Native Americans, the Mainline Church, and the Quest for Interracial Justice.* Chalice, 2016.

Horsman, Richard. *Race and Manifest Destiny: The Origins of American Racial Anglo-Saxonism.* Harvard University Press, 1981.

Hughes, Richard T. *Myths America Lives By.* University of Illinois Press, 2004.

Jones, Robert P. *The Hidden Roots of White Supremacy: And the Path to a Shared American Future.* Simon & Schuster, 2023.

Keller, Robert H., Jr. *American Protestantism and United States Indian Policy, 1869–82.* University of Nebraska Press, 1983.

Madley, Benjamin. *An American Genocide: The United States and the California Indian Catastrophe, 1846–1873.* Yale University Press, 2016.

Miller, Robert J. *Native America, Discovered and Conquered: Thomas Jefferson, Lewis and Clark, and Manifest Destiny*. Native America: Yesterday and Today. Praeger, 2006.

Miller, Robert J., Jacinta Ruru, Larissa Behrendt, and Tracy Lindberg. *Discovering Indigenous Lands: The Doctrine of Discovery in the English Colonies*. Oxford University Press, 2012.

Nagle, Rebecca. *By the Fire We Carry: The Generations-Long Fight for Justice on Native Land*. HarperCollins, 2024.

Newcomb, Steven T. *Pagans in the Promised Land: Decoding the Doctrine of Christian Discovery*. Fulcrum, 2008.

Prucha, Francis Paul. *American Indian Treaties: The History of a Political Anomaly*. University of California Press, 1995.

Saunt, Claudio. *Unworthy Republic: The Dispossession of Native Americans and the Road to Indian Territory*. Norton, 2020.

Slotkin, Richard. *Regeneration Through Violence: The Mythology of the American Frontier 1600–1860*. University of Oklahoma Press, 1973.

Snyder, Howard A. *Jesus and Pocahontas: Gospel, Mission, and National Myth*. Cascade, 2015.

Stephanson, Anders. *Manifest Destiny: American Expansionism and the Empire of Right*. Hill and Wang, 1995.

Tinker, George E. *Missionary Conquest: The Gospel and Native American Cultural Genocide*. Fortress, 1993.

Treat, James, ed. *Native and Christian: Indigenous Voices on Religious Identity in the United States and Canada*. Routledge, 1996.

Woodley, Randy S., and Bo C. Sanders. *Decolonizing Evangelicalism: An 11:59 P.M. Conversation*. Cascade, 2020.

GENERAL INDEX

Abbott, Lyman, 152
Aberdeen Saturday Pioneer, 84-85
Adams, John Quincy, 43, 112
Affiliated Tribes of the Mandan, Hidatsa, and Arikara, 68-70
Alexander VI, 32-33
Alfonso V, 31-32
American Board of Commissioners for Foreign Missions, 140-41
Anglo-Saxons, 174-75
Apess, William, 193-94
Arapaho, 62, 91
Army Corps of Engineers, 67-68, 220, 221, 222
Articles of Confederation, 26
Atlantic Monthly, 137
Baker, Eugene, 100-102
Barker, John Nelson, 181
Baum, L. Frank, 84-85
Big Springs, 107-8
Bird, Robert Montgomery, 183-85
Black Hills, 61, 62-63, 95
Black Kettle, 93-99
Blackfeet, 100-101
Board of Indian Commissioners, 84, 101, 151
Bosque Redondo, 127-29
Boudinot, Elias, 115, 122
Bowles, Samuel, 43-44
Bozeman Trail, 60, 91
Bradford, William, 36, 88, 185-86
Brainerd School, 140
Brish, Henry, 11-12, 37
Brown, Orlando, 60

buffalo, 59, 91, 92, 96-97
Bureau of Indian Affairs, 102, 132, 133, 134, 135, 136, 147, 157, 158, 223
Bush, George, 192-93
Cabot, John, 33
Calhoun, John C., 115, 141, 143
Carleton, James, 127-30
Carlisle Indian Industrial School, 148-50, 154-55
Carson, Kit, 127-29
Cass, Lewis, 9, 107-8
Catlin, George, 169-70, 176
Cayugas, 5, 215
Channing, Ellery, 194
Cherokee, 11-12, 77-78, 114-19, 122, 124-46, 140
Cherokee Nation v. Georgia, 117, 118, 174
Cherokee Phoenix, 114, 118, 122
Cheyenne, 16, 60, 61, 62, 91, 93, 95, 99-100, 148, 224
Cheyenne River reservation, 67
Chickasaw, 113, 119, 125
Chief Logan (Tachnechdorus), 6-7, 115, 215
Chief Wahoo, 161-64
Chivington, John, 93, 94, 99
Choctaw, 11, 119-20, 123-24, 136
Christiansen, Vernon C., 131-32
City of Sherill v. Oneida Nation, 45-48
Civilization Fund Act, 10, 141, 143
Clark, William, 12-13, 41, 91
Clay, Henry, 112-13, 194

Cleveland Indians, 163-64
Code of Indian Offenses, 154
Cody, Buffalo Bill, 97, 169
Collier, John, 156
Columbus, Christopher, 32, 162, 213-16
Comanche, 94, 95, 148
Commissioner of Indian Affairs, 59, 134, 151, 156
Congress
  Confederation, 10, 51, 76
  United States, 26-29, 47, 51, 53, 58, 62, 63-66, 69-70, 71, 84, 94, 95, 114, 115, 116, 117, 125, 126, 137, 138, 140-41, 143, 150, 153, 154, 155
contrapuntal interpretation, 209-11
Cooper, James Fenimore, 177
Corps of Discovery, 12, 41, 98
Cotton, John, 30-31
Crawford, William, 4, 186-87, 215, 235
Custer, George Armstrong, 62, 99
Dakota Access Pipeline (DAPL), 220-22
dams
  Garrison, 69-70
  Kinzua, 66-67
  Missouri Basin, 67-68
Dawes, Henry, 64, 153
decolonizing, 209, 211, 228
Division of the Missouri, 94, 97
Dixon, Joseph K., 170-71
Dwight, Timothy, 195-96
Emmons, Glenn, 134-35

Enns, Elaine, 226, 228-29
Executive Order 13950, 218
Finley, James, 107, 235
Flood Control Act of 1944, 67
Fort Defiance, 127-28
Fort Marion, 148
Fort Sumner, 127
Franklin, Benjamin, 76-81
Frost, Meschech, 1-2
Gardiner, James, 10-11
General Allotment Act/
    Dawes Act, 63-65, 153
Ghost Dance, 101-2
Gibson, John, 73, 75
Girty, Simon, 186-88
Good Housekeeping, 157-58
Goshoots, 173
Grant, Ulysses S., 62, 94
Gray, Robert, 34-35
Greeley, Horace, 174
Greentown, 23
Gregory the Great, 192
Grey, Zane, 187-88
Haaland, Debra, 235
Harmer, Ruth Mulvey, 137
Harrison, William Henry, 2, 9, 56
Hayes, Rutherford B., 68
Heckewelder, John, 73, 83, 187
Helena Daily Herald, 101-2
Hobomok, 177-78
Holmes, Oliver Wendell, 14
Homestead Act, 63
Hoover, Herbert, 133-34
Horseshoe Creek, 58
Indian Adoption Project, 157-59
Indian Child Welfare Act, 159
Indian Citizenship Act, 155
Indian Maid of Fort Ball, 1-2, 4, 7
Indian New Deal, 156-57
Indian Princess, The, 181-82
Indian Removal Act, 11, 107, 119, 141
Indian Reorganization Act, 156-57
Irvine, William, 75-76
Jackson, Andrew, 8, 11, 107, 116-17, 119-22, 125
Jamestown, 17, 34

Jefferson, Thomas, 41, 56-57, 97, 110-11, 113-14
Johnson v. M'Intosh, 41-42, 219
King Philip's War, 89-90, 179
Kiowa, 85, 148
Klamath, 66
Knox, Henry, 53-54, 57
Lake Mohonk Conference, 151-53
Lakota, 5, 60-62, 84, 91, 95, 102, 103, 137, 148, 172
land jobbers, 51
land ordinances
    Ordinance of 1784, 27
    Ordinance of 1785, 27
    Ordinance of 1787, 27, 28-29, 53
Last of the Mohicans, The, 177
Lenape, 5, 23, 51, 72-74, 77, 82, 177, 186
Lincoln, Abraham, 63
Locke, John, 38-40, 41
logic of elimination, 18-19, 21, 23, 78, 110
Long Walk, 126-30
Louisiana Purchase, 13, 41, 113
Madison, James, 58-102
man camps, 222-23, 224
Marshall, John, 42-43, 48, 117, 118, 174
Mason, John, 87-88
Massachusetts (tribe), 86-87
Massachusetts Bay Colony, 30-38, 82, 86-89
massacres
    Bear River, 91-92
    Gnadenhutten, 72-75
    Great Swamp, 89-90
    Marias River, 100-102
    Mystic River, 87-88, 102
    Onondaga, 98
    Sand Creek, 93-94
    Turner Falls, 90
    Washita, 99-100
    Whitestone Hill, 92-93
    Wounded Knee, 102-3
    Yellow Creek, 6
Mather, Cotton, 90
Mather, Increase, 172, 195
McElvain, John, 11-12
McIntosh, William, 41-42
Means, Russell, 136

Medicine Lodge Treaty, 95-96
Medill, William, 59
Meriam Report, 155-56
Merrymount, 185-86
Mescalero Apaches, 127-28, 129, 130
Metacom/King Philip, 89-90, 179
Metamora; or, The Last of the Wampanoags, 179-80
Methodists, 9, 10, 22, 93, 107, 142, 231-35
Michilimackinac, 143
missing and murdered Indigenous women and girls (MMIWG), 222-25
missionaries, 20, 72, 83, 94, 115, 118, 139, 141-42, 147, 154, 159, 187, 188
Mississippi River, 8, 10, 11, 26-27, 51, 56-57, 59, 76, 97, 105, 107, 109, 113, 116, 119-20, 123, 169, 193
Missouri River Basin Committee, 67
Monroe, James, 10, 114-18, 140-41
Montgomery, James, 10
Monuments Project, 213-14
Moravians, 72-78, 83, 197
Morris, Robert Hunt, 82
Morton, Thomas, 185-86
Morse, Jedidiah, 142, 143-44
Munnacommuck Swamp, 88
Myer, Dillon S., 134
Myers, Ched, 226, 228-29
Narragansetts, 87-90
nationalism, 8, 165-67
New York Times, 92, 101
Nicholas V, 31-32
Northwest Territory, 51, 53-55, 123
Not One More, 225
Oneidas, 45-47, 58
Onondagas, 5, 98
Oregon Trail, 59
Owl Child, Peter, 100
Pacific Railway Act, 63
Parkman, Francis, 172-73
Paxton Boys, 80-82
Peace Commission, 60, 95, 129

General Index 245

Pease, William B., 101
Pequots, 87-89, 102
Pick-Sloan Missouri Basin Program, 67-68
Pine Ridge Reservation, 102-3
Pittsburgh, 72-73, 75, 78
Plymouth Colony, 85-86, 88, 89
Pocahontas, 181-82, 209
Pratt, Richard Henry, 148-49, 152-54
Public Law 959, 137
racial hierarchy, 112-13
Red Cloud, 60-61
Reimagining Columbus Project, 213-16
reservation
    Fort Berthold (Three Affiliated Tribes), 68-70, 222
    Grand Reserve (Wyandotte), 105-9, 233
    Great Sioux Reservation, 60-61, 65, 95, 220
    Standing Rock, 67, 220-21
Ridge, John, 121-22
Roosevelt, Franklin Delano, 156
Roosevelt, Theodore, 14-16, 44, 66
Ross, John, 121-22
Rufo, Chris, 218
Said, Edward, 209
scalping, 6, 73, 74, 75, 79-80, 93, 184, 185, 187
    bounties, 81-82
Schermerhorn, John, 122
schools, 140-42
    education policy, 147-48
    residential schools, 148-51
scientific racialism, 146-47
Senecas, 186

of Sandusky, 2, 7-14, 215
settler colonialism, 17-19, 226-29
Shawnees, 6, 51, 58, 73, 78, 109, 183-84, 186, 236
Sheridan, Philip, 94, 96-102, 144
Sherman, William Tecumseh, 94-97
slave code, 89
Smith, Anthony D., 165-67
Smith, John, 181-82
Spain/Spanish, 32-33
sports mascots, 161-64
Sprague, Charles, 168
squatters, squatting, 51, 53, 77-80, 82-83, 106, 109, 117
Stewart, John, 107, 234
Strong, Josiah, 174-75
Sullivan, John, 98
Sully, Alfred, 92-93
surveyors/surveying, 27-28, 53, 61, 63, 79, 83, 106, 124, 156
Teller, Henry, 154
Templer, Bill, 196
Termination Act/House Concurrent Resolution, 108, 65-66
terra nullius/vacant land, 31, 35, 37, 39-40, 44
Terry, Alfred, 62
Tiffin, Ohio, 1-4, 238
Tinker, George "Tink," 231
townships, 25-26, 27
Transcontinental Railroad, 63, 91, 94
Treaty of
    Bosque Redondo, 129
    Cusseta, 120-21
    Dancing Rabbit Creek, 120, 123-24

Fort Finney, 51, 53
Fort Harmar, 53
Fort Jackson, 58-59
Fort Laramie (1851), 60, 68
Fort Laramie (1868), 96, 220
Fort McIntosh, 51, 52
Fort Meigs, 9
Fort Stanwix, 51, 52
Ghent, 8
Greenville, 54-55
Hartford, 88
Little Sandusky, 11
Maumee Rapids, the, 106-7
New Echota, 122-25
Paris, 8, 27-28, 51, 53
treaty commissioners, 51-52, 106-7, 119-20, 144
Trump, Donald J., 218-19
Turner, William, 90
Twain, Mark, 173
Vattel, Emer de, 38, 39-40
Virginia Company, 34-35
Volf, Miroslav, 226-28
Wampanoags, 89-90
Ward, William, 123
Washington, George, 53, 76, 97-98, 111, 186, 235
Wessagussett, 85-86
Whipple, Henry B., 61
Wigglesworth, Michael, 36-37
Williams, Roger, 89-90
Williamson, David, 76
Winthrop, John, 37-38
Worcester, Samuel, 118
Worcester v. Georgia, 118
Wounded Knee, 85, 102-3
Wyandottes, 105-10, 233-34
Xenia Torch-Light, 105-6
Yanktonai, 92-93
Zeisberger, David, 72, 73

SCRIPTURE INDEX

Old Testament

Genesis
1, *31*
1:28, *35, 43*
9:1, *35*

Exodus
12:21-24, *207*
19:4, *30*
23:28-31, *202*

Numbers
33:50-56, *202*
33:52-53, *202*

Deuteronomy
1:8, *198*
7:1-2, *198*
11:22-25, *202*
11:24-25, *198*
20:16-17, *198*
28:58, *198*
29:1, *198*
29:1-29, *207*
29:5, *207*
29:11, *207*
31:24, *198*

Joshua
1–12, *197*
1:1-18, *197, 198*
1:2-9, *198*
1:3-4, *198*
1:6, *198*

1:10-11, *198*
1:12-15, *198*
1:16-18, *198*
2–12, *204*
2:1-24, *205*
2:1–12:24, *197, 199*
2:2-3, *208*
2:8-14, *205*
2:14, *206*
6:1-27, *199*
6:25, *206*
7:1-5, *203*
7:1-26, *205, 206*
7:2, *206*
7:2-4, *203*
7:5-6, *204*
8:1-23, *208*
8:1-35, *199*
8:29, *206*
9:1-2, *208*
9:1-27, *205*
9:5, *207*
9:21, *207*
9:27, *207*
10:1-14, *201*
10:1-15, *199*
10:22-36, *208*
10:23-26, *201*
10:28-42, *199*
10:40-41, *199*
11:1-5, *208*
11:1-9, *201*
11:1-15, *199*
11:4, *199*
11:12, *208*

11:14-15, *191, 200*
11:23, *200*
12:1-6, *200*
12:7-24, *200, 208*
13:1, *200*
13:1–21:42, *197*
13:1–24:33, *200*
13:6, *200*
15:63, *201*
16:10, *201*
17:12, *201*
17:14-18, *201*
18:1-7, *201*
18:2-3, *206*
19:28, *201*
19:40-48, *201*
21:43–24:33, *198*
23:1-16, *197, 204*
23:5, *202*
23:7, *204*
23:9, *202*
23:12-13, *204*
23:13, *202*
24:19-22, *206*

Judges
1:1-36, *202*

2 Samuel
7:10, *30*

Psalms
80:9, *30*